ACCOUNTABLE TO NONE

By the same author

A City at Risk
Landlords to London
Companion Guide to Great Britain
Images of Hampstead
The Battle for the Falklands
The Market for Glory
The Selling of Mary Davies
Against the Grain

ACCOUNTABLE TO NONE

The Tory Nationalization of Britain

SIMON JENKINS

HAMISH HAMILTON · LONDON

HAMISH HAMILTON LTD
Published by the Penguin Group
Penguin Books Ltd, 27 Wrights Lane, London W8 5TZ, England
Penguin Books USA Inc., 375 Hudson Street, New York, New York 10014, USA
Penguin Books Australia Ltd, Ringwood, Victoria, Australia
Penguin Books Canada Ltd, 10 Alcorn Avenue, Toronto, Ontario, Canada M4V 3B2
Penguin Books (NZ) Ltd, 182–190 Wairau Road, Auckland 10, New Zealand

Penguin Books Ltd, Registered Offices: Harmondsworth, Middlesex, England

First published 1995
1 3 5 7 9 10 8 6 4 2

Copyright © Simon Jenkins, 1995

The moral right of the author has been asserted

Filmset in 10·5/12 pt Monophoto Baskerville
by Datix International Limited, Bungay, Suffolk

Printed in England by Clays Ltd, St Ives plc

A CIP catalogue record for this book is available from the British Library

ISBN 0-241-13591-5

CONTENTS

PREFACE

The chief sources used in this book, apart from personal observation and interviews, are memoirs and academic studies. Both have their defects. No period of government has been so 'memoirized' by its departed actors as have the Thatcher years. In memoirs, self-adulation is often spiced by malice. The two leading players in the 1980s, Margaret Thatcher and Nigel Lawson, have each written exhaustive accounts of the period. Both are apologists for their own actions and do not always tally on facts (for instance over the NHS reforms). Both have opened quarries from which historians will hack stone for many years. Memoirs by Geoffrey Howe, Nicholas Ridley and Kenneth Baker are lighter but still intriguing. (Howe is better on his Foreign Office years.) There has as yet been no intimate cabinet diary by a participant, though Alan Clark's *tour de force* gives a flavour of the outer fringes of Thatcher's court.

Politicians and officials rarely stand back and examine the implications of what they are doing. Parliament is barren as a forum for exploring the conduct of public administration, being too polarized and theatrical. Select committee cross-examination is poor, as we shall see in the silence on poll tax. Only the House of Lords has occasionally come to life, for instance on police and universities. The same is mostly true even of the serious media. Newspapers give a good account of the surface tensions of government, but rarely have time, space or inclination to plunge deeper. This function falls to scholars, and some rise to the challenge with credit. British political science has maintained a running commentary on the events of the 1980s and 1990s to an extent unimaginable two decades ago. Much of this is irritatingly partisan, but, given the weakness of press and parliamentary scrutiny, academic analysis of the domestic reforms of the late 1980s offered the principal critique of government legislation.

I sometimes witnessed these years as a non-executive participant in government, sometimes as a journalist. I should declare these past interests: membership at various times of the British Rail and London Transport boards, of the English Heritage Commission, the South Bank board, a Monopolies Commission panel and the governing bodies of a state and a private school and a housing association. I am a member of the Millennium Commission. These experiences of the 'quangocracy' have left me particularly critical of the growth of appointed government. There is much good in involving as many lay citizens as possible in administrative oversight. I am convinced that the health of democracy lies in that oversight being based primarily on the ballot box. If the franchise ill serves public administration it should be reformed, not abolished. Appointment should not be a substitute for election.

I am indebted to the research of Liora Lazarus on the departmental chapters. She was formerly at the London School of Economics and is now at the Max Planck Institute in Germany. Her knowledge of the literature of Thatcherism-in-government is unrivalled. Lee Jackson (also of the LSE) helped admirably on housing and London. Many others read and commented on drafts of individual chapters, including politicians and officials mentioned in the text who prefer to remain anonymous. Some disagreed with parts of my analysis. I hope that I have done justice to their argument. I would in particular thank Tessa Blackstone, Vernon Bogdanor, David Bowles, David Butler, Carolyn Fairbairn, Stephen Glaister, Catherine Graham-Harrison, Terence Heiser, David Howell, Kate Jenkins, Jeffrey Jowell, Rudolf Klein, David Lipsey, Margaret Maden, Peter Newsam, Jennie Page, John Palmer, Charles Pollard, Clive Priestley, Daphne Priestley, Robert Reiner, Tony Travers, George Walden, Jim Walsh and Michael Zander. Gill Ross and Elaine Jones at *The Times* supplied invaluable support.

*

I have avoided using personal titles, not out of disrespect but because in a book full of names they become cumbersome and monotonous. British public figures also have a habit of changing their titles, which can be confusing for readers. Male politicians are used to being referred to by surname alone. In the interests of consistency I have extended this practice to women, including to Margaret Thatcher. I also try to avoid spattering the text with capital letters. In particular I do not draw the distinction sometimes made between the (political) Government and the (administrative) government. They are constitutionally inseparable and I find the capitalization of one and not the other confusing.

CHAPTER ONE

ACCOUNTABLE TO ONE

No decade in the history of politics . . . ever contains its own explanation
— JOSEPH SCHUMPETER

The new Tory leader interrupted the seminar by reaching into her handbag and hauling out a copy of Hayek's *The Constitution of Liberty*. Disregarding the speaker, she banged the book on the table and announced, 'This is what we believe.' The theatrical gesture, made shortly after Margaret Thatcher's defeat of Edward Heath in the Tory leadership election of 1975, made its point. Conviction politics had superseded the politics of consensus. From now on the electorate was to be led, not followed. What 'I believe' became what all were to believe, and remained so for twelve years.

Thatcherism was never an ideology. It was not a coherent set of principles to be used as a guide to policy. Its personification was a tense, intelligent, bossy woman who shared with millions of Britons a background in upwardly mobile mercantilism. Hailing from a Lincolnshire grammar school, she found her ambition in the anonymous politics of suburban London, not in some aristocratic or academic forcing-house. She was an intellectual jackdaw. She picked the shiniest stones from the separate strands of English liberalism and conservatism, and carried them back to her nest. She rose to power at a time of disillusion with the tradition of post-war social democracy and for this reason her era is seen as politically distinctive. But her contribution to British

1

political history will, I believe, be primarily one of style and statecraft. In this sense she stands in the tradition of 'strong' Tory leaders, rather than being in any tradition of her own.[1] Her leadership was autocratic, personalized and radical. Doers are rarely thinkers, and she was a doer.

This was the feature of Thatcherism that was widely admired abroad, indeed the one that made Thatcher the first British prime minister since Churchill to be cited in the political households of the world. This book is not a study of that phenomenon but an account of its impact on a range of policies that guided British public administration through the 1980s and early 1990s. My intention is to examine politics in practice, not in theory. I agree with the thesis set out by Richard Rose and Phillip Davies in *Inheritance in Public Policy*[2] that 'policymakers are heirs before they are choosers'. Incoming British ministers are subject to both inherited and environmental pressures. They are bred to the constitutional norms of British politics, and forced by circumstance to accept the policy framework of their predecessors. The Tories in 1979 were no exception to these rules of political biology. Not until the end of the next decade did they begin to carve out for themselves some room for manoeuvre.

There is now a copious literature on both the thesis and the antithesis of Thatcherism. She was a politician who evoked strong responses even in the most reserved scholars. To her supporters, the 1980s were a decade of crusade. Forty years of state socialism, of what Thatcher herself called 'snarling envy and motiveless hostility',[3] were confronted and defeated. Private enterprise was freed and British pride restored. An early acolyte, Jock Bruce-Gardyne, described Thatcher's government as a 're-affirmation by the Party of its confidence in private enterprise . . . a breaking with the politics of post-war Conservative governments'.[4] Nigel Lawson in 1981 defined Thatcherism admiringly as 'free markets, financial discipline, firm control over public expenditure, tax cuts, nationalism, Victorian values, privatization and a dash of populism'.[5] In an erudite eulogy, Shirley Letwin acknowledged the criticism that Thatcherism was just a 'ragbag

2

of ideas', but pointed out that a ragbag stimulating such passion in supporters and critics alike must have some coherence. That coherence was, she said, 'a belief in the purpose of government as To do the Right Thing'.[6]

The antithesis holds that Thatcher simply wanted to do the wrong thing. Hers was a rehash of old free-market dogma and right-wing cabalism, the 'One of Us syndrome'. It was a blind alley, an attempt to take Britain back to an existence detached from its European future and from the necessary compromises of a mixed economy. 'The Thatcherites,' wrote Andrew Gamble in a sustained critique of the breed, 'were the first group to grapple with the problem of turning their criticisms of post-war social democracy into practical programmes and policies.'[7] In doing so, they shattered the tolerances on which the welfare state was built. They searched for a new hegemony and constructed new bases of state power to pursue it, but they, or at least she, ran out of time.[8]

Both favourable and unfavourable standpoints see Thatcherism – a term taken as referring to the period from 1979 to the present day – as a turning point in modern history, a time when the social concordat of the post-war era was torn up. Britain was reborn either as a freer and more hopeful place, or as a crueller and more divided one. Since Thatcher's fall in 1990, time has blurred these opposites. Another group of historians has begun to detach Thatcher from her -ism, pointing out that the reality of her term of office was far from the myths that have subsequently surrounded it.[9] The 'revisionists', with Peter Riddell in the lead, see Thatcher as just a particularly effective and long-serving Tory leader. Her term of office embraced much reform, as would be expected in nearly twelve years of power. On this argument, Thatcherism was a *mélange* of crisis management and U-turns, adapting itself to each twist in the electoral and economic cycle. Stop-go continued as before, more stop than go. Only rarely, as during the Falklands war and the miners' strike, was Thatcher able to rise above the swirl of events and give them a distinctive direction. A different song was sung at the cabinet table from that of the conference speech. To the revisionists, Thatcher's true art was that of keeping power, and she kept it for longer than any leader this century.

This analysis was lent some support by what might be termed the 'disillusioned Right' after 1983. Thatcher as leader in Opposition had drawn heavily on the work of Sir Keith Joseph and his colleagues at the Centre for Policy Studies, and on the Institute of Economic Affairs and the Adam Smith Institute. All these bodies poured out policy documents in the late 1970s, some at least taking root in the leader's always frenzied mind. The CPS group of John Hoskyns, Norman Strauss and Alfred Sherman enjoyed considerable access to Thatcher after she won office, at least in the pre-Falklands period. They were her gadflies, reminding her of her own ideological shortcomings. Each of them became embittered at her caution and her initial lack of interest in radical reform.[10] Hoskyns, who headed her policy unit at Downing Street, wrote to her in 1980 complaining that 'we have been brutal to our friends . . . and gentle with the real problems, trade unions, nationalized industries, lame ducks and public-services pay'.[11] It was ironic that Thatcher picked up these ideas only after the early mentors had departed disgruntled into the wilderness.

The revisionist synthesis is plausible, but only up to a point. As we shall see, Thatcher's government was, until the middle of the 1980s, essentially reactive. Both the 1979 and the 1983 manifestos lacked the idealistic thrust that might have been expected of a conviction politician. Like most manifestos, they promised to govern well, with favours for important interest groups. They were not inspiring. But even before Thatcher got into her stride after the 1987 election victory, patterns in the handling of events can be detected.[12] The turmoils of Thatcher's early years were handled differently from those of the Heath, Wilson or Callaghan governments. She was not so much decisive as emphatic. She insisted on reforming the trade unions and on compulsory competitive tendering. Her strength of personality was crucial in the conduct of the Falklands campaign and the battle against the

4

miners. She drove her ministers forward – and sometimes back again – without sheltering behind them. If she disagreed with them, everybody knew it, especially their private offices. Whether or not she always got what she wanted, it was always known what she wanted.

Thatcher herself thus offered a significant innovation in modern leadership. She re-established in Britain the concept of governability. It is hard with hindsight to recall the decay of that concept at the time of her election. The historian Sam Beer regarded the illness of Britain in the 1970s as an acute clogging of the arteries, a stultifying diffusion of accountability: 'the enormous new powers that government exercises over producer and consumer groups at the same time puts these groups in a position to frustrate those powers by refusing their co-operation and consent'.[13] Writing in that cul-de-sac year of British politics, 1982, Beer presented a vision that was near unrecognizable ten years on, one of untrammelled welfarism, rampant unions, demoralized Conservatism and only the Social Democrats carrying the flag of 'neo-radicalism'. Such was the desperation of the Right that its more drastic theorists wanted to 'un-manage' the economy, to draw government back altogether. Not so Thatcher. Her response was to increase its power over events, to bend it to her will. 'Never let anyone say I am *laissez-faire*,' she said, echoing Hayek's similar cry. 'We are strong to do those things which government must do and only government can do.'[14]

In this respect, Thatcher was reviving a tradition that can be traced back to the Second World War, to the 'can do' conduct of that war and the establishment of the welfare state. I believe that there was much in common between the domestic policies of the 1945 Labour government and Thatcher's administration, despite the custom of contrasting them. In the epilogue to his biography of Attlee, Kenneth Harris suggested that not until Thatcher was the Attlee 'consensus' challenged: 'She began to attack not only much of the Attlee legacy . . . but Thatcherism meant that the individual would be freed from government restraints and allowed to prosper. Out of the new wealth consequently acquired

5

the citizen would be able and willing to pay a proper share of the cost of welfare, education and health.'[15] True, this was what she implied she would do. But, like Attlee, she was interested in the power of government to set goals and achieve them. Both granted Whitehall unprecedented control over the public sector. In this respect, as Letwin pointed out, 'Thatcherites bear a resemblance to full-blooded socialists and are wholly unlike the Conservatives who had earlier dominated the party.'[16]

Thatcher naturally put a different gloss on the 1980s. On the occasions when I spoke to her in office, she conveyed above all a sense of entrapment. Her egotism was of a woman wanting to exert power, not of one actually exerting it. She was perpetually at odds with her political surroundings, like a dog straining at the leash, barking at anybody who came near. She was by instinct a radical. Hugo Young has suggested that Thatcher was rare among British leaders in winning power not from the inner club of Conservative politics but as an outsider, a rebel who fought her way up a hostile male hierarchy. (In fact, her rise was conventional: grammar school, Oxford, a Tory candidate at twenty-four, safe seat at thirty-three and junior minister two years later.) To William Keegan she was the beneficiary of a 'peasants' revolt' against the élitist corporatism that had grown up under Heath and Wilson alike. She was a politician perpetually searching for enemies. When accused of seeking to enhance the power of her office she cited the forces ranged against her. Out there, she would cry, was an accumulation of socialist lethargy, an overbearing state, a grasping and corrupt Europe, a political economy demanding reform. Any amount of power was needed to confront all that.

To Thatcher, British politics had seen two failures since the war. One was the experience of democratic socialism: 'No theory of government was ever given a fairer test or a more prolonged experiment,' she wrote, 'yet it was a miserable failure.'[17] The second was the capitulation of her own party under Heath to the same failed experiment, to its 'centralizing, managerial, bureaucratic, interventionist style'. (As we shall see, this was an ironic

6

list of epithets for her to use.) She admitted that for twenty years she had gone along with the coalition of right-wing Labour and left-wing Tory programmes known as Butskellism. Not until 1975 did she and her mentor, Sir Keith Joseph, discover the truth. That was the year when he told her, in a phrase heavy with revolutionary import, 'I have only recently become a Conservative.'[18]

This was hard on Heath. He too entered power believing in a new Conservative revolution. The 1970 election had been fought under the right-wing banner of Selsdon Man. 'We were returned to office,' he said, 'to change the course of the history of this nation, nothing less . . . to bring about a change so radical, a revolution so quiet and yet so total that it will have to go beyond the programme for a Parliament.'[19] Heath even cited the need for tax cuts, social-service selectivity and the reform of the public sector. Thatcher was a senior member of that government. She sat at the cabinet table, fought to increase her own education budget and was party to the famous 'U-turn' on industrial intervention in 1972. Unaware of any hypocrisy, she later said: 'I could not help noticing a curious discrepancy in the behaviour of my colleagues. What they said and what they did seemed to exist in two separate compartments.'[20] She excused her own role in these events on the grounds of her 'inexperience'.

Yet Thatcher comprehended one aspect of statecraft that had eluded her predecessor. What a leader needs is not ideological conviction – that comes cheap – but confidence in government's ablity both to implement conviction and, more important still, to keep hold of power. There is a circularity in the open-ended centralism of the British constitution, with no entrenched checks and no term limits. The first duty of a leader is to stay leader. Heath's reign ended with the humiliating question, 'Who runs Britain?' The manner of Heath's defeat left a deep scar on Thatcher. In particular she retained a dread of the latent potency of trade unions and student militants.[21] Heath had been weak. She was determined to be strong. She needed power to fight power. 'I will use every means at my disposal,' she said in a conversation with the author, 'to fight socialism, because socialism is never defeated.' When her downfall was imminent I asked her at Chequers about her leadership opponent, Michael Heseltine. She shouted across that dark, bare sitting room that he must not win because 'he will bring back socialism'.[22]

This fixation on the lingering power of the Left holds a clue to the paradox of Margaret Thatcher's rule. Her proclaimed desire to dismantle state power required the fullest exploitation of that power to achieve it. As Gamble put it, 'The problem for the Thatcher government was that its own diagnosis of the crisis of state authority constantly impelled it towards intervention.'[23] She would protest that she wanted to get government out of people's business, out of their life, out of their way. Yet the phrase 'I want' was not the mere will of an individual; it carried behind it the full force of one of the world's most cohesive democracies. Thatcher made politics seem simple. That was her trademark. But politics is never simple. It exists to resolve conflicts that simplicity has failed to resolve. It lives and breathes complexity, which is why it has fascinated intelligent men and women down the ages. Hence John Adams' reflection that, after 3,000 years of experience, the art of politics is no better understood by its practitioners than it was by the ancient Greeks. The same mistakes are made in much the same way, to be admonished by the same quotes from Plato and Aristotle.

Normally politics operates within the confines of a constitution. Practitioners play on a field with the boundaries clearly marked. They contend for power within those boundaries. What makes the British version of this game so compelling, and so dangerous, is that there are no boundaries. The executive in parliament is sovereign. There is no written constitution. Thatcher the rebel, the outsider, the soldier for truth came to office as challenger to, not champion of, the power of government. In a touching anecdote at the start of his book on the British constitution, Ferdinand Mount recalls finding an underlined copy of Lord Radcliffe's stern 1951 Reith Lectures, *The Problem of Power*. The underlinings all emphasized Radcliffe's warning at the direction that centralized power was taking in the constitution. Parliament was becoming 'the instrument of power rather than its holder'; it was a 'meaningless constitutionalism which asserts that anything is all right if it is permitted, nothing is all right if it is forbidden, by an Act of Parliament'.[24] The underlinings, he went on to reveal, were by Thatcher herself, in Opposition. Yet in office she acknowledged few constraints beyond the rudiments of parliamentary procedure and the Parliament Acts governing elections. Her treatment of local democracy, her abuse of the patronage system, her accumulation of statutory 'reserved powers' showed little regard for the spirit of any constitution. Lord Chief Justice Hewart's warning in *The New Despotism* (1929) that laws delegated to ministers under what he called 'Henry VIII clauses' was 'administrative lawlessness' was not for her. As for Acton's maxim on the corrupting effect of power, she would have laughed that that was for wimps.

The 1980s are seen as the decade in which, thanks to Thatcherism, Britain shook off 'the British disease' of industrial strife and uncompetitiveness. For two decades, government attention had concentrated on the public sector. Private enterprise had been despised or ignored. Thatcher set out, if not to dismantle the public sector, at least to free the private sector of guilt. When Thatcher lunched with British Rail executives she treated them (to the author's knowledge) as second-class citizens: 'If any of you were any good you would be in private industry,' she said. There was no doubt who was the favoured guest at the banquet of Thatcherism. As we examine in the next chapter, state industries were privatized. The private sector penetrated the public sector at every level through compulsory competitive tendering. Merchant banks, management consultants, security firms, small-time caterers worked with government as never before. Profit was no longer abused. Exchange control was abolished. The unions were curbed. Enterprise was rewarded. The rich were honoured.

This book is about the unfavoured guest at that banquet, the public sector. It lurked in the shadows of Thatcherism like an awkward and embarrassing relative. Thatcher herself might be

9

'the' government, but beyond the gilded walls of Downing Street was a quite different sort of government, inherited by her from Labour, encumbered with political obligations, always expensive, always detested. Despite her contempt for it, Thatcher failed to reduce the public sector's appetite and barely contrived to reduce the proportion of the nation's wealth that it consumed. On the Treasury's own definition of public spending, it took 43 per cent of Britain's gross domestic product in 1979 and 39 per cent at the end of the boom in 1990. A year later it was up to 42 per cent and recession pushed it back to 43 per cent in 1992 and 44.5 per cent in 1994. Thus Thatcherism (though Thatcher would say not so herself, at least in 1990) failed in its central goal. Maurice Mullard has suggested that for the foreseeable future, 'the boundaries between the private and public sectors are likely to be consolidated. A Conservative government plans to redirect about 40 per cent of national income to the public sector.'[25] This compares with roughly 35 per cent in the 'socialist' 1960s.

Whatever else Thatcher and her successor, John Major, did they did not curb the state's call on the taxpayer. On the narrower definition of government receipts, excluding borrowing and asset sales, the public-sector 'take' from gross domestic product was an astonishingly consistent 40 per cent in 1970, 1980 and 1990 and, on the Treasury Red Book 1995 forecast, will be the same in AD 2000. This one statistic towered over Thatcherism and explains much of its turmoil. It helps explain the constant tension between Thatcher as leader of a cause and Thatcher as custodian of the public sector. The programmes that grew fastest under her were 'demand-led' welfare spending such as health, social security and law and order. Only drastic cuts in spending on public investment and later in defence kept the overall total within bounds. As we shall see, Thatcher wrestled to control these sums. The struggle never abated. At first she employed damage limitation, precipitating one cabinet argument after another with 'the wets'. In her later, radical period she tried to restructure spending programmes to reduce their cost. Yet her spending never stopped rising in real terms. The inflation seemed inexorable. The chant 'Public spending seems out of control' runs monotonously through Thatcher's memoirs. It maddened her and, especially after 1987, became the motor behind her more drastic reforms.

To economists in the 1970s, such growth came to seem no longer a passive beneficiary of prosperity but a potential saboteur. Even Roy Jenkins, when Labour Home Secretary, questioned whether public spending could go above 60 per cent of GDP 'and maintain the values of a plural society with adequate freedom of choice'.[26] Conservative economists such as Douglas Hague put the threshold figure at 40 per cent. Most agreed that there must be some figure at which the public sector becomes so big as to be beyond the capacity of the economy to sustain. Hence Thatcher's determination to curb her new domain, regarding it as a state in which 'the private sector was controlled by government and the public sector wasn't controlled by anyone'.[27] Thatcher managed to withdraw some of her forces from the public sector's outer perimeter and allow some fraternizing with the private sector. But she did more than keep control over what was left: she tightened that control and concentrated it in her own hands.

The Thatcher years seem in retrospect to have been ones of ceaseless running disputes. Memoirs of the time show how crucial personal relations were to the outcome of these disputes. As we shall see, the poll tax owed much to Patrick Jenkin's eagerness to please his boss and to the presentational skill of Kenneth Baker. The caution of the NHS reforms was due to the replacement of John Moore by Kenneth Clarke. Gas was not broken up because Thatcher sided with Peter Walker against Nigel Lawson. Electricity was broken up to make amends for that error. Railways were not privatized because Thatcher hated trains. Her ten-year war against local government had little to do with the reality of its spending, more with the Prime Minister's aversion to political collectives of which she was not a member. Ministers shirked consultation before decisions not because they were averse to consultation but because they knew Thatcher disliked consensus.

She borrowed her politics from Tennessee Williams: the medicine was not working if there were no screams of pain. Ministers wanted to please her more than they wanted to rule well. They made mistakes as a result.

Thatcher is always at the centre of our stage, bobbing, weaving, hectoring, backtracking. She emerges as a different leader from the Thatcher of legend. Letwin describes her fundamentalism as 'inchoate and wholly unselfconscious', so much so that 'she could not communicate it even to her most loyal followers'.[28] She was a fundamentalist in demeanour and often in speech. She was not a fundamentalist in government. As Lawson complains, she 'had to be dragged kicking and screaming' to approve even the mildest radicalism. She wanted to preserve such corporatist dinosaurs as the National Economic Development Council, the National Dock Labour Scheme and the wages councils.[29] She wanted the state to keep its shares in 'Britain's oil' (see next chapter). She was opposed to privatizing the railways, censoring any reference to it from conference speeches by her transport secretaries. She was nervous of the national curriculum, disliked health vouchers and backtracked on civil-service reform. When in 1985 Keith Joseph brought forward his student loans scheme to cover tuition fees, she rejected it as 'political dynamite'. Lawson, who helped Joseph with the scheme in the belief that it had Thatcher's blessing, recalled the resulting cabinet: 'When they saw which way the wind was blowing, those colleagues who had assented in the earlier discussion promptly ratted.'[30] Not for another five years did anybody dare return to the subject.

Not surprisingly this led to confusion over the Prime Minister's commitment to the -ism that bore her name. Insecure ministers (all her ministers were insecure) overestimated her radicalism because they made the mistake of believing her speeches. There was never any coherent statement of what the Thatcher government had as its creed. British politicians are required to 'set out the stall' only twice, in election manifestos and party conference speeches. Both tend to be stronger on abstract pieties than on specifics. Green and white papers, preambles to acts of parliament, may give some theoretical background to reform. But the cabinet, indeed the whole political community, had to navigate the Thatcher years by dead reckoning. Those who thought they could second-guess the Prime Minister frequently came unstuck.

Even as she became less hostile to radical reform in the late 1980s, Thatcher's style was not conducive to general debate. She was scornful of forming policy through such ungainly means as Royal Commissions. She authorized Norman Fowler's great social-security debate of 1984, but her preference was for gathering together a group of ministers, advisers and officials to plan in private. This enabled them to be free-thinking and argumentative. The reforms to health, education, local taxation, the railways and the law were all prepared in this way. Excluding outsiders gave reform a pace and cabinet commitment lacking from the old commissions and committees of inquiry. Opposition was muted. Lobbyists were circumvented. The result was that by the time a plan was presented for 'public consultation' it had developed a momentum within the government machine that made it near unstoppable. Attlee's ministers based their reforms on a mass of wartime and pre-war research and experience. The policy legacy inherited by Thatcher was one to which she was hostile and which was hostile to her. There were to be errors galore. But for a radical government in a hurry, the procedure got things done.

That this activity did not emerge until the second half of Thatcher's term was perhaps not surprising. Hindsight credits her with superhuman dominance over her cabinets. In the early days this was not the case. Her colleagues were deeply sceptical, not just of anything that might be termed Thatcherism, but even of her personal staying power. The 1979 government was largely composed of Heathites who treated Thatcher as on probation. At the Treasury, Howe and Lawson attempted to get the privatization programme on the road but, as they admit, with little success. Howe was fiscally radical and would certainly have tackled the 'supply side' with greater vigour had Downing Street agreed. But he hated fights, and Thatcherism was forged in the heat of conflict. As a result, the 1979 parliament was largely devoid of structural reform, taken up with a prolonged struggle to curb (not cut) public spending, to achieve Rhodesian independence, and then to win the Falklands war.

The 1983 parliament saw a different struggle, with the miners and the local authorities. Both fights were regarded by Thatcher as inevitable, but they exhausted the cabinet and caused deep divisions in the wider political community. Although the groundwork was laid for the privatization of the state trading corporations and utility monopolies, substantive reform of the welfare state remained untouched in this 'middle period'. These were the wasted years of Thatcherism. To Nicholas Ridley, this was the 'window of opportunity which alas she missed'.[31] The turning point came with the 1987 election, a victory which Thatcher attributed to her own intervention in a halting and incompetent party campaign. Afterwards she felt a new invincibility and embarked on what became an extraordinary hyperactive burst from 1987 to 1990. Most of the chapters in this book focus on this period, and on its aftermath under John Major.

Indeed, what might be termed 'the golden years of Thatcherism' covered a relatively short span of time, beginning in 1987–8 and ending with the heavy programme of changes to education, police, railways and the law in 1993–4, well into John Major's term of office. I have treated John Major's administration as a continuation of Thatcherism, because that is what it was. Despite a wholly different leadership style, Major's approach to the public sector analysed in this book was unchanged from that of his mentor. He brought no new insight into policy, announced no change of approach and retained what was generally termed a 'centre-right' balance within his cabinet. That balance held even after the extraordinary incident in June 1995, when Mr Major declared a leadership contest out of the blue, which he went on to win. While that contest was widely seen as a battle between Left and Right in the party, it was hard for advocates of the challenger, John Redwood, to marshal a coherent alternative programme. Since he had supported in cabinet the welfare state

14

and fiscal conservatism, any divergence from Major's policies in the direction of higher spending or swifter tax cuts merely sounded irresponsible. As with most critiques of Major, the emphasis fell on leadership style rather than on substance.[32]

Major's public sector was, if anything, more rather than less 'Thatcherite' than Thatcher's. After 1990, the privatization of state corporations continued into areas that she had specifically avoided. The Coal Board was sold and British Rail prepared for sale. The disposal of the Post Office was halted only by a backbench revolt. More significant, Thatcher's centralization gathered pace. As we shall see, it extended further into the running of the NHS, the new police authorities, housing, the railways, the schools and universities and the administration of justice. The abandonment of the poll tax in favour of the council tax led to a decrease rather than an increase in local-authority discretion (see chapter three). A nationalized lottery was invented. League tables and audit comparability proliferated. Thatcher's caustic references to Major's performances on the European stage and to his borrowing enthusiasm grabbed headlines. But it is hard to imagine she would have behaved any differently in office.

This continuity is not surprising. By the time Major came to power, the cabinet's inheritance and approach to policy had altered. The supertanker was on a new course. The habit of privatizing what could be privatized and centralizing the rest was embedded in ministerial and Whitehall responses. The changes to local-government finance initiated in 1991 and the performance standards for hospitals, police forces and universities were all more centralist than anything conceived in the 1980s. Treasury supremacy over policy had become what Richard Rose would call both genetic and environmental.[33] Unchecked by constitutional balances, those in power tended to accrete power, whether or not they were seen as strong or weak leaders. To this extent, the replacement of Thatcher by Major in 1990 made little difference to the thesis of this book. That elusive concept 'Thatcherism' continued and was, if anything, strengthened by the Tory election victory of 1992. Future historians will be entitled to refer to the period as the Thatcher/Major era.

Both leaders worked with the grain of prime ministerial power in Britain. Both came to office accepting the framework of the welfare state inherited from Labour. When Thatcher left office, for all the 'questioning' that surrounded the future of welfare, it remained intact. Thatcher and Major found themselves spending more on housing subsidies, pensions and law and order. Spending on unemployment relief, family and housing benefit rose steadily in real terms to the recipient over the 1980s and 1990s. When local taxes were cut in response to electoral pressure, central taxes were increased to pay for it. Thatcher in particular was fiercely protective of subsidies to mortgage holders, company-car owners and even students. Regional subsidies to Wales, Scotland and Northern Ireland were likewise protected. As early as 1981, the then Chief Secretary to the Treasury, Leon Brittan, had declared that his expenditure white paper 'disposed effectively of the notion that the government refuses to adjust its plans to circumstances. The decision to increase spending is a conscious and deliberate collective policy response by the government.'[34] As we shall see, time and again Thatcherism was happy to will a general good but not a specific pain. Leaders must above all keep power, and keeping power customarily means spending tax-payers' money.

I am convinced that it was, above all, Thatcher's early failure to contain public spending that determined the whole course of her domestic policy. It was as if she knew she had let down an ideal, a compact reached with Sir Keith Joseph and his wing of the party. To expiate this she invented ever more demonic dragons, and demanded ever more draconian powers to slay them. Public-sector unions, notably at GCHQ and in Whitehall, were early victims of her fury. Enemies had to be created, if only to make room in the budget for necessary friends: college lecturers to make way for farmers, housing committees to make way for policemen, teachers to make way for nurses. Where cuts were made ministers searched desperately for productivity gains to

16

forestall a decline in standards. Public-sector efficiency became the obverse of the 'cuts' coin. Financial planning and value for money were the ruling obsessions of late Thatcherism. The result was an 'audit explosion'.[35] Audit was supposedly non-partisan. Value for money was not left-wing or right-wing but just good housekeeping. Yet it soon became another weapon in the march towards national efficiency and national uniformity. In alliance with Treasury expenditure control, it too was an agent of centralization.

This centralization came naturally to the institutions of governing power. Number Ten Downing Street, the Treasury, the Cabinet Office and the Whips' Office all increased their influence over the government machine in the 1980s, even when their public image was battered. Thatcher was known for drawing forceful aides round her, men such as Clive Whitmore (her first private secretary), Charles Powell and Bernard Ingham. After the Falklands victory her office enjoyed a remarkable dominance over the cabinet. Letters over her signature or that of her aides were obeyed. She ruled by force of argument as well as by fear – British government remains deliberative in character – but fear was often uppermost when she controlled the career prospects of so many under her command. Not surprisingly, her ministers came to rule their own departments and client agencies likewise. But since these were not tight-knit groups of ministers who could be gathered in Downing Street but large bureaucratic empires, the forms of control they employed were inevitably bureaucratized.

At the centre of this web sat the Treasury, subject of chapter twelve. Harold Wilson used to moan that the one institution he should have nationalized was the Treasury, but that such a policy had eluded every prime minister. Thatcher tried hardest and came nearest to success, because only thus could she transmit power directly through the organs of government. Her two principal Chancellors, Geoffrey Howe and Nigel Lawson, were strong if lonely political figures. The donnish Howe and the saturnine Lawson had to play Jeeves to Thatcher's Wooster.

They soothed her political hangovers, brushed her coat each morning and rescued her from innumerable scrapes. Both were committed to the agenda of Thatcherism, but as both make clear in their memoirs they doubted the full commitment of their leader. They tried to implement her wayward outbursts and canalize her dynamism. Yet she fought them incessantly and, sadly for all three, alienated them both. Howe and Lawson were natural centralists, as were Major's two Chancellors, Norman Lamont and Kenneth Clarke. Neither in their writings nor in their speeches did any of them show a feel for the diversity of the British constitution. If they deferred to any external political institutions, it was to the Bank of England, to the European Council of Ministers and the finance ministers' 'union' of the G-7.

Lawson was the more interventionist of the two. 'The Treasury is not simply a finance ministry,' he wrote. 'It is also both in name and reality the central department with a finger in pretty well every pie that the government bakes.'[36] His conclusion on the 1980s is stark: 'The Treasury did not fully recover its pre-eminence among Whitehall departments [since the nineteenth century] until the accession of Margaret Thatcher. This was vital to the overall success of that government. It re-established the truth that just as a company cannot be run successfully without a strong finance director, so the economy cannot be run successfully without a powerful Treasury.'[37] Thatcher was often jealous of the Treasury and taunted it by consulting maverick advisers such as Douglas Hague, Patrick Minford and Alan Walters. But she needed it and used it. As Leo Pliatsky recorded, she knew that without it a revolution was inconceivable.[38] It was the principal agency of the centralization that she believed was vital to the projection of her power.

Thatcher could count for allies on a political community which in Britain is instinctively centralist. Few MPs and almost no cabinet ministers have served on local councils or in the nether reaches of the public sector. Their experience of the private sector is brief and often limited to the learned professions.

Senior civil servants regard terms of secondment 'to the real world' as meaning the City and possibly a public corporation, but not local government or private industry. To them career success still lies in the Italianate palaces of Whitehall or the concrete bunkers of Marsham Street and Victoria Street. While the civil service has been fragmented into agencies and quangos, the degree and character of central control over these bodies meant that public service remains a remarkably homogeneous activity. While privatization reduced ministerial patronage in state industries, this was compensated by the growth of Thatcher's 'sub-national government'.[39] In regional and increasingly in local administration, the 'new magistracy' was on the march. By the end of the Thatcher years, as we shall see, twice as many people responsible for local administration were appointed by central government as were elected by local voters.

The media, on which modern politics feeds as never before, mirrors this centralization. Reporters and commentators live and work in London. Few of them nowadays began life on a provincial newspaper. Political coverage focuses on Westminster – on Bagehot's dignified rather than efficient governors – and on its theatrical pretence of scrutiny. Such politics is based on an amalgam of personality and incident, adding to the pressure on ministers to protect themselves against short-term criticism. To help them, officials must intrude and monitor with ever greater diligence. The closure of a hospital ward, an accident on the railway, a prison scandal is a national story requiring ministerial accountability. Matters that once would have rested with local government or an industry board are subjects of partisan argument in the House of Commons.

This trend will not be easy to reverse. In his speech to the 1994 Labour party conference, Tony Blair set out what he saw as a new vision of British politics. He embraced such fashionable concepts as participation, citizenship, partnership and the social market. The one word absent from his list was decentralization. Nothing in what he said suggested any radical departure from the interventionist tendencies of Labour and Conservative governments since the war. Indeed his specific proposals implied more intervention: minimum wages, rights for the disabled, women and minorities and social legislation under the European social chapter. When challenged on the ending of rate capping, the same Labour party that had vociferously opposed the capping in the first place found itself promising to keep some cap in place on the most 'irresponsible' authorities. Blair's one ostensibly decentralist proposal, assemblies for Scotland and Wales, would increase interference in subordinate local government.

What neither Blair nor his team re-examining public ownership seemed to realize was the legacy that Thatcherism offered them. As we shall see in later chapters, a future Labour government would require little by way of legislation to reassert control over the 'commanding heights' of what had been within the public sector prior to 1979. The reserve powers contained in Thatcher's statutes would give Labour more power over the state sector than any other European government. The centralization of local taxes and the power of direction over schools, hospitals, the police, railways and housing had all been enhanced by Thatcher. Most of her privatizations left in place regulators and golden shares that Labour planners could activate, or legislate to reinstate (see chapter two, pp. 37–8, on Lawson and Britoil). A suspicious mind might even see behind Thatcher's 'reserve powers' clauses a socialist fifth column of civil servants at work, sharpening their tools for an elected dictatorship of the Left under Labour.

Each succeeding chapter of this book is intended to raise and sometimes answer the question of what is the right balance between central authority and diversity, between control and autonomy. This balance is now crucial to the debate on the future government not just of Britain but of the whole of Europe. In each area of public administration the answer is likely to be different, but the same considerations apply. Government will always seek more control. Thatcher claimed to have insufficient powers to effect her anti-socialist revolution. Perhaps the truth is that she only began to find her true self in office after overcoming years of storms, opposition and what she saw as defeats. We often forget the learning curve required to master tough jobs. Thatcher fought to survive two full parliaments before, in 1987, being able to launch her most determined assault on the public sector that she inherited in 1979. Yet no sooner had she acquired the necessary experience, and amassed enough control, than she began to overreach herself with her colleagues. It was a measure of her political dominance that she could contemplate, and introduce, the twentieth century's only poll tax.

Deep in Thatcher's political psyche was a characteristic shared with traditional British socialism: a faith not in parliament but in government. Her instincts were 'democratic centralist', rooted in the legitimacy of a single, all-powerful executive subject only to periodic election. As noted earlier, she was never a believer in *laissez-faire* – any more than was her intellectual mentor, Hayek. She believed in her power to impose a global view on a nation's political economy. As I show in chapter nine, she believed in government as social engineering. Through the extension of audit and the widespread use of league tables she sought a national harmonization of welfare beyond anything attempted by post-war socialism. Her reforms were a relentless pursuit of the equitable allocation of resources – equitable by her own lights. Hers was the apotheosis of the 'efficient state'. In this scheme of things there was no place for layers of accountability. Thatcher brought about a revolution of control within government. This enabled her, notably between 1987 and 1990, to drive through the most drastic public-sector reforms seen since the 1940s. She may have intended to 'take power to cede power', but she never got round to the second half of that remit. We must take our politicians for what they do, not what they say.

I have been asked whether this book is meant as an attack on Thatcher. It is not. It is an attack on aspects of British politics and the British constitution, to which she partly fell victim. If I express a measure of disillusion, it is the disillusion of a believer. Thatcher and her colleagues never promised the nation a bed of roses. They said only that severe medicine was required to restore the British economy. That limited prescription has stood the test of time. There was, as they said, 'no alternative' to the treatment administered by Geoffrey Howe and Nigel Lawson. Tighter expenditure control, wider incentives, privatization and the curbing of restrictive labour and monopoly practices were necessary objectives.

So too was Thatcher's reassertion of political leadership. She proved what Edward Heath and James Callaghan doubted, that British politics could be made susceptible to change. The Thatcher/Major years have been ones of intense political turbulence. The changes to the landscape of domestic government outlined in this book have been real, more than those of any time since 1945. I have tried to show that they liberated some aspects of the British political economy. They also enslaved others. They demolished respected checks and balances on central power and in doing so undermined democratic freedoms. Some of this damage may have been inevitable in view of what was to be achieved, much may have been unintentional. But since the landscape Thatcher was seeking to remould was itself the British constitution, any change to it must be of constitutional significance. The observer cannot shrug and say with Dr Pangloss that all is probably for the best in the best of all possible worlds. Britain's freedom does not necessarily 'broaden down from precedent to precedent'. Broaden has to be an active, not a passive verb. With the growth of shared sovereignty in Europe, freedom must be audited, monitored and sometimes defended. Thatcher and Thatcherism cannot have left so flexible a creature as the British constitution unbent. Indeed they did not.

CHAPTER TWO

The Family Silver

Never be a pioneer. It's the Early Christian that gets the fattest lion – SAKI

Privatization was to be Thatcher's pride and joy. She described it as 'the central means of reversing the corrosive and corrupting effects of socialism'.[1] In 1979 many of the great industries of Britain were still in the government's hands: cars, shipbuilding, aeroplanes, coal, steel, telecommunications, gas, electricity, trains, airlines, ports, airports. The government had a stake in the oil business, in banking, hotels, shipping and road haulage. The agenda of post-war socialism was all but complete. When Thatcher left office the ownership of roughly half of this output had been transferred to private shareholders. Six hundred and fifty thousand workers had left the state's employ, 90 per cent of them holding shares in their own companies. In addition, one and a quarter million council tenants had become home-owners. It was the biggest transfer of assets out of state hands in the history of democracy. In most cases the outcome had been a measurable rise in productivity.[2]

Yet of all Thatcher's reforms, privatization is the most curious. By the mid-1990s the concept, if not all the practice, had turned electorally sour. Less than a quarter of opinion poll samples felt utilities privatization had been a good thing. Two-thirds wanted water and electricity renationalized and there was overwhelming opposition to privatizing the Post Office and the railway.[3] This

23

unpopularity chiefly concerned the utilities (and may have been related to the overall standing of the Tory government). But undoubtedly a reason was the initial motivation and thus the manner of privatization in Britain.

Privatization came to Thatcher, though not to all members of her government, rather as an afterthought. It emerged, like so many of her reforms, from her campaign to reduce public spending and borrowing. Before she came to office the subject was barely mentioned. The 1976 'Right Approach' policy statement merely suggested that 'in some cases it may be appropriate to sell back to private enterprise assets or activities where willing buyers can be found'. This was hardly a ringing ideological crusade. Contributors to Geoffrey Howe's economic policy group in Opposition, including Nigel Lawson, Keith Joseph and David Howell, certainly wished to take denationalization forward. Howell had been an early enthusiast, actually using the word in a pamphlet as early as 1970, influenced by the American management economist, Peter Drucker.[4] The word privatization even appeared in drafts of the party's 1970 manifesto.

Thatcher was not an enthusiast. In the 1979 manifesto the word did not appear, largely because she hated it.[5] Reference was made to selling back some recently nationalized concerns, such as road freight, shipbuilding and aerospace, but, says Howe, 'Margaret had been fearful that a more extensive catalogue might frighten the floating voter.'[6] In her memoirs she excused the slow start of privatization on the grounds of the recession and the fact that nobody really knew whether it would work.[7] Her reaction to proposals from ministers suggested a deeper hesitancy. As Ridley recorded, apart from council houses 'she was adamant she would not start down this road . . . she didn't want to stir up the lobbies in the public sector. She felt we could come to that in a few years' time.'[8]

None the less a cabinet committee was set up after the election under Howe's (not Thatcher's) chairmanship, with the appellation E(DL), for economic (disposal). The earliest adventures took the form of insisting on competitive tendering for many government services previously supplied by the government's own employees. Tendering was made compulsory for local-government services such as refuse and street cleaning under the 1980 Local Government Act. The same applied to the sub-contracting of government catering, Whitehall security guards and Home Office remand centres. These were described as privatized, but remained public services still paid for by taxation. Government did not withdraw and leave citizens to spend their taxes in the market place. The public sector retained control throughout.

What became known as this 'purchaser/provider split' is widely credited with bringing private incentives into many areas of public administration and much increasing its efficiency. The previous inadequacy of public-sector management meant that quality control was likely to be greater where the service was delivered by a competitive private supplier rather than a heavily unionized government labour force. The system embraced competition in the rivalry between suppliers. But as we shall see elsewhere, the relinquishing of ownership over a particular set of assets does not necessarily signify a shift of control – or at least not one of any great constitutional importance. Ministers and officials had been given a choice as purchasers of a service. The providers had been given the opportunity of profit. The consumers might have a better or more cost-effective service, but they had no choice. They still spent their taxes and had to accept government's judgement on quality.

The new government's first steps towards the outright sale of assets were driven not by any manifesto commitment or sense of ideological excitement but by a fixation with cutting public borrowing (see chapter twelve). The cabinet never saw a white paper putting the public case for privatization. As Howe put it, 'The sensible disposal of public-sector assets had grown in urgency, not least as a short-term way of helping reduce the PSBR. I set a target of £1 billion for 1979–80.'9 The money-raising motive was pre-eminent for the cabinet through the first two Thatcher administrations. Sam Brittan pointed out that

25

'selling public assets was politically much easier and more popular than cutting public expenditure'.[10]

Asset sales were carefully separated in the Treasury accounts, but as long as public borrowing was treated as a key economic indicator, it was plain that asset sales relieved it. They brought more money to the Treasury each year without taxes having to be raised or money printed. This added greatly to the ministerial appeal of the programme. As Oliver Letwin wrote in his survey of world privatization, 'Once the anticipated proceeds are written into the budget, failure to realize them becomes a cause of serious financial embarrassment. This keeps up the impetus at times when the will might otherwise flag in the face of difficulties.'[11] Some states, such as in the former Soviet Union and Latin America, gave shares to every citizen: they took the view that these industries, assuming they were worth anything, were already owned by the public. That was not the British way. State industries were owned by the Treasury on behalf of a different entity, the taxpayer. By the time of the Major government any conceptual distinction between asset sales and other public revenues had all but evaporated. The sale of the nuclear industry to the private sector announced in 1995 was openly described as 'yielding' £1–1.5 billion for tax cuts in the years before the next election. The sale of Railtrack was also expected to bring a similar windfall.

In the light of subsequent history, Thatcher's ministers were eager to proclaim their early commitment to the privatization cause. Yet in the early years, enthusiastic 'privatizers' were confined to a small group on the party's right wing. The Treasury's institutional interest was in raising money. The cabinet's economic committee in the early 1980s was deluged with Treasury papers demanding a departmental search for cash. What effect such 'fire sales' might have on the longer-term profitability of the industries concerned was of no interest to the Treasury. In the case of the transport and energy utilities, asset sales took the form of stripping out profitable activities, such as retail and property development, even if this made the industry less attractive for eventual sale as a whole. At British Rail, Treasury ministers showed no interest in privatization, but an obsession with swift property disposals.

Early sales were unspectacular. They included a tranche of shares in BP followed by Cable and Wireless, Amersham International, National Freight, British Aerospace, and British Rail hotels. Widest publicity went to the staff buy-out of National Freight in 1982 and the privatization of Britoil in the same year. Howe was keen for more. In a speech to the right-wing Selsdon Group in 1981 he remarked that 'since the election the issue of privatization has moved to the very forefront of politics'.[12] Yet to the public this was a marginal issue, as indeed it appeared to be to Thatcher herself. Within the Treasury, Lawson as financial secretary became principal campaigner for the cause. While his fellow-ministers were struggling to find new ways to control and cash-limit nationalized industries, Lawson had one answer: sell them. To him there was no such thing as a private-sector discipline for a public-sector enterprise. He described it as painting stripes on a mule and calling it a zebra.

What is strange about this timid beginning is that the early Thatcher cabinets had every incentive to get shot of nationalized industries. They occupied extraordinary amounts of ministerial time and effort. The financial and industrial troubles of British Leyland, British Steel and British Coal dominated the cabinet agenda. Their borrowing and subsidy requirements were a perpetual drain on public finances. In 1979, they were costing each taxpayer an average of £300 a year at 1995 prices.[13] Costs dominated all discussion of their future. Sponsoring ministers tried hard to sustain the tradition of arm's-length autonomy for the industry boards if only because the more 'commercial' they were the easier it might be to cut subsidy. A nationalized board under early Thatcher probably came nearest to the 1945 Morrisonian ideal of a public corporation: declared objectives backed by financial targets but not under the aegis of ministers or directly accountable to parliament.

'Arm's-length' proved as transient as its comrade 'hands off'.

27

It met the expectations neither of politicians nor of the public. Nationalization, as we saw in chapter one, was not the same as control. By declining to meddle, at least publicly, in the affairs of the industries, ministers found that they had responsibility but no power. The Treasury attempted to use 'chairman's letters' to lay down financial and policy objectives for the industry boards. Yet as the Attlee government had found, ministers hated these letters as much as did the chairmen. Nobody wanted to publicize a directive for fear of being blamed for its results. All had a vested interest in not revealing the criteria by which an industry was being run, so they could pass the buck in a crisis. The chairman would be invited to lunch, or the whole board to dinner. Furious argument would surround the fixing of the annual borrowing limit, the subsidy or fares or prices. At times of strikes and price rises, ministers would nudge and wink and even plead. But relations were always said to be 'deteriorating'.

In 1981 the Central Policy Review Staff produced a document aimed at 'transforming the relationship between government and the nationalized industries' by means of tighter targets and performance monitoring – the cash limit and the value-for-money audit. On a different tack, Howe set one of his officials, William Ryrie, to draw up rules whereby private investment could contribute to public-sector industries. They became a standing joke. Ryrie drew them so tightly as to make them inoperable. Not a pound of private/public investment was allowed through under the 'Ryrie Rules'. Other ideas along similar lines proliferated from ministers, including BT 'Buzby Bonds' and North Sea oil bonds. All were beaten to death by the Treasury as mere gimmicks either for avoiding privatization or for redefining government stock.

The debate over privatization received new impetus following the 1983 election and Lawson's move from the energy department back to the Treasury as Chancellor. He regarded tinkering with nationalized industries as fundamentally misguided and a distraction from the central task of privatizing them. The sale of half of British Telecom had been postponed to 1984, as had the sale of

British Airways. The BT sale was a huge political success. At £3.7 billion, it was by far the biggest equity offering ever made anywhere in the world.[14] The 1983 manifesto was bold, pledging shipbuilding, airways, steel, cars and airports to the private sector, with tentative mentions of gas and electricity.

Political enthusiasm for privatization now found itself riding in happy tandem with fiscal necessity. Lawson found it significant that Treasury officials who worked on nationalized industries, 'whatever their political views . . . nearly all ended up convinced that nationalization did not work and in practice was positively harmful'.[15] But that did not take their collective eye off the ball. The nationalized industries were not just to be tightly controlled and stripped of profitable assets (British Rail lost its hotels, ferries, harbours, hovercraft, advertising sales and most non-operational property at this time). They offered a more tempting prospect, as a source not just of once-off capital but of on-going revenue. The result was one of the most extraordinary incidents in the short history of public industry, the Treasury's consultative paper of December 1984.[16]

The normal financial target for most of the industries was that they should 'break even over time', an objective seldom realized. The Treasury wanted this replaced by specific financial targets, adjustable each year and backed by statute. The paper treated the public utilities as no different from government departments. In this respect, the industry boards and their chairmen were obstacles to more efficient oversight. Lawson saw the Treasury as a holding company with the nationalized industries as subsidiaries. Ministers should be able to sack their chairmen more easily, and to break up or privatize all or part of the industries without legislation or argument. More radical still was the suggestion that external finance (borrowing and subsidy) could be 'negative' as well as positive, provided industry prices were driven high enough. Since any surpluses could be seized by the Treasury at will, the nationalized monopolies offered a potential source of Treasury revenue.

In the 1985–6 public-spending white paper, the industries

29

were expected to cost the taxpayer £3.2 billion that year. The Treasury proposed that this loss be converted into a cash surplus by 1988 by means of above-inflation price rises. Electricity was set a 'negative external finance limit' of £1.3 billion in 1987 and again in 1988, rising to £1.8 billion in 1989. Similar surpluses were to be removed from gas and the Post Office. The Commons energy committee protested at rises in energy prices being syphoned off by the Treasury. 'Despite the strenuous denial of Treasury witnesses,' it said, 'we cannot avoid the conclusion that the only plausible motivation for the large increase in the electricity supply industry's negative external finance limit ... was to raise additional revenue in order to reduce the PSBR.'[17] A sceptic might judge that the Treasury was using the monopoly pricing power of the nationalized sector to reduce taxation – as it was using nationalized industry asset sales. It had discovered what in technical terms was its own private 'fiscal adjustor'.

One of the few analysts to notice the constitutional significance of this proposal, Tony Prosser, pointed out that it would give the Treasury a source of revenue by executive action. This was taxation without specific legislative authority. The Treasury proposed that its new powers be subject only to negative parliamentary order, the mildest of all forms of oversight. British Gas, also targeted as a milch-cow, protested that 'the Corporation's board would, to all intents and purposes, be reduced to the role of a management committee acting at the ultimate behest of the Treasury'.[18] The Treasury argued, not unreasonably, that years of ill-discipline on the part of these industries justified the taxpayer in claiming some return on his past outlays. But that saw the industries as merely spendthrift enterprises, not as public services. Monopoly pricing and the seizure of the resulting surpluses was public-sector profiteering, unrelated to the needs or long-term planning of the industries themselves.

In chapter twelve we examine the pressures that were leading the Treasury down this road. Those on both taxes and borrowing were intense. But Lawson was right. The only way of avoiding such pressure affecting every area of public spending was privatization. In the event, the rising pace of privatization, coupled with the furious reaction of nationalized industry chairmen, led Lawson to withdraw the Treasury paper. He learned that the best way to proceed with a policy of stealth was by stealth. The Treasury had been unnecessarily frank. The concept of 'negative external finance' was imposed on the industries individually rather than as a general policy. (As we shall see, the concept of surplus seizure was to have far wider application in the 1990s.) By 1987 gas, electricity and the Post Office were all having surpluses taken by the Treasury, while rail fares were rising well ahead of inflation to reduce BR's subsidy. This stripped industries of all control over their capital programmes and caused that control to revert to the Treasury. In 1989 the nationalized sector overall yielded a surplus. The implication to the Public Accounts Committee was that in future, 'wider considerations of government economic policy would probably take precedence over the economic efficiency and welfare' of the industries themselves.[19]

The early privatizations had been transfers of ownership from the state sector into the competitive market place. Many of the enterprises concerned had previously been acquired by government, like the British Empire, 'in a fit of absence of mind'. Cable and Wireless, Amersham and National Freight slid back into private ownership with little fuss, British Airways with slightly more. But as the 'natural monopoly' utilities such as gas, electricity and water came forward new concerns came into play. They were not internally competitive. New forms of regulation were needed. The government might divest itself of ownership, but it could not divest itself of a degree of control. These industries were to remain 'political' entities.

The novelty of what the government was doing continued to invite admiration and confusion. John Moore was minister in charge of privatization at the Treasury in the mid-1980s. He wrote in 1986 that 'privatization means power, the kind of power that matters to ordinary people, the power to make choices, the power to control their own lives'.[20] That is true where privatization leads to choice. But the conversion of utilities into private

31

companies did not necessarily lead to choice, merely a new name on the top of the bill. Corporations such as British Telecom, British Gas and the water companies were being rushed to market to relieve public borrowing. Little thought was given to the philosophy of their regulation and even less to injecting into them competition or other market disciplines.

Moore and Lawson at the Treasury acknowledged this and sought to break up state monopolies into potentially competitive units before sale. Lawson failed over British Telecom and British Gas, the latter after a fierce battle with the then energy secretary Peter Walker and his 'craggy, overbearing chairman', Sir Denis Rooke. Telecoms and gas were privatized as monopolies (some competition was introduced later). Thatcher claimed that she took sides against Lawson 'in order to achieve privatization in the available time-scale'.[21] She implausibly pleaded lack of parliamentary time to make gas more competitive. But she recognized the strength of Lawson's case when it came to electricity, though it cost her the resignation of the electricity chief, Walter Marshall. She recalled that in conversation with him, 'I again and again insisted that whatever structure we created must provide genuine competition.'[22] The water industry was divided geographically, with regulation and inspection passing to a National Rivers Authority and tariffs fixed by a regulator, Ofwat.

Thatcher's chief concern was to derive a political return from privatization. In meetings with the Treasury she stressed the need to sell fast, and if necessary cheap, to the widest number of shareholders. This led to many undervaluations which cost the taxpayer dear. British Ports was thirty-four times oversubscribed, electricity ten times oversubscribed, Rolls-Royce nine times and British Airways twenty-three times.[23] At the end of the decade the National Audit Office calculated that the manner of privatization cost the taxpayer £2.4 billion in expenses and asset values forgone, half of it on electricity and water.[24] The economist John Kay, who was a constant critic of privatization, concluded that 'the conflict between privatization and liberalization is no longer a conflict but a rout'.[25] Lawson himself admitted that 'the most serious criticism is that the government concentrated too much on ownership and not enough on competition',[26] though it was not a criticism he shared.

Hindsight on this subject risks distortion. Britain was treading uncharted territory in privatizing such huge companies. The learning curve was steep. By the late 1980s monopoly utilities were tumbling into the private sector, dragging behind them regulatory chains of varying degrees of strength. This regulation became controversial and, by the mid-1990s, was subject to real strain in the case of water, electricity and gas. Under Attlee the 'public interest' in the utilities had been expressed simply. His new public corporations kept their managers, factories and head-quarters buildings, from which they conducted guerrilla warfare on ministers.[27] The public was expected to rest content that what it owned must, by that very fact, be run in its best interest. Accountability was axiomatic rather than systematic.

The argument for Thatcher's privatization of monopoly indus-tries was that it brought regulation out into the open. The franchise granted to the privatized companies exposed the public obligations of the monopolies, and did so the more emphatically because they were privately owned. Government thus divested itself of ownership and of any concern in the management of labour and capital. But it did not divest itself of often detailed contractual obligations on the industries, or of regulation of pricing policy and thus of the availability of investment resources. Indeed by exposing these matters to public view, regulation had the effect of increasing both public interest and public control. The new regulators – such as Ofgas, Ofwat, Ofrail and Offer (for electricity) – were instantly battered by covert and overt pressure.

These factors were diverse and their interpretation increasingly politicized. BT had been given a 'universal service obligation' under its licence, to maintain callboxes in remote places and offer services to the blind and deaf. Similar obligations were imposed on the gas, electricity and water companies. They had to help the elderly and infirm, maintain supplies to rural areas and, in the case of water, worry about access to land and water sports.

Energy and landscape conservation were a source of constant friction between regulators and industries, as they had been under nationalization. The rail regulator had to worry about helping the franchising director to sell his operating franchises, code for keeping track charges down. On this he had initially to 'take into account' directions from the Secretary of State. There was even confusion over whether the regulator or the minister had responsibility for the number of stations that would sell through tickets or the fate of the Fort William sleeper. Responsibility no longer lay within the industry.

These requirements could be both onerous and subjective. The profitability of a company or an entire industry might turn on what many industries saw as 'a regulatory whim'. Yet the regulators' constitutional status was curious. Given the monopoly character of the utilities, the public interest and the interest of consumers had to be expressed statutorily rather than in the market place. In place of a minister answerable to parliament was a regulator, also answerable to parliament but not (directly) through any minister. The regulators were defined as 'non-ministerial departments', as if they were governments outside the government. They were creatures of the British civil-service tradition, chosen secretly as reliable and well-meaning individuals, not institutions or boards. The regulators did not hold public hearings and they reached decisions in private. In 1995 the director of Ofgas, Clare Spottiswoode, gave a candid speech in which she admitted that she felt wholly unaccountable. Neither the public nor parliament could take her to the Monopolies Commission if she was thought to be in the pocket of the industry (as some did think). She admitted her reports to parliament were 'not worth the paper they are printed on'. She was scrutinized by the National Audit Office and was subject to judicial review. But as for 'What is our accountability? . . . In truth very little.'[28]

There was no guiding philosophy for this new form of control, any more than there had been for nationalization itself. The terms of reference for telecoms and water regulation, suggested by Stephen Littlechild in the mid-1980s, implied that regulation should be a proxy for private-sector competition. Prices should be fixed so as to suppress costs and release money for investment. As we have seen, competition was not uppermost in the cabinet's mind as privatization proceeds poured into the Treasury from the mid-1980s onwards. Instead the interests of the environment, the consumer and political lobbies became more dominant, especially after the hostile reaction to water privatization, due to large rises in bills to meet new investment. The regulators were soon caught between public and consumer pressure to act toughly against monopoly abuse, and no less fierce pressure from industries whose share price (and executive share options) the regulator could determine. The former head of Thatcher's policy unit, John Redwood, wrote that 'the more detailed regulation becomes, the more the other benefits of privatization in terms of management freedom and innovation are likely to be lost'.[29] Redwood's predecessor, Ferdinand Mount, wrote in 1987 that 'it has become increasingly clear that the regulators have no teeth and the operators no conscience'.[30]

As the 1990s progressed, the privatized monopolies found themselves unable to shake off the incubus of politics. In October 1994, after the water regulator had reduced charges in the South-West area, it was Tory MPs and ministers who congratulated each other on bringing this about.[31] When Spottiswoode arrived at Ofgas in place of Sir James McKinnon the industry felt that a change of government had occurred. McKinnon had fought it tooth and nail on price. Spottiswoode was more concerned with injecting competition and resisted conservation costs being loaded on to gas bills. Small wonder the industries were soon complaining of whim. John Baker of National Power called in 1994 for a 'college of regulators' to draw up common criteria and give consistency to decisions. The Institute for Public Policy Research called for public hearings, as in America.

Early in 1995 the rail regulator, John Swift, decided, apparently off his own bat, to change the basis on which Railtrack would charge for access to its infrastructure. This transformed the value of Railtrack as a private company and the value of the

35

railway operating franchises. In March of the same year the electricity regulator, Stephen Littlechild, acted 'in response to widespread public concern'[32] at what were seen as large cash reserves built up by the distribution companies. Despite having just fixed prices, it was thought for five years, he announced that he would be cutting them and tilting the balance away from the shareholders. This devastated share prices and undermined the government's recent flotation of the electricity generating companies. Littlechild appeared to be behaving in a way as arbitrary and vulnerable to politics as any minister had in the days of nationalization. Small wonder one observer held that Britain's privatized utilities were really parastatal hybrids, which elsewhere in Europe would be counted as public enterprises.[33]

In part these were inevitable teething troubles of a completely new form of government, that of private monopoly regulation. At the same time it was naïve to think that these monopolies were not still regarded by the public as in the 'public domain', if not the public sector. Neither the electorate nor politicians were going to leave them in peace. The political row over the pay of senior executives in the gas and water industries showed as much. These were not just private companies. Nor had the government really believed it. The Electricity Act vested regulation 'jointly' in both the Secretary of State and the regulator. We shall see in chapter eleven how railway privatization proved to be more a redrawing of the boundaries of public-sector control. Bidders for government railway contracts were soon milling about with regulators, ministers and Treasury officials either in cahoots or in contention. As Prosser concluded, 'the regulators have had to take precisely the sorts of discretionary judgements which the system was intended to avoid ... reflecting social as well as economic objectives'.[34]

This applies beyond the utilities. As we saw above, Thatcher's early reaction to privatization had been cautious. She was nervous about giving up control over any 'flagship' British industry. She resisted the privatization of coal, railways and the Post Office to the last. She was no less concerned about oil. Lawson referred to 'Margaret's acute sensitivity that privatization of the British National Oil Corporation's operating arm would somehow lose control of part of her oil. She rejected a number of BNOC privatization options on these grounds.'[35] Lawson's response was to create what he called a 'golden share', to be kept by the government after a sale. This, he said, was to 'enable [government] to prevent control of the company from falling into unsuitable hands ... The term "unsuitable" had to be used, rather than foreign, to avoid falling foul of Community law; but everyone knew what it was likely to mean.'[36]

These shares were retained not just in the case of Britoil (as BNOC became) but in the majority of commercial privatizations. They were held in British Aerospace, Cable and Wireless, Jaguar, BT, Rolls-Royce, British Gas and the water, electricity and airports companies. BA has a version of a golden share. The powers granted by these shares were not puny. They were designed to prevent hostile takeovers by foreigners and encompassed powers over share issues, voting rights and the disposal of assets. The golden shares in water and regional electricity companies expired in 1995, but remained open in gas, telecommunications and electricity generation. The Britoil golden share enabled the government to pack the board should a hostile bidder stage a raid on its shares, and to exercise a veto on any AGM vote.

This is precisely what happened in December 1987, when BP staged a bid for Britoil. BP was not a foreign bidder and Lawson's original purpose in taking a golden share in Britoil did not apply. BP was simply stronger than Britoil and wanted to buy it. In theory, the matter should have been left to the Monopolies Commission. But the golden share lay enticingly on the table and ministers were unable to keep their hands off it. The politics of Britoil was the politics of Scotland. The Scottish secretary, Malcolm Rifkind, warned the cabinet that this was a 'sufficiently sensitive issue' to justify activating the golden share. The Britoil golden share was duly used as a negotiating card. BP would be allowed to take over Britoil on a number of detailed conditions. These included continued North Sea exploration; the company remaining in Glasgow; research and development moving north of the border along with 'between fifty and seventy senior executives'; and Aberdeen staying as the operating base for the North Sea. The barter was a classic of 1970s government corporatism.

The Britoil case was a one-off. The company was Scotland's biggest and Scottish politics had a logic of their own. This was the only time a golden share was openly activated under Thatcher, and it was specifically not activated to stop Jaguar being sold to Ford. But the incident does illustrate the vulnerability even of privatized companies to political pressure where any weapon is left in the hands of ministers. Golden shares were a loaded gun which any left-wing politician or central planner could pick up and point at a recalcitrant company. If Lawson could use them to buy off political criticism in Scotland, what might Labour do?

To most observers, the new structure was unquestionably an advance.[37] The exposure of regulatory judgements to publicity was better than the secret protocols that used to govern relations between government and nationalized industries. As Thatcher wrote, 'regulation which had, when in the public sector, been covert now had to be overt and specific'.[38] Pricing decisions were publicized by regulators and could be more clearly related to performance standards. Politicians and the media could make more informed comments. The freeing of the industries from Treasury investment control enabled them to take a more dispassionate view of their needs, and ended the risk of the 'surplus seizure' planned for them in 1984. The consumer might no longer be 'owner' of a utility, but the consumer as lobbyist and voter probably had more leverage on them than ever before. In addition, the 1990s saw real attempts to bring some competitive pressure to bear on the gas and electricity generation industries, while technology was doing the same to telecoms.

That said, there was never any likelihood of government relinquishing dominant control over the public utilities, whether implemented through statute, minister or regulator. They were too big, too important to the public and too monopolistic in character. As Christopher Foster wrote, the industries were originally nationalized by Labour because regulation in the private sector had not worked. Ministers had no ownership and inadequate control. Now nationalization had not worked either, so private ownership with extra control was to be tried again.[39] This was the basis of Nicholas Ridley's celebrated boast that 'utilities which we have privatized or intend to privatize are more easily controlled when they are in the private sector'.[40] Thatcher put it more succinctly. Privatization with regulation, she wrote, 'provides a clearer and better discipline'.[41]

By the mid-1990s the new regime was yielding increases in efficiency without glaring examples of monopoly abuse. *The Economist* reported in 1995 that 'total factor productivity' had risen in all industries while prices had fallen.[42] It questioned whether, in the absence of real competition, private ownership had made the crucial difference. Non-privatized corporations such as the Post Office and British Rail had also seen big advances in productivity over these years. The magazine's answer was that the difference was real. Tory utilities privatization might be no more than a sophisticated subcontract, a licence to deliver a service to the public at a fixed price. But it had invigorated the industries' investment policies and exposed government control to public view.

What was not resolved was the basis of accountability. To whom were the regulators answerable? Although any body established by statute is answerable in some sense to parliament, Clare Spottiswoode pointed out in 1995 that this meant nobody (though she in part answered her own question in June 1995, when she demanded and won a 22 per cent pay rise from the government). Most industry chairmen felt themselves at the mercy of an individual regulator's judgement of the state of public opinion towards their policies, and indeed their pay. There was no formal accountability to parliament via ministers, only informally through appearances at select committee meetings. Ministers controlled regulators' terms of reference and were free to pass laws changing them. Yet ministers denied any further responsibility. They had declared the regulators 'non-ministerial', independent, agents of the state yet responsible to it only in some metaphysical sense. Of all the institutions of Thatcherism, the utilities regulators were the least coherent or democratic.

CHAPTER THREE

THE FIRST CASUALTY

If I be served such another trick, I'll have my brains ta'en out and buttered, and give them to a dog for a new year's gift – SHAKESPEARE

Margaret Thatcher detested local government as much as she detested the trade unions and the Labour party. There is no reference in her memoirs that is not pejorative. Her colleagues were frequently shocked by her vehemence on the subject. She saw local councils as irresponsible, left-wing and profligate. Government departments and nationalized industries she thought she could control. 'Local government as usual is overspending' is the comment that litters her memoirs, whether or not it was true. Local councils were holes not just in the public-spending bucket but in the whole Thatcherite political economy. Worse, they imposed a tax that was to Thatcher a fixation, a tax on property known as a rate.

Rates were regarded by most fiscal experts as robust taxes. They were simple to calculate, mildly progressive and easy to collect. Houses owed rates and houses could not move. Houses were wealth, and a property tax was a rough proxy for a wealth tax, estimated on what a property could theoretically rent for in the open market. Yet to many Tories the rates were demons. They appeared to penalize home-owners, the elderly in large houses and those who improved their property: the 'little old lady living alone'. Worse, they were a particular burden in left-wing cities, where councils used them as a weapon of redistribution

41

from rich to poor. In autumn 1974 the Tory leader in Opposition, Edward Heath, had ordered Thatcher as environment spokesman to promise to abolish the rates, very much against her judgement at the time. She recorded in her second volume of memoirs that she felt 'bruised and resentful to be bounced again into policies which had not been properly thought out'.[1] The pledge duly appeared in the party's October 1974 election manifesto. The election was lost but the rates-abolition pledge haunted Thatcher from then on.

The saga of the poll tax would be tangential to our theme were it not for the motive and manner of its introduction and the consequence for local democracy of its collapse. It has mesmerized contemporary historians for its role in Thatcher's eventual downfall.[2] But poll tax was not a passing folly. It was more a wrinkle in the demise of pluralist democracy in Britain. It accelerated that demise, an acceleration that was not reversed with its abolition. For central government it was merely expensive. For local democracy it was a catastrophe. At the moment of its introduction, local government retained control over roughly 60 per cent of its total revenue. By the time of its abolition that percentage had shrunk overall to 18 per cent.

On taking office in 1979 Thatcher was, as we have seen, pre-eminently concerned with cutting public spending and thus borrowing. Narrowly defined, this did not include local spending, except insofar as the latter was covered by grants and loans from the centre. But the wider definition of 'general government expenditure' embraced all local-government activity, including that totem of the politics of the early 1980s, the public-sector borrowing requirement (PSBR). Any politician intent on cutting government's 'total take' from the economy had therefore to worry about local government. How far they needed to worry is the subject of controversy. Economists are inclined to take a more sophisticated view of the contribution to national wealth of government investment and trading activity and distinguish it from, for instance, transfers between taxpayers and social-security recipients. In Germany and the

United States central government exercises no control over local spending.

What is most extraordinary, in view of what was to occur, is that the Tories inherited from Labour a more or less disciplined local financial scene. Under Thatcher's first environment secretary, Michael Heseltine, councils maintained that discipline. The 1970–74 Tory government had upheaved local councils in an expensive reorganization. Bureaucratic reorganization is always costly, both immediately and over time as new patterns of accountability bed down. The 1974 changes led to rate rises of up to 30 per cent in 1974–75 and a fierce battle between the subsequent Labour environment secretary, Tony Crosland, and the local-government lobbies. Central grants, paid on a percentage basis, were at the time supplying two-thirds of local spending. New town and county halls, housing estates, swimming pools and theatres blossomed across the land. In Manchester in May 1975 Crosland gave his celebrated warning that 'the party is over'. The councils heard him. Most were Tory-led and, backed by cuts in central grants, held current spending roughly constant in real terms for the remaining three years of the Labour government.

Heseltine continued that discipline. Encouraged by the Treasury, he demanded real cuts of 1 per cent a year over the next two years, with central-government grants falling accordingly. This was at a time when central-government spending was rising strongly, not least on public-sector pay, which had a direct impact on local spending. The effect of the cut in central grants was to hold down spending but inevitably to push up rates. This combined with the early unpopularity of the Thatcher government to devastate Tory support in local elections. The Tories lost half the council seats they fought in 1980, and then lost half the ones they fought in 1981, when the Greater London Council also fell to Labour. By 1981 the stage was set for confrontation between the government and local councils across the whole range of the latter's activities. The war was to last for almost ten years.

The first stage of the attack was like a cat playing with a

mouse before the kill. Heseltine had first hoped to reduce local spending by castigating 'overspenders'. Then came statutory 'transitional arrangements' whereby he could adjust central grants to penalize those councils declared to be spending more than they needed to. Then in 1981 the old rate-support grant, calculated by a complex formula of needs and resources, was replaced by a single block grant, which was to prove even more complicated. This included penalties that meant a council losing grant for every pound it spent above what Whitehall thought it should have spent. This doubled the rates cost of any 'extravagance'. Since rates to poor people in the high-spending councils were rebated (by government), the impact of doubling was felt most sorely by businesses and by better-off householders. Government penalties thus had the bizarre effect of hurting mostly Tory ratepayers.

Heseltine was initially successful. Local spending was restrained. It actually fell in real terms over the first three years of the new government, making six years of restraint since Crosland. If from the total we remove police spending, where the Home Office was encouraging swift rises in budgets, local expenditure in 1985 was still more or less where it had been in real terms when the government took over. In view of the propaganda used by Thatcher and her colleagues throughout the 1980s, this point should be stressed. In 1980, local authorities were spending £24.5 billion, which was 28.3 per cent of the public sector and 10.5 per cent of gross domestic product. By 1983, according to CIPFA, real-terms spending had fallen to £23.9 billion (10.1 per cent of GDP and 26.3 per cent of the public sector). Even at the end of the 1980s and after the surge that preceded the poll tax, local government's share of public spending was lower than when Thatcher took office. The original policy had worked. There was no case in overall macro-economic terms for the upheavals that eventually led to the community charge. Indeed, since upheavals invariably cause more spending, rises in local budgets in the late 1980s can in large part be put down to the introduction of the charge.

44

Thatcher, her cabinet and her party ignored these figures. 'Ministers might exhort, bewail and threaten but local-government spending grew inexorably in real terms, year after year,' she declared, with no supporting evidence.[3] She fastened her gaze on a dozen left-wing councils where a combination of profligacy and reduced central grants had indeed sent spending and rates bills soaring. Councils such as Liverpool and Camden had embarked on a long and costly campaign of defiance. The new Labour GLC cut bus fares and levied a supplementary rate to do so, as it was legally entitled to do and with the indubitable support of its electorate (albeit on Britain's notoriously low turnouts). These councils bit deep into the Tory soul. The obvious answer, let them spend and let them face their electorates, was unacceptable. So too was the answer, let them spend and let us hold them up as an example of what Labour government really means. Leaving the high-spenders unpunished implied a sign of lack of control. It was bad government. Thatcher was appealed to by 'our people' in these cities and she felt she had to respond.

The Treasury, and in particular its Chief Secretary, Leon Brittan, duly declared war on the environment department as defender of local autonomy. The concept of 'target' spending, fixed for each council, was introduced by the department, to be a benchmark against which both central grants and, later, capping were to be set. The department offered to cabinet various devices to make the target regime bite, to make high-spenders more directly accountable for their supposed profligacy. These included referendums, 'town polls' and mid-term elections. One such referendum was held in Labour Coventry and it went against a higher rate. This greatly appealed to Thatcher, but she curiously abandoned the idea when told that her backbenchers were opposed to it.[4] Had she been more robust she might have saved herself a deal of trouble.

The next stage in the battle was similarly modest. It took the form of a revival of the idea of abolishing the rates. A green paper from the environment department had the beguiling title of *Alternatives to Domestic Rates*,[5] but it covered territory familiar to

45

all inquiries on the subject since the Redcliffe-Maud report of 1969. An inquiry with an identical remit had been conducted by Sir Frank Layfield in 1976. All flitted through the garden of local autonomy before slamming up against the wall of Treasury control. A classic statement of the latter's antagonism towards local democracy came in response to Layfield's call for a clear decision to be made between, on the one hand, local taxation and accountability and, on the other hand, the centralization of both. An environment department green paper in 1977 had mused that 'the disadvantages of both the centralist and the localist approaches are clear and the Government does not think there is a case for the adoption of either'.[6] In other words, there was a case for the confusion of both.

The trouble with property taxes was not so much the principle – every Western country has them – as their application to British local government. The rates has become wayward and therefore unfair. They lacked 'accountability bite'. Ministers constantly claimed that of 35 million local voters only 18 million paid rates and three million of those had them reduced. Rebating in the poorer parts of inner cities meant that too few voters felt the famous 'bite' before going to the polls. In addition, some London boroughs were deriving as much as 75 per cent of rate income from (voteless) businesses. The argument was wildly overstated. The bulk of 'non-paying voters' were spouses of rate-payers. To imply that they were voting for profligacy without it costing them a penny was as absurd as to imply that wives of income-tax-paying husbands were equally unaccountable voters. As for businesses, they paid corporation tax to government without getting an extra vote. The debate over local government at the time rarely saw reason at a premium.

Heseltine's 1981 green paper read like an inquiry going through the motions. The ambition was clear. All those pondering local taxation at the time had as their central concern the enhancement of local accountability. They were not out to kill democracy but strengthen it. The old central rate-support grant, based on something called 'stepwise multiple regression analysis', was felt to be subsidizing profligacy at the expense of economy. Yet the system was incomprehensible. The existing tax and grant system had eroded the link between taxing and voting. 'Over-spending' was a metaphysical concept understood only by a handful of experts in the environment department in Marsham Street. Local treasurers, local politicians, let alone local electors, could not understand how their grants were calculated. They waited aghast each year to be told what seemed a wholly arbitrary figure before they could fix their rate.

Officials rehearsed what were now well-known options, reject-ing each in turn: local income tax, sales tax, capital value rating and poll tax. The last was dismissed cursorily. 'Try collecting that in Brixton,' one member of the drafting team is reported to have said.[7] Similar rejections of poll tax came from Tory research-ers, from respondents to the green paper and, conclusively, from the Conservative-led Commons environment committee. This last 'recommends strongly that a poll tax, even at a low level, should not be introduced'.[8] Meanwhile the Treasury pressure was becoming ever more intense. In July 1982 Brittan remarked that 'overspending will soon force any government to take further steps in the direction of central control'.[9]

This overspending was confined to about a dozen councils and it was more than balanced, overall, by restraint elsewhere. At the time the cabinet was having great difficulty holding back its own expenditure. It therefore turned to local spending that it half-controlled and demanded that it be cut by more than the cabinet was prepared to accept for itself. When this local cut was not fully achieved (though it was in part) the cabinet accused local councils of 'overspending'. This was explained by Nigel Lawson, then a junior minister at the Treasury, as 'local irresponsibility in exceeding government forecasts'. The cabinet's own overspend-ing, on the other hand, was due to 'conscious Government priorities' for defence, unemployment and the NHS.[10] Local councils were not allowed priorities of their own, whether or not they had put them to their electors.

There was little doubt who would win this struggle. The

47

outcome was the constitutional innovation of rate-capping, the legal limitation of local tax-raising power. This was a step so draconian and so counter to customary deference towards local democracy that not a single minister outside the Treasury was prepared to endorse it in cabinet at the time. Yet Thatcher ordered a plan for capping to be drawn up as a 'foolproof alternative to abolishing the rates'.[11] I recall Terry Heiser, the environment department official charged with the task, asking at the time, 'What would you do if your minister had just ordered you to abolish local democracy?' Rate-capping was duly added to GLC and metropolitan county abolition in a 1983 election manifesto that was universally hostile to local government. With the Argentinians out of the way and Arthur Scargill not yet over the horizon, 'loony Left' local councils were Thatcher's public enemy number one.

Patrick Jenkin now took over from Heseltine at environment. Not a sophisticated politician, Jenkin was on his way out rather than up. He was, like many in that position, eager to ingratiate himself with his boss. The department had followed up its previous green paper with a white one entitled simply *Rates*.[12] This stated baldly that 'the Government have concluded ... that rates should remain for the foreseeable future the main source of local revenue for local government'. Indeed the paper gave a hostage to fortune. Rates might not be popular, it said, but 'they are highly perceptible to ratepayers and they promote accountability. They are well understood, cheap to collect and very difficult to evade.'[13] Instead there would be selective rate-capping, introduced in the Rates Act of 1984. Capping galvanized local democracy as nothing had done in years. The sense of constitutional outrage within local government was echoed by the clarion calls of Livingstone's London battalions trying to save the GLC. The latter's 'Say no to no say' was an effective and popular campaign, drawing to the colours many (including Tories) whose distaste for Livingstone was outweighed by their concern that London should be stripped of any democratic voice (see chapter eight).

48

The government's local-government policy now slid with extraordinary speed towards chaos. A number of cities and London boroughs defied Whitehall by passing budgets above target or, if capped, by refusing to set any rate at all. Whitehall decisions on targets and grants were so opaque as to be easy meat for judicial review as 'unreasonable'. Camden council won a case against Whitehall's penalty. Derek Hatton's Liverpool refused to set a rate. Officials at the environment department were seriously worried that the cabinet had bitten off more than it could chew. Hardly a year went by without another local-government finance bill, as Marsham Street wrestled to implement the *dirigisme* demanded by Howe and Brittan at the Treasury. One count gave fifty acts of parliament on local government in the government's first decade in office.[14]

A miasma of overspends, targets, penalties and caps left even the most responsible local treasurers mystified as to what was expected of them. From every meeting and conference in London they brought back to their town and county halls nothing but a Whitehall antagonism bordering on hatred. Downing Street had terrorized local government's one-time allies in Marsham Street. Everybody not of the Treasury faith was tarred with the brush of Liverpool's Militant Tendency. In September 1983 Jenkin had declared that the old consensus by which local and central government had respected each others' wishes had broken down. 'The government has a duty to heed the increasingly bitter complaints of domestic and commercial ratepayers. There can be no room in our unitary state for unilateral declarations of independence by individual local authorities relying on claims of a local mandate.'[15] Thatcher was roaming Downing Street looking for someone to fight. As David Butler commented in his joint history of the poll tax, 'None of her ministers, least of all the beleaguered Jenkin, could mistake her views on the town hall barons.'[16]

Jenkin was desperate to find a way to rid his mistress of the 'turbulent priest' of local finance. There followed a sequence of incidents, each of them markers along the otherwise puzzling path to poll tax. Rate-capping was on the statute book in 1984, meeting Thatcher's need to bring the worst overspenders to heel. Norman Fowler at the social-security department was to propose that everybody liable for rate rebate nonetheless had to pay 20 per cent of their liability. Local referendums were still on the agenda. Yet in the autumn of 1984 Jenkin persuaded Thatcher to let him return to the barren larder of an alternative to the rates. She was reluctant. She made this plain and restated her reluctance in her memoirs.[17] Had she not been entering the toughest phase of her campaign against the miners, the instinctive caution she was later to show towards health service reform might have won through. As it was, she was receptive to any passing triumph.

The resumed search for an alternative to the rates was an object lesson in the inadequacy of British government. It achieved the precise opposite of what the instigators of reform originally intended. Jenkin delegated the task to his junior ministers, Kenneth Baker and William Waldegrave. Both had reputations as being on the Left of the party. Both had spurs to win in the court of the boss. Waldegrave set up a team of officials and outside advisers, none of whom had first-hand experience of local government. Most of the officials had previously drafted white and green papers rubbishing poll tax. They saw little point in restating such opposition against the express demand of ministers for fresh thinking. They started work after the traumatic 1984 party conference (hit by the IRA bombers), where their existence was announced by an eager Jenkin. A six-month target was agreed. The result, Waldegrave later claimed, 'was a model of how modern policy should be formulated. There was a project team. There were outsiders. There was published analysis and enormous consultation. There was modelling of outcomes using the latest technologies.'[18]

In the event there was little consultation, at least until after the dynamics of Thatcher's cabinet had made the tax all but irrevocable. Such reaction as took place was not so much hostile as incredulous. Most significant was the lack of debate among other cabinet ministers involved. Many have later sought to distance themselves from poll tax, but they were kept fully informed and while some asked hostile questions, they could not complain they were not warned. The Prime Minister held a special Chequers meeting for at least half the cabinet in March 1985 to discuss nothing else. Present were the Welsh, Scottish and Ulster secretaries and the Home Secretary, as well as the environment and Treasury teams. Of these only the Chancellor, Nigel Lawson, was absent. 'I never liked giving up my Sundays in this way,' he reflected. He 'foolishly' sent his Chief Secretary, Peter Rees, in his place after briefing him 'to register my firm opposition to poll tax and [giving] him the arguments to use'.[19]

Lawson's arguments were no different from those previously marshalled against poll tax but came with the authority of a Chancellor. As he pointed out in his memoirs, all his criticisms were vindicated and all his predictions for the tax proved true. Yet he was not persuasive. Perhaps he was too much of a loner. Perhaps the Treasury had made too many enemies to find support in what seemed at this stage largely an intellectual dispute. To a cabinet hostile towards local government, poll tax's chief virtue was that it would punish local councils. Local income tax would, so Thatcher thought, be an invitation to local irresponsibility. She was anyway trying to cut income taxes. Local sales tax would have shoppers moving back and forth across local boundaries. New forms of property tax (such as was finally introduced) were too much like rates. For a brief moment poll tax seemed a magic elixir. It was the tax that nobody knew, and therefore no experience or evidence could be marshalled against it.

Thatcher was initially a sceptic. As we shall see through most of this book, she was rarely on the radical side of policy innovation, preferring to let others go out on a Thatcherite limb before deciding whether to join them or chop it off. But once she felt politically committed she was adamant. She had already been badly jolted early in 1985 by the political impact of rates revaluation in Scotland, with a marked shift from commercial to domestic uprating. Throughout 1985 Scotland was to fuel the reformist zeal – as it later led opposition to its manifestation in the poll tax. In the case of poll tax she persuaded herself to abandon an instinctive caution and become an enthusiast. To be against the tax after the spring of 1985 was to be against her. Cabinet reservations were expressed – Leon Brittan at the Home Office worried about the tax seeming a tax on voting – but there was no cabinet revolt. A cabinet sub-committee met regularly through the summer on poll tax details with, round the table, Douglas Hurd, Willie Whitelaw, Norman Fowler, Norman Tebbit and John Wakeham. Poll tax was a matter for the environment department, the Treasury and the Prime Minister. If they could sort out their differences, other cabinet ministers were reluctant to intervene. When poll tax was abolished five years later, its executioners were mostly the same ministers who had framed and implemented it – as Thatcher bitterly pointed out.[20] Nobody thought to resign.

The backers of the poll tax presented it, above all else, as an exercise in strengthened accountability. They held this position even when local accountability had been stripped from the tax by capping, rebating and other centrally financed reliefs. They also declared it fairer than rates, though from the moment of its implementation this was patently absurd. Rates might have become distorted in their incidence, largely through rebating. Poll taxes are regressive and unfair by their very nature. Rich and poor alike, slum dwellers and dukes, all paid the same. That is why poll taxes were, as Nigel Lawson pointed out, 'notorious throughout the ages'. They were the earliest taxes to be abandoned, after peasants' revolts in the fourteenth century, to be replaced by taxes on property and eventually on income. But in theory a local poll tax was a decentralist measure. It had the famous 'bite'. Once a council fixed its poll tax, everybody had to pay it and either approve or resent it come the next election. It put nettle into democracy's grass roots.

Everything that subsequently happened to poll tax neutralized the sting. The tax that evolved over the course of 1985 was termed a 'graduated residents' charge' that would run alongside the rates. It would be rebated for the poor, but everybody would have to pay something. The tax would be harder to collect than the rates, but not much harder, ministers were told. Round it was constructed a wider package of reforms to local finance. These included ideas on annual elections, wider charging for services and a new central grant formula. The non-domestic, or business, rate would no longer be fixed by local councils but would be nationalized. Two-tier local government would be eliminated and replaced by 'more efficient' single-tier councils. This would wipe out the counties as separate political entities.

No package could have been more full of constitutional dynamite. Yet only Lawson registered sustained opposition. In a memorandum (quoted in full in his memoirs)[21] he welcomed parts of the package, including nationalizing the business rate, but dismissed poll tax as 'completely unworkable and politically catastrophic'. On the environment department's own figures, a London couple on low income but not destitute could pay 22 per cent of their income in poll tax, while a rich suburbanite would pay 1 per cent. How anybody could describe such a tax as fair was, to Lawson, astonishing. He was deeply suspicious of Waldegrave bringing into the study team his mentor, Lord Rothschild, a man who 'prided himself on having no political judgement: he was above that sort of thing'. The tax's other outside enthusiast, Sir Christopher Foster of Coopers and Lybrand, was actually summoned by Lawson and berated for his support for Waldegrave's proposal. Foster had been involved in energy privatization. He was to add poll tax and the railways to his portfolio as Thatcherism's Dr Strangelove. Foster sensed the Treasury was about to experience a rare defeat and decided to differ from Lawson.

Lawson himself proposed what amounted to a new property tax, with single-person rebates and a nationalized business rate. He also wanted education, which took half of all local spending, removed totally from local government. Aware of the original terms of the debate, Lawson pointed out that this would leave local councils raising virtually all their revenue from local sources to spend on matters over which they had real discretion, such as street cleaning, parks, libraries and the environment. Electors really would 'vote the rate'. That was the best route to accountability. Lawson emerges from the poll tax saga as one of the few Thatcherites able to stand back and take a detached view of the localist/centralist dichotomy. He was unashamedly for centralism, but at least had a model for a new agency-based local government, looking after parks and drains with a capped property tax to pay for it.

The cabinet committee approved the 'dual running' of the so-called 'residents' charge' and rates at the 1985 Tory party conference. The charge would be presented by the new environment secretary, the same Kenneth Baker who had been party to its invention. Lawson continued his opposition, but was content at least that the rates would stay in being under dual running. The original studies had intended that the rates would wither and poll tax take over; Lawson hoped the opposite. The debate still seemed open as the study team continued to refine its proposals.

More significant, Lawson secured a concession: Treasury capping would continue to be available for the new tax as it had for the rates. This sleight of hand subverted the central point of the tax, that it would expose profligate councils to accountability at election time. A capped poll tax meant a capped council. Blame for reduced services would pass up a different accountability route, to central government. This duly happened. Each year the Tories lost more seats at local elections as odium was heaped on their heads by local Labour and Liberal Democrat politicians for any curtailment of local services. Thatcher noticed this inconsistency. She wrote that in an ideal world the poll tax would have meant an end to capping, 'but the world which years of socialism in our inner cities had created was far from ideal. I was determined that capping powers would remain. Indeed before the end I would find myself pressing for much more extensive community charge capping than was ever envisaged for the rates.'22 Her aversion to local government thus led her to abandon the central purpose of the poll tax adventure, greater accountability. Capping was a savage blow to poll tax. Baker and Waldegrave should have abandoned the tax there and then: it was holed below the waterline. No council would be permitted to be truly profligate. Central government, not local electors, would stop it.

The poll tax green paper, *Paying for Local Government*,[23] passed full cabinet on 9 January 1986. It was the cabinet from which Heseltine walked out over Westland. He thus avoided collective responsibility for a tax that he was to abandon as environment secretary in 1991. The following year was spent by ministers and officials in a frenzy of revisions and increased doubt as the tax was adjusted to make it less unfair. Safety nets, rebates and transitional reliefs proliferated. By the end of the year the transitional dual running of the tax alongside rates had been abandoned by yet another environment secretary, Nicholas Ridley. It was, he felt, 'two taxes for the price of one' and therefore doubly unpopular. Local authorities, whose political nous outstripped that of the cabinet, realized that now was the time to spend. Restraint was cast to the winds. Whatever poll tax they fixed could be blamed on the government. A private Tory survey showed that as many as 80 per cent of householders would be worse off under the first year of poll tax.[24] An initial estimate given to the cabinet was of £50 a head with dual running in 1990, rising to £250 a head in 2000. This grew to an initial £200 a head, then £278 a head, then to an actual £363 in the first year of operation. Three adults in one house might thus have to find £1,100 in local tax in a year. This was the grim arithmetic of poll tax down the ages. Central government was held accountable for local taxes as never before.

Environment secretaries now came and went with bewildering frequency: Baker handed over to Ridley, who handed over to Chris Patten. The last two began as sceptics but were trapped by Thatcher's commitment. Ridley saw the opening of the accountability gap and tried to get Thatcher and the Treasury to abandon capping. Thatcher refused. She was adamant that 'local people' looked to her for protection from socialist councils.[25] Ridley had the unhappy task of passing the Local Government

55

Finance Act in 1987–8. Its passage was dominated by nervous and unconvincing predictions for the new creation. Clouds were gathering on all sides, including on the backbenches. There were now some hundred 'doubters', with forty rebels on some votes and seventeen voting against the government on second reading. No rebellion that faced Major on Europe was as great as Thatcher experienced on poll tax.

Poll tax was now beginning to cost the government serious money. Ridley's successor, Chris Patten, demanded £2.6 billion in additional subsidy to local authorities to reduce poll taxes for the 1990 start. As Butler points out, this was a greater rise in Treasury support to local government than in the entire decade of Thatcher's government so far.[26] The steady drift to put more of the burden of local spending on local taxpayers was abruptly reversed. No sooner had the Treasury conceded this sum than Patten demanded another £2 billion on top. Lawson was furious. 'While [Patten] was well aware that the poll tax was a political disaster he made no effort whatsoever to abort it, even though he was in a strong position to do so.'[27] This was unrealistic, but Lawson's anger was understandable. He alone had fought the reform and was now expected to pick up the tab for it.

Lawson continued his scathing comments both on the tax and on Patten's pusillanimity. In reviewing the Butler book for the *Spectator* in 1995 he again attacked Patten for making 'not the slightest attempt to abort the tax'. He was also critical of environment department officials. He felt Waldegrave's team approach had infringed the separation of officials and ministers. 'A committee formed of ministers who have lost their political judgement and officials who have abandoned their scepticism and objectivity is unlikely to produce a happy outcome. And so it proved.'[28] I know that many officials were subsequently worried at the role they played in the débâcle.

As 1990 approached, poll tax was so distorted by safety nets and rebates as to be as incomprehensible as the rates. The Treasury was forced to find another £400m to reduce bills (and twice as much a year later). I calculated at the time that half those eligible to pay poll tax would not do so for the three years of transition and that a third never would pay in full.[29] This was apart from the 10 per cent of likely evaders: a huge leakage for any tax system to sustain. Poll tax would have a lower incidence per household than the rates, a reversal of its intention. Patten used his reserve powers to cap the poll taxes of twenty of the highest-spending councils, relieving the most irresponsible councils of accountability to their electors.

In March 1990, with the tax on the point of imposition, Thatcher held a private meeting with her public relations advisers. They pleaded with her to find a way of cutting the tax even further. Present was Kenneth Baker in yet another incarnation, as party chairman. Baker was already distancing himself from a tax that he saw as wholly changed from what he had originally proposed.[30] Thatcher was forced to acknowledge that some drastic innovation was essential to avert a political catastrophe. Her 'flagship policy' of the 1987 election was in danger of sinking. Yet the cabinet had run out of options. Scotland, where the tax had been introduced a year early at the bidding of Scottish Tories, was in uproar. The tax was now causing real political panic in the Conservative party and riots in many parts of the country. The ghosts of medieval populism were roused from their graves.

In June Thatcher tried to get the cabinet to approve a complete central cap on all poll taxes. This final humiliation meant abandoning all faith in the tax as a tool of local accountability. 'I pressed with the Treasury and Environment Department my ideas for wide-ranging direct controls over local-authority spending combined with more extensive use of central grants,' she recorded.[31] This was *de facto* nationalization of all local finance. Lengthy legal advice suggested this was only possible – which appears to have meant only constitutional – if councils were given enough warning of what government considered 'excessive spending'. Otherwise the presumption was in favour of local democratic choice over 'reasonable' budget setting. This was

57

good enough for the cabinet. It duly announced a general capping for the following year. This legal judgement, made not by any court but by the government's own lawyers, was a constitutional innovation. It took capping well beyond the selective scope of the 1984 Act. Thatcher fell in November of that year and poll tax two years later, but this capping power lived on, a power far more significant in its impact on local democracy than the tax itself. The Treasury may have lost a battle over poll tax but it won a bigger victory in its campaign for a fiscally centralized Britain.

The poll tax was Thatcher's biggest political blunder. Whether it was crucial or merely contributory to her fall is debatable. Her style of rule had already begun to exasperate her colleagues. In my view poll tax was actually an exception to the normal conduct of Thatcher's reforms, a moment when she took her eye off the ball, ignored caution and allowed others in her government to drive her down a road to disaster. She lent the argument her commitment rather than her intelligence. She had no particular feeling for the three ministers who had 'sold' her poll tax, Jenkin, Baker and Waldegrave. She had been a sceptic over rates abolition in 1974[32] and over the Jenkin initiative in 1984. She was distracted over the formative months of the reform by the aftermath of the IRA Brighton bomb, the Westland affair and the miners' strike. Yet the contrast with her handling of health service reform is stark.

Thatcher suffered, like most of her political generation, from a lack of grounding in local government. She ignored the adage that 'all politics is local'. To her, local government should implement central government's wishes at minimum cost. Councils were not there to legitimize local discretion. 'She expected them to be agents of central government,' wrote Kenneth Baker.[33] Her affection for the two 'flagship councils', Westminster and Wandsworth, was entirely due to their severe cuts in local spending. She was proud of rate-capping as 'enabling us to curb the extravagance of high-spending councils in the interests of local ratepayers and the wider economy'.[34] I know from conversations with her at

58

the time that she regarded the resulting loss of accountability as a small price to pay for this boon. She was unconcerned at the toll she was taking on local Conservative activists.

Her colleagues followed her lead in what was a parody of collective responsibility. To Thatcher, councils needed punishing for being local and for being Labour. Her overspending rhetoric, the emphasis on 'hard-left' extravagance, the restless search for new controls, all indicated a resentment that a quarter of the public sector was beyond her direct control. The frenzy of her colleagues was more synthetic. Ministers deceived themselves about the new tax's fairness, size and collectability. They were content to cap it, to subsidize it, to graduate it, to rebate it. They would do anything just to get it imposed. As Geoffrey Howe recorded, 'A huge amount of political goodwill and energy was expended on the destruction of the Greater London Council and other citadels of the loony left. Yet local government seemed always to elude control.'[35] The eel kept slithering from the cabinet's grasp.

Thatcher still believed that the tax was 'beginning to work at the very moment it was abandoned. Given time it would have been seen as one of the most far-reaching and beneficial reforms ever made in the workings of local government.'[36] Its abandonment, she wrote, 'will mean that more and more powers will pass to central government, that upward pressures on public spending and taxation will increase accordingly'. Yet she also claimed that the tax needed one further improvement: 'It would have been necessary to introduce the much more far-reaching controls over council spending to which my mind had anyway been turning.'[37] Never did she or anybody round her properly debate this garbled contradiction. The tax is estimated to have cost the Treasury a colossal £1.5 billion just to set up and then abolish. This was dwarfed by the rebates, safety nets, transitional and Exchequer subsidies which, by the time of poll tax abandonment in 1993, were calculated by Butler and his co-authors to total £20 billion. This is money that would otherwise have been raised from the rates or remained in people's pockets. That means that 4p could have been cut from income tax or there could have been a commensurate reduction in VAT instead.[38]

Major's decision on taking office to 'review' local finance was greeted with sighs of relief. Heseltine, whose opposition to poll tax had been consistent and public, was sent back to the environment department. His job was to slay the poll tax dragon, preferably with one swoop of his sword. The appointment drew the sting of poll tax within the Conservative party but it initiated an extraordinary debate within the cabinet on the future of British local government. With so much of its revenue now under Treasury control, some ministers felt that the time had come for a shift of functions (as well as powers) to Whitehall. Observers felt that local government in the early months of 1991 came nearer to total abolition in Britain than at any time under Thatcher. Instead, as we shall see in chapter six, a further attack on education authorities was immediately launched. Michael Howard, who succeeded Heseltine at environment, encouraged the Local Government Commission to abolish county government, while Kenneth Clarke at the Home Office sought to bring police authorities under direct ministerial control.

Heseltine responded by promising yet another 'review of the structure' of local government, a review that was to stagger on for five years. He mischievously asked the Labour party to join him in his search for a new position to defend. His official team set about the task of 'finding an alternative to the poll tax' with the same grim loyalty they had devoted to finding an alternative to the rates. Many cabinet ministers were appalled at merely returning to the rates. The environment department suggested various forms of tax, part personal, part property. Once again, the Treasury, Number Ten and a spending department were wrestling to rush through yet another significant alteration to the British constitution. The cabinet eventually produced a version of the old Lawson scheme, a property tax banded according to capital value and rebated for single occupants. Seldom can a new tax have had such an easy passage into law as the council tax. The rates had in effect been restored.

Poll tax gave one final kick before it died. Terrified at the likely bills in the tax's second year of 1991–2, Major had asked the Treasury to find £4.5 billion to cut the tax to £140 a head. The year would be a general election one. Norman Lamont's Treasury capitulated, raising VAT by 2.5 per cent to 17.5 per cent to pay for the subsidy. This was one factor in its insistence that the new council tax have a predominant property element. Here was another shift of resources from local to central taxation. Local taxes would now cover barely 20 per cent of local spending. The necessary legislation was rubber-stamped by the Commons in just one day, 26 March 1991. The quid pro quo for this was no surprise. Even at just 20 per cent of budgeted spending, the council tax too was to be capped by the Treasury. Michael Howard, the latest environment secretary to fret his hour upon this painful stage, announced that the general cap would still apply to the new tax, based on a standardized assessment of what each council ought to be spending. For 1992–3 only three councils defied him and incurred the cap. Local government had learnt that submission was the better part of valour. Butler concluded, 'Local government survived, but in so emaciated and withered a form that some doubt whether it deserves the name.'[39]

Most commentators took the view that the death of poll tax returned matters to the status quo ante. This is not true. With hindsight poll tax was merely a bizarre incident on a road that government had been travelling ever since Crosland's 1975 speech. The highpoint on that road was not poll tax. The highpoints were the standard spending assessments now set for each local council; the capping of local revenue and after 1990 of budgets overall; and the abolition of local business rates. All these controls on local democracy, either *de jure* or *de facto*, emanated from Crosland's speech and the 1976 trauma of IMF supervision. The spending assessments implied that in local as well as national administration, Britain is a politically homogeneous entity. Its people 'ought to have' the same level of local service nationwide. Deviation from that standard should be considered a matter not of local choice but of political perversity. The contribution of taxation should be calculated on the assumption of uniformity. Within the central corset, spending might shrink in response to local efficiency, but not expand in response to local franchise. By the 1995–6 local finance settlement, local treasurers were estimating that, on average, their discretion to vary from the centrally determined budgetary norm was down to under 5 per cent. This was less discretion than in any other democratic country.

This standardization was a new concept in public finance. It concluded what I suppose should be seen as the honouring of the Tories' original 1974 rates-abolition pledge. Discretionary local taxes were all but abolished. In the mid-1980s the rates covered half of local-government spending and roughly 11 per cent of total public spending. By 1995 the council tax covered barely a fifth of local spending. The Treasury, which had campaigned so fiercely against local government in the early 1980s, found by the end of the decade that it was having to accept extra tax-borne expenditure in the form of higher grants to local authorities, beyond any of the burdens of social security or housing benefit. Nor were councils any longer inclined to restrain their spending below the central target. Local spending rose and continued to rise more strongly after capping than before it.[40] Those who persistently try to subjugate 'distant provinces', as Macaulay warned, have to pay for it in the end. By nationalizing this large area of the public sector the Treasury had to carry the can for it.

While the finances and politics of the poll tax attracted intense debate, its constitutional significance attracted almost none. Despite a brief Tory revolt, poll tax passed parliament with ease. The much-vaunted select committee system was toothless. After the bill was published, neither Lords nor Commons environment committees looked at the tax. The Commons committee chairman, the Tory MP Sir Hugh Rossi, gave an odd reason for this. The committee decided 'as an act of conscious policy not to become involved in topics which are the subject of major political

62

controversy'.[41] As Hayek pointed out, elected assemblies are always the last institutions that seem inclined to curb dictators.

Yet standardization, capping and parliamentary impotence were not the only legacies of poll tax. The least noticed but most emphatic change initiated by the Waldegrave–Baker reforms was the nationalization of all business rates. At a stroke this wiped out roughly half the discretionary income of local treasurers, replacing it with a business property tax, fixed by the Treasury, collected and redistributed to councils on a per capita basis. Business rates had featured prominently in writing on local taxes prior to the poll tax debate.[42] Businessmen had no vote. Though this applied in most countries where property taxes are levied, the business rates had in many urban areas grown to outstrip domestic rates as a percentage of local-government income. Though they were related to domestic rates, they were exploited by city Labour parties in the knowledge that the domestic rates of most Labour supporters were rebated. They thus diluted local accountability and distorted industrial location. Such objections undoubtedly called for reform.[43]

The new 'uniform business rate' of the 1988 Act did not reform local business rates, it abolished them. Businesses instead experienced a new national tax related to the capital value of their property. Since parliament was distracted by the wider issue of the poll tax, MPs were unaware of the significance of the new business tax until it was imposed. It was almost as painful as the poll tax. The government decided to revalue all business premises for rating purposes at the same time as introducing the new tax. This led to 'losers', mostly small businesses in the rural south, howling loudly. Given the temper of the times, they demanded and got costly transitional relief from central government.

In 1994–5 this tax brought £12.3 billion into the hands of the Treasury, to re-emerge as 'central assistance to local government' (as against a mere £8.8 billion to local authorities in council tax).[44] Although it was given to local authorities, the allocation was within central government's control and entered as such in

63

the public accounts. The Treasury promised to increase it by no more than inflation each year – for the time being – but this in itself offered the Exchequer a completely new index-linked source of revenue. This seizure of what had been one half of the revenue available to local government was a drastic extension of the fiscal power of a British cabinet. Taken together with the introduction of budget-capping and standard spending assessments, it constituted the biggest single act of nationalization undertaken by any government since the war.

Nobody in Westminster or Whitehall batted an eyelid.

CHAPTER FOUR

NATIONALIZATION AT LAST

You will find that every man is the worse for being poor; and the doctor is a specially dangerous man when poor – GEORGE BERNARD SHAW

The National Health Service was an implausible candidate for 'nationalization'. It was supposed to have been nationalized by Labour in 1946. The NHS introduced by Nye Bevan over the 'bloody corpse' of medical opposition was as centralized as the most enthusiastic statist could ask. Every general practitioner, hospital doctor and nurse was accountable to the Minister of Health. In a celebrated phrase, Bevan remarked that 'when a bedpan is dropped on a hospital floor its noise should resound in the Palace of Westminster'. The managers of the service, he said, 'will be the agents of my department'. That was his ambition.

As with most of the emergent welfare state, the reality was different. Bevan's NHS only narrowly survived a bruising battle with Herbert Morrison, who had wanted socialized medicine to be under local-council control.[1] Herbert Morrison pointed out that the majority of hospitals had their origins in the municipal corporations, from which the government had no mandate to take them. He lost the argument largely because Ernie Bevin had an aversion to Morrison's municipal enthusiasm and sided with Bevan. Yet the new health service was a hard-fought compromise between the minister and local and professional interests. Local councils continued in charge of community health beyond the ambit of hospitals and GPs. This left them with midwifery,

65

childcare, public health and preventive medicine. More important, both the hospitals and the GP service were run by doctors, not civil servants. Government's role was to give them the money, no more and no less.

Bevan was reduced, as he often said, to throwing pound notes at doctors to get them to offer a full medical service to the public. He explained that he had 'deliberately come down in favour of a maximum decentralization to local bodies, a minimum of itemized central approval . . . relying for economy not so much on a tight and detailed departmental grip but on the education of the bodies concerned'.[2] Beveridge had even supposed that a healthier nation would mean a reduced need for doctors and hospitals, and some doctors feared that nationalized medicine would reduce medical employment. Nowhere in the literature of the time is there any inkling that people would make unlimited calls on health care. The fitter and richer they are, the more they demand care and the higher the cost of supplying them.

These principles underpinned the NHS for four decades. A reorganization in 1974 took certain community health services from local government and brought them and the hospitals under new regional and area health authorities. The intention was the familiar one, of containing bureaucracy and ensuring 'a maximum of delegation downwards matched by accountability upwards'. The confusion of objectives was equally familiar. The white paper promised 'a national strategy with national objectives, standards and priorities. It is, however, equally important to encourage variety and flexibility in working the strategy over the country.'[3] The dominant role of doctors in running the service and fixing priorities continued. Regional and area committees continued to include local-government and medical representatives, but the latter tended to call the tune. The bill was, after all, sent to London for payment. The general practitioner service was run through local GP committees, though the 'contract' was negotiated nationally. Nowhere else in the public sector was there a service in which both producers and consumers

66

could call forth expenditure so directly on demand. This could not last.

On coming to office in 1979, Margaret Thatcher was even more timid towards the NHS than she was towards the rest of the welfare state. She admitted she was 'much more reluctant to envisage fundamental changes than in the nation's schools ... I always regarded the NHS and its basic principles as a fixed point in our policies.'[4] Her health secretary, Patrick Jenkin, adhered to this admonition. He steered through yet another reorganization of the NHS, albeit one planned by the outgoing Labour government. Implemented in 1982, this abandoned any link between health and other local-government boundaries and instituted 14 regional and 191 district health authorities (DHAs) in England, with similar changes elsewhere in the United Kingdom. The purpose of this change was the same as that of 1974: to devolve 'as many decisions as possible to the local level ... with the minimum of interference by any central authority'.[5] Jenkin's white paper wanted to see local health authorities 'using their own initiative to respond to local needs rather than being a conveyor for detailed orders and advice from the centre'.

Jenkin's approach was rare among Thatcher's ministers. When he said he wanted to devolve power he appeared to mean it. In Opposition he had stridently criticized the bureaucracy of Labour's NHS. His white paper proved to be one of the few truly decentralist documents to emerge from Thatcher's government. He accepted a loss of Whitehall control and demanded in return a 10 per cent cut in local administration costs.[6] He remained deferential to the medical profession and accepted its established role in running the NHS. Talk of 'chief executives' for health authorities was rejected as 'not compatible with the professional independence required'. Bevan's compact remained strong. According to Gerald Wistow, 'there were now to be no detailed standards by which the rate of progress towards objectives could be assessed ... However, the approach was not only consistent with the commitment to localism and the removal of detailed central controls. It also made sound political sense.' By strengthening the status of local health authorities, the government aimed to deflect criticism for poor delivery on to them. Rudolf Klein, a seasoned observer of NHS reform, refers to this as the 'decentralization of blame'.[7] Jenkin's successors were to be painfully bad at it.

The devolutionary policy lasted less than two years. Jenkin was chivvied to abandon it by parliament, his colleagues and the Treasury. The new culture of Westminster and Whitehall was against him. The new Commons Social Services Committee accused his department of 'not being in a position to measure its actual achievement'.[8] This theme was taken up by the Public Accounts Committee, which declared that the department was not in control of its budget. Thatcher herself recognized that health spending was being impelled upwards by public demand and by managers resistant to budgetary control. The slightest attempt to curtail spending would lead to claims of empty wards, lengthening waiting lists and dead babies: a practice known as 'shroud waving'. As Nigel Lawson pointed out, a centrally provided health service would always require rationing. 'The consequence of this in terms of human suffering will all too often be held to be the direct responsibility, if not the deliberate policy, of the Government.'[9]

The Jenkin hands-off strategy was abandoned with his replacement in 1981 by Norman Fowler, who promptly initiated 'an era of unprecedented central control and intervention'.[10] Like Archimedes leaping from his bath – and with little respect for his predecessor – Fowler announced that 'the real problem with the NHS is a lack of management'.[11] Management it must have. Most of Thatcher's reforms needed at least two bites at the cherry. At health the first came with the arrival as adviser in 1983 of the managing director of Sainsbury's, Sir Roy Griffiths. He offered Fowler a brisk twenty-four-page opinion of the NHS that swept aside forty years of custom and practice. He called for an end to the medical veto and damned the tradition of 'consensus management' of local health authorities. In a memorable phrase he said that 'if Florence Nightingale were carrying her lamp through the corridors of the NHS today, she would almost certainly be searching for the people in charge'.[12] He proposed that new non-medical managers should be inserted into every regional and district health authority, some two hundred in all.

Griffiths' executives came from outside as well as within the health service. Many were to be criticized by medical colleagues as 'failed doctors'. They were to be the praetorian guard of the new managerialism in the health service. They were not intended to assist or monitor the work of the medical committees. They were to override them. Conflict over priorities must be brought to the surface and openly resolved. Resources were to be allocated on the basis of a centralized decision, not just last year's budget plus inflation plus a bit more. At the apex of the NHS in London was to be a supervisory board, deploying a battery of indicators holding districts and hospitals accountable for the burgeoning cost of the service. These controls grew in complexity as the decade progressed. Each region had to lodge 'action plans' in the Commons library. A package of national performance indicators was issued to every authority in 1983. As information flowed back to London it revealed, in the words of one manager, 'that 191 different National Health Services existed in the country, rather than one single NHS operating in 191 districts'.[13] The government's competitive tendering policy for local government also applied to the NHS and had similarly traumatic impact on union featherbedding in hospital laundries, catering and cleaning.

As the new managers installed themselves in their offices after 1984, they found themselves trapped. On the one hand were cash-limited budgets set by the health department in London, on the other was a barrage of vociferous local pressure groups. As Rudolf Klein pointed out at the time, neither ministers nor managers had yet gained real control of spending or of priorities. The regional and district health authorities remained in place, as did the hospital boards and GP committees. Medical staff dominated policy decisions, such as over new equipment or the balance between acute and geriatric wards. 'It is doctors who are responsible for the clinical policies which determine whether or not resources are used efficiently,' wrote Klein, 'but doctors are not answerable for their clinical performance to their employers, only to their professional peers.'[14] This crucial confusion would have to be resolved.

The Griffiths intention was to smash the custom and practice of deferring to doctors. It was to bring to the surface the natural tensions in any bureaucracy over the allocation of resources and get more value for money for taxpayers and consumers. The managers were to circumvent the medical stalemate. They would be battalion commanders of a New Model Army at the head of which was the health secretary and the NHS management board. In a study of this quasi-military operation, Mark Exworthy has shown how inadequate the plan was to meet the task expected of it.[15] The managers rapidly saw that their interest lay in establishing local alliances with doctors rather than in confronting them. They realized that their lay boards could be used as lobbyists for money, indeed as shroud-wavers-in-chief. In other words, many decided that a quiet life depended on re-establishing the old consensus.

The regional and district board chairmen were to be selected by the Secretary of State as having 'business experience'. Whitehall had great difficulty finding such people, especially as they were expected to support the Griffiths reforms against the medical professions and trade unions. Many a Tory constituency chairman or MP's wife was 'sounded out' at a cocktail party for service on a health board. Yet even after this political screening, chairmen and members found their loyalties in conflict. Were they committed to localism or to nationalism, to a bottom-up view of regional or district health, or a top-down one? When a general manager came pleading for support in winning more cash for his district, consultants at his side, the inclination of most board members was to sympathize. Klein found that most health authorities saw accountability to the Secretary of State as largely nominal. They took seriously their role in bringing a lay view to bear on clinical priorities, but in practice they were at

70

the mercy of their professional and managerial staffs. Chairmen of my acquaintance felt themselves caught between the Whitehall devil and the medical deep blue sea. Most opted for the sea.

The Department of Health searched desperately for ways to convince the Treasury that it was in control. The pressure to find something, however marginal, to measure was overwhelming. Visits, consultations, referrals, 'medical incidents' were logged. Health care had to be quantified so as to prove productivity and somehow validate escalating public expenditure. But was more treatment a sign of success or failure? Were shorter hospital stays and shorter waiting lists a sign of efficiency or merely of callousness? (There was an outcry when one Midlands waiting list was found to include many patients already dead.) Should greater life expectancy – presumably incurring more care – be regarded as a good thing irrespective of cost? The NHS was never sure whether it was meant to be supplying care on demand or creating a healthier nation.

Ministers travelled the land, making speeches and pretending that their finger was on every pulse. Every time a ward closed or a renal unit was postponed, they had to find out why and answer for it in parliament. Edwina Currie's memoir of her time at the health department is of constant 'visits' and meddling in local management. 'We've got to make that kitchen easier to clean,' she said in a Birmingham hospital, 'and then we've got to insist that they clean it and keep it that way.'[16] Each public-health issue publicized in the media was used to obtain money from the Treasury, but the money obtained had to be 'ring-fenced' before being passed on to health authorities. One week ministers were finding money for cervical cancer smears, the next for AIDS, the next for anti-smoking campaigns, the next for shorter waiting times for hip replacement. Local priorities were shot to pieces. The NHS that Bevan invented and early Thatcherism prodded with a stick was anything but 'nationalized'. The health department's ugly citadel at Elephant and Castle was at this stage like a command centre with no lines out to the troops. It relied on

71

mercenaries whose loyalty was unreliable but who had a voracious appetite for ammunition.

By 1987 it was clear that Griffiths was not delivering what the cabinet most yearned for: relief from political pressure. Many causes are given for the sudden collapse of political confidence in the NHS. Some were long-term. Advances in preventive medicine and in high-cost treatment for cancer and heart disease were outstripping capacity. No less costly were treatments such as hip replacement and renal dialysis, regarded as unusual in the 1970s but as an entitlement in the 1980s. The hospitalization of the elderly and mentally ill, all living longer, was also escalating costs. Public support for doctors' and nurses' pay kept this part of the budget well ahead of inflation. In addition, the new emphasis on better management was revealing large areas of waste and thus of potential saving. But the savings took time to show, while the pain of eliminating the waste was politically instantaneous.

With the approach of the 1987 general election, the Labour party moved health to the top of the agenda. NHS spending shot forward as if in response. It had risen over the first seven years of the Thatcher government by 30 per cent in real terms. It was clear to both Thatcher and the Treasury that some sort of crisis lay ahead. Norman Fowler had discussed various options for changing the basis of health care with Thatcher in January 1987. But Fowler was no radical, nor at this stage was Thatcher. She was so hesitant that she even pondered what was normally anathema to her, a Royal Commission. Reflecting later on the 1987 election manifesto, which made no mention of the impending upheaval, she wrote, 'I was reluctant to add the health service to the list of areas in which we were proposing fundamental reform.'[17] This did not stop her claiming later that she had an election mandate for 'the most far-reaching reform of the NHS in its 40-year history'.[18]

Election victory brought no relief. By the winter of that year the cabinet was in the midst of a fully-fledged 'underfunding crisis'. A score of hospitals put out closure warnings. Shrouds were waving the length and breadth of the land. Birmingham children's hospital announced it was denying new admissions. The cabinet was powerless to respond, except in the only way it knew. An extra £100m was thrown at the NHS shortly before Christmas. Health was now dominating each week's Prime Minister's Commons question time. Thatcher recorded her despair at this 'bottomless financial pit' that yielded nothing but trouble.[19] She seemed baffled at what was happening round her.

The final months of 1987 proved a turning point, for health as for so much of Thatcherism. The Prime Minister was already in search of new enemies to replace Scargill's miners and Ken Livingstone's GLC. The health enemy was hard to define but it had sorely wounded Thatcher and seemed intent on continuing to do so. Suddenly the NHS was no longer untouchable. It was firmly in Downing Street's sights, for reasons not of ideology but of politics. Thatcher did not abandon Griffiths but took him to his logical conclusion, that of a super-efficient nationalized industry under central management command. She thought even the media might be sympathetic: 'If we acted quickly, we could take the initiative, put reforms in place and see benefits flowing from them before the next election.'[20] In December 1987 she decided to set up a small study group under her chairmanship to chart a new course for the NHS. To the amazement of her cabinet and the nation, she announced it on a BBC *Panorama* programme the following month. It would be complete, she said, within a year. She made no mention of prior consultation.

The review team was similar in approach to the one that produced the poll tax and the education reform bill (see chapter six). It was secret and strictly goal-oriented. No use was made of parliament or the health service associations as sounding boards for advice. There was, and is, no deliberative forum for Britain's NHS. If there was to be change, change would depend on the initiative of the centre. Besides, the question was at root political: how to contain NHS spending without appearing to deny treatment. Committed ministers, officials and 'sound' outsiders brainstormed for six months. Answers only were wanted. Nothing

73

could have been further from the elegant deliberations of a Royal Commission.

There was one crucial difference between the health review and that on poll tax. In the case of poll tax Thatcher had left Patrick Jenkin, Kenneth Baker and William Waldegrave to go in search of an alternative to the rates. She had allowed ambitious ministers to confront her with a radical proposal – and do so in front of her cabinet. Her instinct for caution put her at a disadvantage. In contrast, Thatcher personally chaired the health study group. There would be no reckless going back to first principles. The team comprised the two Department of Health and Social Security ministers, John Moore and Tony Newton, together with the Chancellor, Lawson, and the then Chief Secretary to the Treasury, John Major. Griffiths attended as an adviser, as did John O'Sullivan, Thatcher's political aide. Advice arrived from a wide range of sources. British government may be singular, but thinking about it is plural. Thatcher's announcement prompted six swift studies into the future of the NHS. High in the frame was the American consultant Alain Enthoven's idea of setting up internal trading markets for health care, put forward for the NHS in 1985.[21] He suggested that money be injected into the system at a given point, whether the patient or the GP, and then follow demand through the system. Doctors would buy beds off hospitals as and when required, hospitals would buy equipment or drugs or consultants' time.[22]

The review began with the defeat of Moore's attempt to convince Thatcher to opt for radicalism, such as health charges, subsidized private insurance or health vouchers. When at one point the Treasury supported a proposal for across-the-board charging Thatcher stamped on it as politically illiterate. She said it was characteristic of that department's espousal of unpopular reforms, on the basis that some other minister would carry the political can. 'It would have discredited any other proposals for reform and ditched the review,' she wrote scornfully.[23] The review saw Thatcher at her most street-wise – and her memoirs at their most engrossing. 'Moore and the DHSS strongly favoured a hypothecated tax model for the not very mysterious reason that it would have guaranteed them a large, stable and increasing income . . . contracted out of the annual public spending round.' Baffled that the Treasury should be supporting Moore's scheme, she concluded that its motive 'may have been to strike an alliance with the DHSS in order to get control of the review and curb any radicalism of which it disapproved'. Thatcher guessed that the Treasury would then ditch the DHSS and plough some other furrow. This is exactly what it did. Nor did her own policy unit get far with a scheme for devolving all NHS spending to general practitioners alone, in effect a GPs' voucher scheme. Edwin Griggs concludes that, apart from David Willetts' Centre for Policy Studies, most right-wing think-tanks were disregarded, including Thatcher's old favourite, the Institute for Economic Affairs. Even the party's own research department was left in the cold.[24]

An early victim of the study was John Moore himself. His health was unsound and his ability to argue his corner weak. By May the review was suffering from the one thing its lean structure was designed to avoid, 'ideas overload'. Moore had deluged the group with no fewer than eighteen options. Meetings at Chequers in March and April 1988 – as we shall see, the springtime of Thatcherism – heard views from health professionals known to be 'of the faith'. (Poll tax meetings at Chequers never tested the water with public-finance professionals.) Then in a July reshuffle John Moore and Tony Newton were supplanted by a new health secretary, Kenneth Clarke. Clarke was no radical on health. He was against drastic change to the NHS and formed a natural alliance with Thatcher's aversion to 'dismantling the NHS'. From being a drag on radicalism, she could now switch roles, to one of complaining about the caution of others. For her, this was far happier.

Thatcher's strategic decision was to go for changing the structure of the NHS rather than alter the principle of central funding. She decided to make enemies of the medical lobbies, few of whom were now her friends, rather than threaten the public's belief in free health care. The Treasury now moved to centre stage as Thatcher became increasingly enamoured of the idea of hospital independence and money following the patient. The Treasury (through Lawson and Major) was fiercely opposed to this for the most archaic of reasons. The idea of freeing hospitals to compete for health authority contracts conjured up images of pricing chaos and overcapacity in some areas. It was inefficient, an abandonment of planning and a loss of control. Hospitals might invest in new units to attract business and find themselves bankrupt. Who then would pick up the bill? (This is precisely what happed to a new hospital built on Clydeside.) It was a pseudo-market of the sort that Lawson abhorred within the public sector.

The Treasury was scarred from years of what it regarded as profligacy and duplicity from NHS hospitals. It came back with one scheme after another to keep hospital budgets under its tight control. One participant told me the Treasury shuddered at any mention of the phrase 'money follows the patient'. The only money it wanted to see following the patient were charges, a view dismissed by Thatcher as 'a characteristic Treasury device to assert its central control of spending and disguise it as extending consumer choice'.[25] She wilfully infuriated the Treasury with a demand for tax relief for BUPA and other private insurance premiums, reflecting her long-standing enthusiasm for 'middle-class subsidies'. This would be costly, and met the concerted opposition of both Lawson and Clarke. She compromised on tax relief only for the over-60s. She scored other victories over the Treasury. It had opposed fund-holding for general practitioners as uncontrollable, and demanded that 'trust status' for hospitals be only for an experimental period. (Lawson and Thatcher give contradictory accounts of this stage of the review: Thatcher's account is rather more credible.) The review conceded only that the 'self-governing trust' hospitals should not be independent entities but remain part of the NHS and thus inside the public-sector borrowing pale, at least for a 'transitional' period. (That period is still in being at the time of writing.)

76

Thatcher had here secured a real change in the management of the NHS without undermining its principle of 'free at the point of delivery'. To her the proposals set out in the white paper of January 1989, *Working for Patients*, 'simulated within the NHS as many as possible of the advantages which the private sector and market choice offered but without privatization'.[26] She worried whether the DHSS was up to the job of implementation 'as we moved from one system of finance and organization to another'. Yet the virtue of the NHS reforms was that, unlike poll tax, the concept was robust. Any administrative reform must win the consent of its handlers down the line. British bureaucrats do not mutiny. They do not kill reform. They merely 'do not strive officiously to keep alive' the lunacies imposed on them by politicians. Poll tax won no friends. The NHS reforms singled out efficient hospitals and fund-holding GPs as beneficiaries. Nor was it intrinsically about privatization, whatever its political opponents tried to maintain. From the smoke of battle, allies gradually emerged. An organization that boasted it was second only in size to the Red Army did change. As an exercise in structural reform, Thatcher's 'new' NHS was in my view her most emphatic public-sector achievement.

The white paper was sensational. For the whole of 1989 the NHS was in uproar, but the 1990 NHS and Community Care Act made its way steadily on to the statute book. It continued the trend away from local government that had been a feature of all post-war health reform. All local-authority representation on regional and district health authorities ended and lay members of these bodies had to be recruited, straining Conservative head-hunting to the limit. Roughly 700 new health authorities and hospital trusts in England, Wales and Scotland required some 4,000 lay appointees, who by definition needed to be supportive of the reforms. Chairmen were appointed personally by the Secretary of State. The Act was seen as highly political. The medical profession displayed collective apoplexy. It was furious at what it saw as the calculated snub of lack of consultation, and this almost ended the political career of Kenneth Clarke.[27] 'He's a thug and a bully who will be loathed by GPs till time immemorial because he produced a completely cock-eyed scheme moved by pure political dogma,' commented the leader of the British Medical Association, John Marks.[28] Doctors who had fought the setting up of the NHS now fought what they claimed was its dismantling.

The doctors saw the Act as a threat to their professionalism. In this they were right. At the core of the 1990 reforms lay the 'self-governing hospital trust'. At the level of individual hospitals, this entrenched Griffiths' managerialism: it unashamedly declared that management and financial functions were now to be dominant in running NHS hospitals. The trust concept was gradually to embrace almost all of the United Kingdom's 550 hospitals. They would no longer receive the bulk of their money direct from Whitehall. They had to bid for patients from district health authorities or fund-holding doctors. The DHAs and fund-holders thus became the basic spending units of the NHS, known as the 'purchasers'. They decided what use, if any, to make of hospitals, who became the 'providers'. GPs used to plead with hospitals for beds: hospitals now pleaded with GPs for patients. The most self-important of Britain's professions, hallowed in fiction and film, was apparently to be reduced to a sub-contractor. As power seeped away from the consultants, the bellow of James Robertson Justice (the fierce consultant in *Doctor in the House* and its six successors) could be heard across the land. (The bellow was not ineffective: medical staff retained considerable power through hospital consultative committees and often subverted attempts to impose external medical audit on their work.)

Yet once again, the reality of Thatcherism was not quite as it seemed. In stating her intention at the start of the review, Thatcher said it was to ensure that 'responsibility whether for medical decisions or for budgets should be exercised at the lowest appropriate level closest to the patient'.[29] (Every previous NHS reform had said the same.) Her intention was that the government would now merely inject cash-limited quantities of money into one NHS vein, that of the family doctor, and see it flow

78

smoothly round a reinvigorated body. But the motive for the 1990 reform was the need to bring under control a service that had been unresponsive to government priorities as well as to cash limits. The DHSS at the time was desperate not just to contain NHS spending, but to show the world that it was delivering more value for money. Tipping cash into the coffers of general practice was a most uncertain way of ensuring that delivery. As the department's permanent secretary, Sir Kenneth Stowe, later admitted, the devolutionary aspect of the Griffiths reform had been a near-disaster. 'Freedom for health authorities to cut loose and pursue their own paths at the taxpayer's expense was the last thing in any of our minds,' he wrote of that period.[30] The improved monitoring and information flowing up to London were not enough. The department had to have more control.

Attention now focused on the concept of the 'NHS contract'. This totem of the new managerialism implied a free association of two parties in an open market. As a tour operator would contract with a hotel or airline, so a fund-holder would contract with a hospital for operations and beds. One hospital might offer cheaper hips, another cheaper cataracts. The private sector might even enter the public-sector market (as it did for hernia operations, complete with radio advertising). But these contracts were not what they seemed. They were not contracts in the legal sense. The word was more a metaphor for a way of allocating resources between tiers in a bureaucratic system. NHS contracts were not enforceable at law. Local hospitals mostly enjoyed geographical monopolies in hospital services. After an initial flurry, the purchasers and providers quickly settled into what were euphemistically termed 'constructive longer-term relationships'. The chief areas of sustained competition were London and some other big cities, with a variety of hospitals and often an over-supply of beds.

What mattered over time was flexibility. It was debatable how far GPs and DHAs would be able to keep their contracts fluid, as hospitals struggled to re-establish local monopolies and thus

79

plan their capacity with the care expected of them by government. As it was, hospitals were required to supply health districts with 'core' services, including beds for the acutely ill and local accident and emergency services. These were not contracts. The Act laid down that they may be determined by the reserve powers of the Secretary of State, which meant by the NHS executive hierarchy. As Kenneth Clarke told a Commons select committee, DHAs 'have a duty to provide a full comprehensive service reasonably accessible to their population ... Where the district has no choice but to take part of its service from the self-governing trust [hospital] it will probably declare that part of the service to be a core service, so there is no messing about.'[31] Such a declaration would have to be backed by money ordered up from the NHS centrally. Accident services could not be allowed to go bankrupt.

A body of sceptical literature has built up round these reforms, notably among lawyers. David Hughes pointed out that the scope for NHS executive interference undermined the contract principle: 'The power to impose or vary contract terms ... goes well beyond what is common in arbitration.'[32] He concluded that NHS contracts would in time 'simply become an exercise in the skilful manipulation of a different vocabulary in essentially the same bureaucratic environment'. In remarks to a Commons select committee, Clarke appeared to agree: 'One of the arts at the moment is making sure that argument is kept to a minimum.'[33] He had earlier warned MPs against any 'over-legalistic interpretation' of an NHS contract, which he said was a loose term for what were in reality 'administrative arrangements'.

Confusion was not confined to contracts. It extended to the concept of the 'self-governing trust' applied to an NHS hospital. As we noted above, the Treasury fought to gain control of these wayward public-sector institutions. Under the 1990 Act they were not to have the status even of public corporations. The trust boards were appointed directly by the health secretary, who could also sack them. They were in no sense free agents. They could not wind themselves up or opt out of the NHS. Their buildings might be disposed of as the health secretary decided. He or she could close them and merge them with another hospital – as happened in the case of Bart's and other London hospitals. To call such institutions self-governing was absurd. They were run by their managers and governed by the Secretary of State. Autonomy was confined to their dependence for part of their revenue on attracting fund-holder agreements.

In the months following the passage of the 1990 Act the Treasury drove home every advantage. It kept control over hospital borrowing and investment, delegating limited discretion to health department regional officials. Staff grading, negotiations and pay remained firmly with the Treasury, with the strong support of the medical trade unions guarding their national negotiating rights. Here as elsewhere, the unions proved powerful agents of centralism. Their own negotiating strategy and status depended on limiting local discretion and promoting central power. (In 1995 the Treasury did attempt to introduce a decentralized element into nurses' contracts, an attempt furiously opposed by the public-sector unions.) Under section 10 of the Act, trust hospitals had to work to individual financial objectives set by the health department with the consent of the Treasury. Most severe, any profits made by efficient hospitals could be appropriated by the Secretary of State and passed to the Treasury. This Treasury 'seizure of surpluses' was a characteristic of neo-nationalization: we saw it with public utilities in chapter two and shall encounter it again with railways.

Certainly this was confirmed by the language of the white paper: 'The overall effect of these changes will be to introduce for the first time a clear and effective chain of management command running from Districts through Regions to the Chief Executive and from there to the Secretary of State.' This was odd since the regional authorities were supposedly autonomous statutory agents. To analysts such as Hughes all subordinate autonomy in the NHS was now spurious, existing 'only so long as the decisions of local managers remain in line with policy objectives and financial targets set from above'.[34] He went on to draw a comparison with the system of pseudo-contracts that Stalin offered Soviet enterprises under Gosplan. Soviet law established the enterprises as distinct managerial units linked by contracts. 'Their capacity to enter contractual relationships was subordinated to a central planning agency concerned to regulate terms and conditions in relation to national rather than immediate interest.'[35] Disputes between Moscow and the corporations were resolved not by law but by special Gosarbitrazh, or state arbitration boards. They began efficiently, but over time became by-words for delay and corruption. (The Stalinist comparison was also to be drawn with Thatcher's reforms to the university sector.)

The experience of the first five years of the reform suggests that this analysis was over-gloomy. As in any study of Thatcherism, we must distinguish between reserve powers taken by Whitehall and the use of those powers in practice. The tenth anniversary of the Griffiths reforms in 1994 was the occasion of retrospective surveys of NHS managerialism. Although the British Medical Association and political critics of the government held to the view that fund-holding had produced a 'two-tier' NHS, studies by the King's Fund and the London School of Economics found a closer bonding of resources to needs. The LSE's Julian le Grand reported that most people in the health service saw the reforms as a success. 'If forced to choose between the new quasi-legal market NHS and the old command economy NHS, they would unhesitatingly prefer the new,' he wrote.[36] Those most in favour were, not surprisingly, DHA managers and fund-holding GPs; those least in favour were the wing-clipped consultants and many who saw individual patients slipping through the fund-holding net. The latter became an increasing worry as doctors became better at judging the most cost-effective use of their contracted hospital space.

As the new system settled down, the concentration on general practitioners as the primary 'purchasers' for public-health services was seen as a success. It forced them to think before they spent money on expensive hospital treatment. It forced hospitals to think before they opened (or closed) wards, recruited staff and conceded investment to their medical staff. In an important sense, decisions on medical priorities had been devolved down the professional hierarchy and closer to the patient. What was not yet clear was how far success in cutting waiting times – regarded by ministers as the overriding performance indicator – was due to hospital managers gaining a once-for-all benefit from 'disempowering' their medical staff. Might their next step not be to turn self-empowerment into yet another entrenched NHS bureaucracy?

The answer was swift in coming. Most estimates were that administrative costs overall roughly doubled in five years after the reforms. Each hospital saw lengthening corridors of administrators. The NHS Consultants Association (admittedly an anti-reform group) reported in March 1995 that average administrative costs in the NHS had risen from 5–6 per cent of total NHS spending to 11 per cent. Two administrators in Northampton General Hospital had been replaced by seventeen.[37] The *Spectator*'s medical correspondent reported that three nursing administration offices in his hospital had increased to twenty-six. There were twelve medical auditors checking his work, occupying a tenth of his time with their questions.[38] In a detailed analysis of the 1990 Act, Diana Longley of Sheffield University accepted that its underlying purpose may have been decentralization, but in practice it was 'primarily concerned with extending the predominance of management processes'.[39] A health department circular announced that relations between DHAs and hospitals would in future be 'structured as contracts but enforced through the normal management process'.[40] The contracts were no more than management agreements, governed by the deals always struck between higher and lower tiers in any bureaucracy. They were reinforced by demands for extra information flows, audits and monitoring. The NHS had always prided itself on being relatively free of paperwork. No longer.

In 1993 the new health secretary, Virginia Bottomley, found herself under attack (as did the Welsh secretary, John Redwood, responsible for hospitals in Wales) for administrative inflation.

Redwood used his reserve powers to impose an immediate freeze on new administrative recruitment – with no mention of local autonomy. A National Audit Office report was severely critical of the internal market concept. It pointed out that, for all the money spent on financial information, there was no database of hospital treatment prices to which fund-holders could turn. The market was largely dependent on individual doctors telephoning round their local hospitals. It remained near-impossible to determine whether the rise in spending on management had yielded either a healthier nation or more customer satisfaction.

Meanwhile the ever restless Whitehall initiated yet another NHS reorganization. In 1994 a health service bill was presented to parliament, the fourth since 1979. This time the lay regional health authorities were disbanded and the old regions recast as eight administrative outposts of the health department. The family health authorities (governing GPs) were merged with the district health authorities and renamed just health authorities (HAs). There was now one tier of lay involvement in NHS care beneath Whitehall, at the level of districts and their neighbouring hospital trusts. The regional authority chairmen fought against their sacking and secured an extraordinary concession: while their boards vanished they were allowed to live on in limbo with their pay intact. They had no function but to attend policy meetings in London. This appeared to be cowardice on the government's part. Most chairmen were prominent local Tories and it was clear that the party had no stomach for disappointing them.

Explaining the move, the health department still felt obliged to protest its decentralizing enthusiasm: 'The changes continue the process of devolution stimulated by the NHS reforms.'[41] Yet it stated categorically that the new health authorities would be accountable to the health department's regional offices. Their priorities and 'corporate contracts' – that is, operating instructions – would be set by the NHS executive. Compliance with ministerial policy would be reflected in 'standing guidance'. The hospitals would be commercially dependent on their client fund-holders but answerable direct to the 'provider' wing of the NHS regional offices. These offices would continue to have a central role in 'performance management, and important developmental responsibilities in the areas of education and training, research and development and public health'. To call this devolution was bizarre.

As for the litmus test of decentralization – control of staffing and investment – at first no quarter was given by the Treasury. The guidance promised that 'trusts and other employers will become increasingly responsible for determining pay for their own employees'. On the other hand, 'NHS Executive Headquarters will continue to liaise with Treasury on public-sector pay policy.' From 1995 the Treasury did make an effort to decentralize pay to hospitals, though, as we have seen, this was resisted by the other great agencies of public-sector centralism, the unions. As for Treasury control over hospital investment, this appeared entrenched. Treasury external finance limits continued to apply, administered by regional offices 'on the basis of national criteria and local knowledge'. As the new management began to bite, hospital medical staff became restive and in many places took direct action. Hospital doctors who had once ruled the roost now became trade unionists, passing 'no confidence' votes in their managers. One chairman, Roy Lilley of Holmewood Hospital in Surrey, provoked an outcry in 1994 by telling his consultants to remember that their first responsibility was to the hospital not to individual patients.

In these circumstances, the role of the 4,000 or so lay men and women scattered through the NHS structure became problematic. Whether sitting on hospital trusts (as 'providers') or on health authorities (as 'purchasers'), they felt increasingly marginalized from the noisy grinding of gears taking place round them. They were the butt of much criticism, given the crudeness of the politics that surrounded their appointment: lists of names had gone up and down the Conservative party hierarchy. More to the point, they seemed to have no discretion or 'accountability' role. When a controversy over the treatment of a girl leukaemia

85

patient saw a High Court hearing in March 1995, it was the district health authority director who carried the can.

Chris Ham of Birmingham's health management centre commented on the 1994 changes: 'Over a period of years the management of the NHS has been increasingly centralized, and the latest proposals simply bring the formal position into line with reality.'[42] He wondered how much longer lay people would continue to have any role in the NHS, either on health authorities or in hospitals. If the regional committees could go, why not the local ones too? If hospitals were really accountable to the 'provider' section of the new regional offices of the health department, trust boards could have little long-term function. Managers were expected to deliver on performance indicators laid down by the centre. The centre held the money and intended to see it spent its way. The department even made a symbolic move from Elephant and Castle into handsome offices directly across Whitehall from the Treasury. Accountability was now solely to ministers. By 1995 the health secretary, Virginia Bottomley, even found herself being summoned to appear before judges for the judicial review of individual decisions on bed allocation. This was centralization reduced to absurdity.

Bevan had recognized that a health minister could not run the NHS. It was too big and depended on too diverse a web of local institutions and pressure groups. His health service was concerned simply with offering doctors and nurses an administrative apparatus 'for them freely to use in accordance with their training for the benefit of the people of the country'.[43] This was the profession-led NHS that had broken down in 1987. It was attuned to a simple task, that of paying one huge bill. The anchor of nationalization had worked loose and the ship was drifting on to the rocks. Right-wing theorists suggested that the anchor chain be cut. Public money for health should 'follow the patient' direct through vouchers or subsidized insurance systems. Only thus could the producer-domination of the health service be turned into consumer-domination. Thatcher regarded that option as politically unsustainable, choosing instead to reform the NHS structure rather than its financing. If both the Treasury and the health department were to be kept happy, this could be done only by gathering the NHS's disparate institutions under clear central discipline. Constitutionally, a confederation was replaced by a managerial autocracy.

The new health service emerging from the 1994 changes was a quest for the ultimate goal of all large bureaucracies, the best value for a given level of expenditure. The 191 all-purpose health authorities, working to the new administrative regions, would be expected to plan health care according to some measure of need. This planning function was the essence of their power. It was hard to see how the 'contract' principle could long survive such quantitative planning, since the essence of quantitative planning is the predetermining of inputs and outputs. Contracts are by their nature short-term. They may shift resources at the margin and subject some hospital departments to 'market testing'. But sophisticated health care is long-term. As Bottomley put it to the House of Commons in 1991, the NHS 'is not a market where the outcome is allowed to fall where it will, because it is a managed public service'.[44] The achievement of the Thatcher reforms was to make that management centralized and supreme.

The Thatcher NHS was fashioned as a concentrated national-ized industry. The 1990 shift in the emphasis of the NHS from hospitals to health authorities and fund-holders was undoubtedly sound management practice. It began what would be ten years of squeeze both on inefficient hospitals and on pockets of waste in general practice. It exposed the public's demand for health, as distinct from 'need', and forced patients and GPs to confront the cost of meeting that demand. Apologists for this centralization argue that it was essential. There was no other way of taming health spending or securing value for money.

As we have seen, nationalized industries have been inherently unstable political entities in Britain. They have an apparently unavoidable tendency to bureaucracy induced by their confused lines of accountability. Ministers run the NHS, answerable to parliament and subject to the most short-term of pressures: the generosity of the Treasury each year, the state of the party in the opinion polls and the political vulnerability of the minister him- or herself. The minister thus became drawn into what has been termed the league-table culture, the obsession with defensive statistics of quantifiable outputs. Thatcher truly completed what Bevan began: the nationalization of the health service. His bed-pans were not just heard in the Palace of Westmister. They were picked up, emptied, cleaned, counted and given a numbered place on the Whitehall shelf. But the centralization of the service left an uneasy feeling that a professional relationship of trust between patient and doctor and hospital and community had been broken. A new and cruder accountability had been put in its place, to a vague concept of national efficiency and to a nervous minister to parliament.

CHAPTER FIVE

ARRESTING CHANGE

Never, ever have you heard me say we will economize on law and order
— MARGARET THATCHER

The story of the police in the 1980s and 1990s is this book in a nutshell. Ever since the establishment of a statutory constabulary in the reign of Queen Victoria, responsibility for police had been a tug-of-war between local and central government. Slowly central government edged ahead. In 1994 it justifiably declared itself the winner.

Defenders of constitutional pluralism have long resisted moves towards a state police force. To them the British police officer embodies the ideal of a service 'accountable at the point of delivery', an accountability enshrined in local democracy. The British people have offered consent to the authority of police forces partly because they accept the need for law and order, partly because traditionally policemen and women have been answerable to a local political entity. However inadequate that entity, it has the overriding virtue of not being the central state. To localists, this is the key to policing by consent. Together with lack of weapons and non-military uniforms it has made British police forces famous for their popularity. Transfer accountability to the centre and consent is endangered. A police officer enjoys a unique licence to coerce other citizens. His job is to enforce Westminster's laws, but he does so always with a glance over his shoulder to his local community. Block that glance and an implied check on the abuse of state power is gone.

To the centralists this is nonsense. Modern law enforcement demands co-ordination and central command that can only come with a nationally organized structure. Local policing has meant rising costs and poor productivity in fighting crime. The days of Constable Dogberry and Dixon of Dock Green are over. Crime is not a matter of local democratic choice, nor of party debate. Citizens demand domestic security from their government, as they demand proper defence. To the centralists, the police have no more to do with local government than does the army. Central government must deliver efficient policing. That is the message of all national elections and opinion polls.

Police policy has seen three constitutional changes over the past 150 years. London's Metropolitan Police and the provincial forces were set up by parliament, in 1829 and 1856 respectively, in response to fears that law and order were declining as a result of the growth of cities and of social mobility. The cohesion and self-discipline of small communities were no longer holding. Sir Robert Peel as Home Secretary in 1828 wanted a national police to respond to what he perceived was a national demand for a constabulary. He failed to achieve this, in the face of strong parliamentary opposition from local interests. Initially the most he could get through parliament was a 'national' force for London (outside the old City), that is one run by himself directly and not through local parishes. Outside the capital, it took another twenty years to set up police forces under local watch committees. Central government could only inspect and monitor them. Even in London, where the fragmented and undemocratic parishes were unsuited to police administration, the principle of non-intervention by the Home Office was explicitly recognized by the operational autonomy of the chief constable.

Opposition to Peel's police force was a forewarning of the opposition to police centralization under Thatcher and Major. Peel confronted a wide coalition of magistrates, gentry, borough leaders and radicals. The Right saw a police force as a first step to revolutionary dictatorship. The Left saw it in much the same terms, with the police as a para-military agency at the command of government. As a result the early police were ill-paid, unarmed, working-class and closely restricted by law. (Hence the much-ridiculed punctiliousness of police terminology.) Policemen owed such power as they had, not to state authority or force of arms, but to consent. Legal accountability was not to a minister in parliament, but to the law, as administered by magistrates, boroughs, county councils and watch committees, ultimately by citizens. The British police were kept weak and, I believe, were strengthened thereby.

For a century the Peelite local/central compromise proved stable. The police enjoyed widespread public support and even affection. Characters such as Fabian of the Yard and PC49 found their way into popular hagiography. As recently as the 1950s British bobbies were, as they frequently told themselves and others, the envy of the world. According to Robert Reiner, 'they had come to be regarded as the embodiment of impersonal, rule-bound authority, enforcing democratically-enacted legislation on behalf of the broad mass of society rather than any partisan interest'.[1] This may have been an accident of the manner in which police forces were introduced but it was a happy one. British policing had to run with the grain of political and economic change in the nineteenth and twentieth centuries. With exceptions (such as the Chartist riots and the suffragette movement), it was never seen as an agency of state authority but as a manifestation of communal self-discipline.

By the 1960s this state of grace was coming to an end. Accusations of corruption and brutality led to a series of inquiries culminating in a Royal Commission in 1959 and a new Police Act in 1964. This Act began a shift in accountability. Forces outside London were made answerable to police committees composed two-thirds of councillors, one-third of magistrates. Chief constables found their loyalties bifurcated between their local police committees and the Home Office in London. Small forces were amalgamated, with 123 forces in England and Wales coming down to 47. Much of this made sense – borough forces being merged with their surrounding counties – but it began a distancing of local police forces from those elected to represent the policed. The 1964 Act gave the Home Office specific powers. It could insist on force amalgamation in the interests of efficiency wherever and whenever the Home Secretary chose. The Home Secretary took reserve powers to veto the appointment and dismissal of senior policemen and introduced rules requiring chief constables to have served in at least one other force. The Home Secretary could even sack a chief constable 'in the interests of efficiency'.

In a commentary on the 1964 Act, the historians Tony Jefferson and Roger Grimshaw reflected that it was now 'hard to discern what prevents the Home Secretary from assuming overall responsibility and control for policing in this country'.[2] However, as they pointed out in 1984, there was an important distinction to be drawn between administrative control on the one hand and the 'execution of a constable's duties' under law. The latter was 'operational', and Jefferson and Grimshaw took the view that a court would uphold a police officer's right to disobey an 'unlawful' political instruction. The division was thought to be clear: chief constables were responsible for operations and local government for giving them 'adequate resources'. Besides, the Home Office at the time was disinclined to take on the immense burden of a centralized police force. Whitehall and local government respected each other's spheres of authority. The police were local. The 1964 structure was termed a tripartite partnership, with the Home Secretary, local government and chief constables in equal harness.

The equality did not last. As we have seen, the 1964 Act gave the Home Secretary statutory responsibility for police 'efficiency'. Her Majesty's Inspectors of Constabulary, an independent corps of police professionals, were charged with 'such other duties for the furtherance of police efficiency as the Secretary of State may from time to time direct'.[3] None of these terms was defined. The word efficiency thus became a Trojan horse that could be driven by the Home Office into every police station in the land. From it poured an army of inspectors, regulators, consultants and officials.

In the late 1960s and 1970s, the police became more professional and confident. The zest for modernity took the bobby off the bicycle and made him a 'crime-buster' in a Z-car. Spending on training and equipment rose. The street constable lost status. 'Going back on the beat' was a feared demotion for the new tele-cop. Occupational introversion distanced the police from their communities. They developed a contempt for local councillors, especially the more militant Labour ones. Like doctors and teachers they developed a cohesive professional ethos under such bodies as the Police Federation, the Superintendents' Association and the Association of Chief Police Officers. To many observers this led to a decline in public respect. 'The tacit contract between police and public, so delicately drawn between the 1850s and 1950s, had begun to fray glaringly,' wrote Reiner.[4] The police image changed 'from plods to pigs'. Embarrassing incidents were ever more frequent, many suggesting a diminution of external accountability. These included the paramilitary handling of the Notting Hill riots in 1958, CND disturbances in the 1960s and the Kelaher and Countryman scandals of the 1970s.

Troubles were most noticeable in the Metropolitan Police, operating under the direct authority of the Home Secretary. One Commissioner after another would come to office promising his Home Secretary to 'clean up the Met'. The most controversial was Sir Robert Mark from 1972 to 1977. London criminal investigation was regarded by Mark as institutionally corrupt. His fight to smash it was ceaseless.[5] His experience was a warning to all who believe that a large police force can be left accountable either to itself or to ministers and Whitehall. London might have the most intractable policing problems in Britain. But it was seldom out of trouble, and fared worst on all productivity measures throughout the 1980s. As Mark himself recalled, 'It was the failure of the Home Office to discharge its duty in relation to [the

93

Met], for which the Home Secretary was responsible, which provided the weightiest ammunition for the reformers.'[6] That the 1990s Home Office should claim some unique insight into administering policemen was surprising.

By 1979 the British police were declining in both income and public reputation. The Police Federation made a remarkable decision to enter the political arena, the first union to do so on the Tory side. It supported the Conservatives with advertisements and lobbying. 'Give us the tools and we will do the job,' was the slogan. Thatcher was overjoyed. After her victory she promptly kept her side of the bargain. She more than honoured her promise to pay the award recommended by Lord Justice Edmund Davies. As she later boasted in her memoirs, she topped it by bringing the increases due in November forward to April. (She juxtaposed this boast with a reference to the cabinet beginning 'the painful but necessary process of shrinking down the public sector'.[7])

Police pay and resources now rose in line with those devoted to the NHS. They increased by 40 per cent in real terms over the next decade and by 1994 the rise was almost 90 per cent. The police could thumb their noses at their supposed employers, the local authorities, since central grants met their rising incomes. They had friends in the highest places. At police conferences, chiefs from forces covering one local-authority area envied the greater freedom enjoyed by colleagues under less interventionist joint authorities. What had once been 'subordinate and obedient' accountability was becoming merely 'explanatory and co-operative'.[8] Chief constables would talk of 'keeping their committees in good order'.

This new-found freedom came at a price, a price that was to grow over the years. While policing was still a charge on local rates, the police grant was 'ring-fenced' and enhanced by the Home Office to meet the favoured status accorded police pay. It was inconceivable that the Treasury would not seek to bring such rising expenditure under more direct control, with the police as with the NHS. As the police saw oversight by town and county halls diminish, they found that ahead lay not the ivory tower of professional autonomy, but the grim fortress designed by Sir Basil Spence overlooking St James's Park, the Home Office.

Parliament imposed ever greater burdens on the police in the 1980s. It was not just that the Tories expected them to deliver an improvement in what was vaguely termed 'law and order'. The occupational disease of ministers long in office is to intervene in the private and communal lives of citizens, and the police were directed at matrimonial violence, dog control, child abuse, narcotics, vehicle safety, race relations, noise and pollution abatement (see chapter ten). This brought them increasingly into contact, and possible conflict, with the middle-class, the middle-aged and wide sections of the once-respectable young. The Police and Criminal Evidence Act of 1984 and the Public Order Act of 1986 both aggravated police relations with dissident sections of the community and focused new attention on accountability. Sceptics judged the insecurity of a Home Secretary by the catalogue of new powers he felt obliged to boast to his party conference each year. Michael Howard in 1993 promised to extend government into new trespass laws, new stop-and-search laws, new anti-terrorist laws, new powers to collect DNA samples, new witness laws, new bail laws and new urine test laws. Not one of these laws led to a reduction of government power or reduced the burden on the police.

The consequence was a widening of what is nowadays termed the 'democratic deficit'. There was no surprise at what was to fill it. The police soon found that, in escaping the devil they knew in the town hall, they came up against the devil they didn't know in Whitehall. The Treasury's quid pro quo for Thatcher's Edmund Davies largesse on pay initially took the form of a Financial Management Initiative (FMI: see chapter twelve) originating from Lord Rayner's government efficiency unit. It sought new ways of controlling public spending and introduced the police to the alarming disciplines of calculating their value-for-money. The Home Office's FMI went out to police forces in 1983 as Circular 114. It accompanied the growing barrage of

95

rate-capping and expenditure targets for local government, described in chapter three. Half the money spent by police forces came from the Treasury in direct grant, the other half from local police authorities. Since the latter half was capped either *de facto* or *de jure* by the Treasury from the mid-1980s onwards, scope for local discretion in spending soon shrivelled. Police chiefs were constrained ever close to a nationally determined norm.

The Home Office now found itself controlling the number of police officers per force, their pay, grading and promotion. This accounted for 80 per cent of police expenditure. In addition the Inspectorate was given wide powers to scrutinize accounts, comment on efficiency and determine 'suitability for grant'. A typical Whitehall circular was No. 106/88, entitled 'Applications for Increases in Police Force Establishment'. This stipulated that no police force would be allowed to hire more policemen unless it could prove to the Home Office that this would 'improve effectiveness', for instance by thinning of supervisory ranks. For three years after permission for more staff was granted, evidence of value for money had to be delivered to Whitehall. As a former Home Office official, Barry Loveday, pointed out, this 'removed any lingering vestiges of police authority responsibility for manpower levels'.[9] The same controls were applied to equipment and capital spending. All works costing over £1m were to be subject to appraisal in London. Even minor works costing less than £200,000 and, most contentious, the amount spent on vehicles and equipment required London's approval.

The Whitehall 'Matrix of Performance Indicators' laid down what the Home Secretary expected of each police force. Inspectors, themselves former policemen, would assess how effective chief officers were in working with the local community, in identifying problems, setting objectives and using money and equipment. This information was used to determine future grant. Conforming to this implied standardization was thus crucial for local forces. All returns were forwarded by the Home Office to the public-spending division of the Treasury. The approval of a computerized fingerprint service, for which criminal investigation officers pleaded throughout the 1980s, was held up by the Home Office for a decade. As burglary rates rose and with it public concern, police forces were denied the technology which they saw as the key to curbing it. (Needless to say, the Home Office saw only feuding local forces unable to agree on what national system they wanted.)

What happened to Britain's police now paralleled the government's experience with the health service. Thatcher became increasingly annoyed that a professional group on which she had showered money and favours was not giving her a political dividend. Crime was not falling. The police were demanding more resources. On every measure, efficiency was declining. The result was a growing disenchantment among Home Office ministers, in particular Willie Whitelaw and Douglas Hurd, reflected in less sympathetic speeches to police gatherings. The police had embarked on the most dangerous course in politics, of taking Tory patronage for granted. Like hospital consultants and local authorities, they risked being seen as 'out of control'.

The government's first response was to create new police authorities after the abolition in 1985 of the Metropolitan counties and the Greater London Council (see chapter eight). The police, fire and ambulance services in these areas passed to new joint boards. Although composed of local district councillors, the boards immediately had their revenue from these districts, known as precepts, capped by central government. Having abolished a 'wasteful' tier of democracy, ministers dared not let their newly created joint boards appear spendthrift. As a Home Office official frankly told a Court of Appeal hearing at the time, 'For the purpose of setting the maximum precepts the Secretary of State must determine ... a level for each authority's total expenditure.'[10] The phrase became the guiding light of government policy towards the police.

These new boards were in theory free to decide on the size and scope of policing in all the big cities outside London. In practice any decision involving money was vulnerable to Home Office oversight. The joint boards could snap occasionally at the feet of

97

their chief constables. A much-publicized case was the running dispute between the Greater Manchester board and its egotistical chief constable, John Anderton. The chiefs seldom lost these disputes. Their real employers were not local councillors but officials and ministers in Whitehall. As long as they had the support of the latter they were safe. Another Home Office official, Mollie Weatheritt, suggested that Whitehall had contrived to assume precisely the role ascribed in the 1964 Act to the old police committees. Under the 1983 FMI circular, the Home Office inspectors were to become 'arbiters of the effectiveness of not just the managerial but also the political processes involved in performance review'.[11] The screw was tightening.

By the mid-1980s a combination of rate-capping, FMI and reinforced inspection gave substance to the claim that Britain had a nationalized police in reality if not in appearance. In 1984 the public had an opportunity to ponder the pros and cons of this nationalization with the outbreak of the confrontation for which Thatcher had long prepared, the miners' strike. The strikers' particular weapon, the flying picket, demanded a high degree of police co-ordination. Unlike terrorism or serious crime, the government's battle with the miners affected public order both intensively and extensively. It required numbers of constables on the ground, including mounted police, larger than most local forces could muster. 'Policy' emanated from an emergency unit within the Cabinet Office in London and operational co-ordination lay with a 'National Reporting Centre' at New Scotland Yard. For the sake of form, the latter was put under the command of the president of the Association of Chief Police Officers. Whitehall was on a war footing.

Many police forces disliked being asked to intervene in an industrial dispute outside (and even inside) their areas. They also disliked being told by the Home Secretary, Leon Brittan, that they could spend 'without limit' and without recourse to their police authorities.[12] Yet they knew that any opposition would be overridden by the government under emergency powers in the Police Act. Thatcher was aware of the strain that the strike imposed on the relationship between government, police chiefs and local police committees. But she saw the strain essentially as financial. It could be resolved, she said significantly, by the government 'steadily taking more and more of the burden on to the Exchequer'.[13]

The police, too, were sensitive to the threat that the strike posed to their relations with central government, and to their political impartiality. Police officers at the time talked of little else. The Home Office was intimately involved, through Scotland Yard's reporting centre, in the day-to-day handling of police operations on the ground. Indeed chief constables in strike areas were told to report direct to the Home Office.[14] Newspapers and politicians debated whether the strike showed the need for a national police force. Even a decade later the president of the Association of Chief Police Officers, Sir John Smith, could warn his members that the police were still bearing the scars of being 'Maggie's boot boys' during the strike. There was a real danger, he said, in policemen being turned into tools of government: 'I am inclined to the view that we are witnessing a move, perhaps unintended, for national control of the police by central government.'[15]

In retrospect most senior police officers felt the *ad hoc* structure set up during the strike in 1984–5 had stood up to the challenge. It proved that inter-force co-operation was compatible with operational autonomy. The Home Secretary had not been required to use emergency powers. For all the media imagery of battle, the strike had been kept an industrial rather than a political dispute. Evidence of this was the embarrassment it caused the Labour party. There was no national uprising in defence of the miners, despite widespread sympathy for their plight from the media, churchmen and public opinion. There had been no need to call in troops. To some on the Left the police had been dragooned into behaving as a national force under tacit threat of emergency powers. A more reasonable view is that the 'implicit compact' between centre and locality rose to the occasion and was not broken.

As soon as the strike was over argument continued between the police and government over how best to measure efficiency and relate it to public money. Policing the strike had been expensive, and government had paid. But now spending had once again to be justified. Value for money in policing is not easy to define. Throughout the 1980s the local-government Audit Commission, the Commons home affairs select committee and many academics searched for quantifiable definitions to which performance indicators could be attached. Crimes cleared up were measured, as were response rates to 999 calls and expenditure per citizen and numbers of police per citizen. Any task comparable was compared. Huge amounts of time and paperwork went into such measurement. Police journals described it as a bureaucratic craze. Performance inevitably became subject to the same falsification as police-station reports of crime statistics.[16] As we shall see throughout this book, the growth of value-for-money audit and of performance league tables was an effective weapon against bureaucratic inefficiency. Wide divergences between police-force costs and manpower levels were bound to be of concern to chief constables and, once upon a time, to police authorities. But what was being measured was what was most easily measurable. How much security, peace of mind, community relations or victory for good over evil was delivered in each area was not measured. To the Home Office gripping the purse-strings, what was measurable was what mattered. It set off down the road to a uniform pattern of policing.

With the coming of John Major to Downing Street, the Home Office no longer enjoyed Thatcher's protection from the Treasury. The police were floundering. They appeared to have lost both their accountability to local ratepayers and their political patron in Margaret Thatcher. Neither had been adequately replaced. The two-yearly British Crime Survey began to show not just rising crime but eroding public confidence in the police's ability to contain it. Home Secretaries stopped flattering the police and became ever more critical of their performance. Kenneth Baker, Major's first Home Secretary, was surprised at how dismissive his colleagues were of the police cause. A former Home Office minister, David Mellor, told him to remember that the police were grossly overpaid: 'We've thrown money at them and we have the highest level of crime in our history.'[17] Kenneth Clarke and Michael Howard were frigidly received at police conferences as they reminded the police that 'resources were not unlimited'. Police policy became a wholly centralized concept. The size of a truncheon, the wearing of body armour, the question of guns, the future of the 'bobby on the beat' were all matters for announcements by the Home Secretary.

Each push towards centralization tended to rely on the advent of an activist minister at a crucial moment in the evolution of policy. That was certainly the case with Kenneth Clarke's arrival at the Home Office in 1992 and the subsequent report of the 1993 Sheehy inquiry into police pay and conditions. Clarke was spectacularly unsympathetic, opening every sally against police inefficiency with such phrases as 'With all respect to my police friends, I have to say to them . . .' He set about doing to police authorities what Baker and then John Patten did to education committees: emasculate them to the point of irrelevance. Clarke was shameless in his contempt for local government of any sort. He left no chief constable in any doubt that he wanted a nationalized police force. He set about trying to construct one.

The door at which Clarke pushed was loose on its hinges. Local budget-capping had left police authorities already subordinate to the Home Office in budgets and inspectoral intervention. The 1993 local elections stripped them of any political sympathy from ministers. Not one of the forty-one English police authorities was left in Tory control; just five were left in Wales and Scotland. The authorities had no access to any Tory party network to defend their corner. Chief officers professed to value force autonomy but now seemed ready to accept any degree of supervision that offered an assured national career structure and access to resources. Like other professions, the police had become more introverted, more supervised, more reliant on the good offices of Whitehall. In its 1990s review of police efficiency, the Audit

Commission was critical of the role of local police authorities. They should have 'a higher profile in representing their forces to their communities', it said, but stressed that police officers were nowadays 'accountable for their actions through a performance review mechanism'. The contribution of laymen to this mechanism was little more than advisory.[18] The Commission was unaware that the standardization and nationalization of which it was an agent was what stripped the authorities of the sense of accountability it said they lacked.

Clarke's reforms were less drastic than those proposed for health, education or transport, but were of constitutional significance. He decided on yet another reduction in the number of forces and a change in the character of their committees. These would be formally removed from the control of local government and brought under his direct authority. The existing forty-one forces in England would be reduced to about twenty-five. He would appoint the chairman, who would be paid a salary, and half the members. These should be persons 'with business experience' (a code for 'Tory supporter' that became a standing joke in Whitehall). The rest might come from local government. The Home Secretary would set the authority's 'national key objectives' and put all chief constables on fixed-term contracts. In a Commons debate in March 1993, Mr Clarke declared that he had no faith in 'putting [elected] people in position to run the management and be solely responsible for the day-to-day decisions in the police service'. He seemed unaware that police authorities had never been responsible for operational decisions. He said, oddly, that one of his objectives was to 'encourage devolution of responsibility within police forces to local police units which will be directly accountable to their local communities'.[19] It was not clear how this accountability was to be manifest, though in some forces it took the form of 'local consultation'. Three months later Earl Ferrers, a minister in the House of Lords, was more straightforward. He assured peers that 'in future all police authorities will be independent of local councils'.

Clarke's proposals were set out in a white paper in 1993. They were a rare instance of the government misjudging parliament's centralist enthusiasm. Clarke's radicalism was too much, if not for Tory MPs, certainly for Tory peers. He succeeded in reviving the ghosts that had cursed Robert Peel in his bid for a national-ized police force. Most remarkable was the united opposition of former Home Secretaries, both Labour and Tory. One of them, Lord Whitelaw, questioned why Michael Howard (who in an-other general post had taken over from Clarke as Home Sec-retary) should be seeking so much power, 'with all the risks which his predecessors have deliberately and carefully avoided over the years'. Whitelaw was particularly insistent that the chairmen of the new authorities should be elected by those authorities, 'to ensure their independence and, crucially, the operational independence of chief constables'.[20] Whitelaw carried his opposition into the voting lobby.

Lord Jenkins of Hillhead was equally adamant. He said Howard had 'mixed dogma and hubris with a reluctance to consult and a determination to legislate at almost any price'. He felt the bill should be a case of the second chamber refusing automatic consent on a matter of constitutional importance. Lord Carr, a Home Secretary in the 1970 Tory government, was even more forthright. 'If I were still Home Secretary,' he said, 'I would not accept the offer of powers of this kind. I would resign rather than accept them. I believe that they are totally inappropri-ate for any Home Secretary to hold.' Howard was surely aware of the power he was putting in the hands of a future Labour holder of his office. Yet another former Home Secretary (and Prime Minister), Lord Callaghan, said that there was no great national or local pressure for the new authorities to be under the direct control of Whitehall, 'only the desire of the Home Secretary to strengthen his influence over them'. He added in a definitive comment on fifteen years of police reform, 'We all know that democracy does not just consist of electing a national parliament once every five years. We know that the strength of democracy comprises a web and complex of local institutions and local bodies made up of people serving in different ways.' As one peer after another rose to oppose centralization, the relevant minister, Earl Ferrers, protested that the old three-legged structure of police accountability was still in place. He was merely adjusting 'the milkmaid's stool'. He did not contest that he was making the Home Office leg a little stronger than the others.

Later that month, Ferrers was authorized by the cabinet to retreat on the composition of the authorities and the selection of chairmen. The government reduced its proposed appointees from a half to a third of the new authority members, five people in all. These, however, were to be selected by an absurdly convoluted procedure. The authority (on which there would now be a majority of local-government members) would advertise for members and itself send a long list of twenty names to the Home Office. Ten would be returned and the authority could select five of the ten. It was an open secret that the ten were vetted by the government whips' office for political reliability. Many Tories were deeply embarrassed by the crudeness of the party intervention, which was clearly intended to counterbalance any non-Tory majority on the new authorities.

The government stuck to the rest of its aggrandizement. It insisted on setting and assessing more stringent performance targets for the police through an expanded inspectorate. Senior officers had to move regularly between forces to prevent them 'going native', if they wanted promotion. This meant that their careers depended even more on the good opinion of the Home Office rather than on their relations with any one police authority or community. The procedure enabling swifter amalgamation of forces also remained as a reserve power in the bill. This defied evidence from the Audit Commission and from American research that forces do not become more cost-effective as they get larger, often the reverse.[21] Larger forces were easier for government to control. A proposal to give London a police authority with some elected members was abandoned in favour of a purely advisory committee, which itself remained a dead letter.

The Home Secretary sought to head off criticism of centralization by giving the police forces greater discretion over manpower levels and minor capital spending within approved budgets. Since overall revenue remained capped and standardized performance objectives were in place, this was modest freedom. In 1995, for instance, a Home Office cash increase of 1.6 per cent was more than wiped out by a Home Office concession of 3 per cent to the police unions for pay. Ministers tried to protest that as a result of delegation, any resulting cuts in police numbers were the 'responsibility' of the local police authority. By the mid-1990s the conclusion drawn by all observers of the British police was unanimous. A public service whose independence of central government had long been a pillar of the British constitution was within the Whitehall pale. Labour's then home affairs spokesman, Tony Blair, remarked after the passage of the 1994 Act that it was 'driven not just by cost-cutting but by ideology which resents local freedom with an aversion bordering on paranoia'. Whether he would later 'denationalize' the police was a question he left open. In a devastating survey of the implications of the legislation, Vernon Bogdanor pointed out that 'the police are not simply another professional pressure group, but a constitutionally independent body charged with securing obedience to the law'.[22]

By mid-1994, despite the Lords revolt over police authority membership, the government had centralized authority over the police on almost all fronts. The tripartitism of the 1964 Act had been ended. The Audit Commission had concluded that even before the 1994 Police and Magistrates Courts Act, 'the balance has now tilted so far towards the centre that the role of the local police authorities in the tripartite structure is significantly diminished'.[23] Clarke had said in March 1993 that he would in future be setting 'key national objectives for police activity ... and publishing results so that the public knows what their force has delivered'.[24] National league tables of police performance would be published, as for hospitals and schools. The new police authorities came into existence and struggled to give themselves a purpose. Under the Act, the Home Office promised that 'detailed Home Office central control of police force establishments will no longer apply'.[25] But what replaced it was a cash-limited budget based on a detailed central assessment of what needed to be paid for. Chief officers had some added managerial flexibility within their budgets and retained 'operational control'. Police authority members were left with little more than an advisory and consultative role, preparing local plans to 'monitor the performance' of a service over which they had no real authority.

In a detailed balance sheet of the centralizing versus devolving features of the 1994 Act, Barry Loveday acknowledged the devolution of managerial responsibility to chief constables as local executives.[26] But this was no more delegation than would be expected of any sensible national corporation. The key phrase in the white paper that preceded the Act was that its purpose was to 'refocus police priorities and direct them to those things which the government considers the police should be tackling as priority tasks across the country'.[27] A combination of objectives setting and monitoring and the fixing of budgets, said Loveday, had given Britain another National Health Service. The 1994 Act was a major step in the direction 'by which the police will cease to be a local service and will become effectively a state police'.

The Home Office might have won, but had the Treasury? The answer, as with health, must be yes and no. The motive behind Clarke's attempt to bring police authorities directly under Whitehall was to reduce the call on public expenditure without endangering value for money. Yet the Treasury had won this battle through its control of local government generally, well before the 1994 Act. It hardly needed more detailed control over police budgets or constant Home Office reviews of police functions. The Act and its attempted emasculation of police authorities had to do with asserting political as well as budgetary sovereignty. Ministers criticized for rising crime felt the need to take ever greater powers to answer that criticism. The irony is that these powers have not necessarily led to savings in public spending: if anything, the reverse.

We have seen with the NHS and the Metropolitan Police that direct Whitehall responsibility for a service does not in itself make it cheaper. What almost doubled police spending in real terms in the 1980s was not spendthrift local government but the generosity of Margaret Thatcher. She and her Chancellors took a political decision to win votes by spending more on law and order. The Treasury might have its hands on the levers of public finance, but if politicians refused to use those levers, indeed moved them in a reverse direction, there was nothing the Treasury could do. The Home Office employed a total of 34,000 staff in 1979. The figure had risen to 53,000 by 1994. It added 1,000 civil servants to its central (non-prisons) activity in 1990–94 alone. Spending on the police rose in real terms by a quarter over the same four-year period.[28]

The Treasury had argued with some justice that the culture of British policing had been wasteful. Many local forces in the 1960s and 1970s had become inefficient. A survey in Merseyside in 1985 concluded that more policemen on the payroll actually yielded fewer officers 'available for police duties' than in 1975 or 1964. The rest were on leave or doing paperwork. Each police force tried to squeeze as much money as it could out of the government each year, and then a bit more the next. As a result there were wide divergences between forces, with some of the worst in the Audit Commission tables being the largest, notably Manchester and London. The increase in central controls on police forces were 'more detailed than those on almost any other local authority service', according to the Audit Commission.[29] This probably reduced corruption and eliminated some of the worst areas of waste. But with crimes recorded by the police rising and public confidence ebbing, any true measure of value for rising resources and increased efficiency was hard to discern.

At no point did Whitehall have at its disposal performance indicators that more than scratched the surface of what the public expected of the police. Crime work, for instance, is estimated to occupy no more than a third of most police officers' time. Yet it dominates monitoring, because reported crimes are the simplest 'output measure'. In its 1995 review of police performance indicators, the Audit Commission used 'recorded crime' as the basis for its clear-up rate league table.[30] This is a notoriously unreliable indicator compared with the British Crime Survey, but was used because it is the only crime statistic available by local-authority area. Most police (and any sensible statistician) would regard a clear-up rate figure as near worthless for comparative purposes. As to how far such measures indicate public satisfaction with the police, nobody could say. In summer 1994 Howard announced yet another fundamental review of police functions. The headquarters disease of restless reorganization had infected the Home Office. The intention, an official told a police conference, was to 'free the police from unnecessary burdens' so as to fight crime[31] – or at least so as to perform better on Whitehall's indicators.

The centralizers were being hoist with their own petard. As police raced in their cars to improve their '999 call response times' the public did not necessarily feel better protected. A feature of the 1990s was a public beginning to doubt the virtues of the police monopoly. Neighbourhood Watch proliferated. Businesses turned to the private sector for security. Local councils recruited private guards to protect their buildings and housing estates. Non-police vigilantes, night-time citizen patrols and other irregulars emerged, notably among insecure ethnic groups in cities. At a press conference in September 1994, Michael Howard sought to bring the vigilante movement under his sponsorship, if only because of police concern that they might lose control of part of their work. He called a proposal for Neighbourhood Watch patrols 'walking with a purpose', a phrase much ridiculed.

There was no disguising what was happening. As nationalization and performance monitoring increased, so police 'supply' seemed to drift further from 'demand'. Encouraged to adhere to national standards, forces were by the same token less inclined to look over their shoulders to their communities. By the mid-1990s, despite efforts in some areas towards community policing, there were signs of divergence between the 'Home Office' police and more informal security forces. The prospect was of an increasingly mechanized and even armed government police force concentrating chiefly on crime, and a ragbag of *ad hoc* community-based irregulars of the sort found on the Continent. This was precisely the divergence that a century of British policing had sought to avoid. Robert Peel's ambition to establish a national constabulary might have triumphed, but at the cost of putting Dogberry and PC Plod back in business.

Whether or not this prospect is realized, Thatcherism had here constructed yet another nationalized service out of a once-local one, a service over which its consumers had little discretion or control. Policing may have been regarded as a neighbourhood function and police officers seen community relations as an important part of their work. It was one which no performance indicator was able to measure. Nor was local democratic accountability, or discretion over finance, any longer available as a proxy for public approval. Of that accountability, as the Home Office minister proudly told parliament, 'all police authorities will in future be independent'.

CHAPTER SIX

OPTING IN AND OUT AND IN

The greatest millennium of public office is when Commissioners shall rule the earth – CHARLES DICKENS

All the great measures of Tory centralization had a premonition, a forewarning of what was to come. In the case of schools in England and Wales, the moment was a speech on 18 October 1976 by the then Prime Minister, James Callaghan, at Ruskin College, Oxford. In it he called for a 'Great Debate' on the future of the school curriculum. 'There is no virtue,' he said, 'in producing socially well-adjusted members of society who are unemployed because they do not have the skills.' He suggested 'a basic curriculum with universal standards' and indicated that there was now 'a strong case for the so-called core curriculum of basic knowledge'.[1] The schools, he implied, were failing the nation. Standards were not rising but falling. Britain needed the same jolt that had been given to American education by the Russian sputnik.

Lord Callaghan's speech transformed morale within the Department of Education and Science in its tawdry headquarters overlooking Waterloo Station. Teachers had long regarded classrooms as consultants regarded operating theatres, as no-go areas for laymen or civil servants. Civil servants often referred to the curriculum as the 'secret garden' into which they were not admitted. Under the Butler Education Act of 1944, which still guided education policy in the 1970s, curriculum was delegated to local education authorities, who in turn delegated it to governors and teachers. Grammar schools worked to a rough and ready curriculum laid down by examination boards. The only mention of the content of teaching in the 1944 Act concerned religious instruction, part of the deal bringing church schools under local-government sponsorship. Every report on schooling in Britain referred to curriculum in the most tentative terms. Certainly Her Majesty's Inspectors of schools (HMI), working within the department, were heavily involved in classroom monitoring and curricular reform. But inspectors were within the professional pale and regarded as such by teachers. Like doctors and lawyers they expected to go about their business immune to influence from politicians.

The 1944 Act was a pillar of the welfare state, outcome of a wartime consensus that education had to be free and available to all. Like post-war reform of the police and health services, it was rooted in compromise. The central government had a duty to 'promote' education, but the agents of this duty would be local councils answerable to local electorates. The cost of national education was to be divided roughly 50:50 between central and local taxes. This partnership – tripartite between government, councils and schools themselves – was first assaulted by the strong central encouragement of comprehensive secondary schools in the 1960s. The 1964 Labour government was committed to end 11-plus selection and its circular 10/65 'invited' schemes for reorganization, though it was careful not to impose its own pattern. The view was that this reorganization was no more or less centralist than the 1944 Act's grammar/technical/modern distinction. Although some Tory councils refused to conform, most did so. Powers to impose non-selective schooling on recalcitrant Tory areas were only taken in the late 1970s, though still not implemented in a number of areas (such as Kent) even by 1979.

The Callaghan speech may have been no more than kite flying. But it brought curriculum out of the professional realm and into the political one. Officials in the education department had already produced what became known as the 'yellow book', for internal consumption.[2] Its phraseology gave an insight into the objectives of Whitehall at the end of the Wilson–Callaghan era. Officials, it said, should try to 'get on record from Ministers and in particular the Prime Minister an authoritative pronouncement on the division of responsibility for what goes on in schools'. Such a statement might usefully imply that the department should give a firmer lead. It 'should firmly refute any argument . . . that no one except teachers has any right to any say in what goes on in schools. The climate for a declaration on these lines may in fact now be relatively favourable.'[3] The department was jumping the gun by at least a decade, but its officials could sense the opportunity that politics might soon offer them.

The outcome of the Callaghan speech was a circular (14/77) from the education secretary, Shirley Williams, asking local education authorities a series of questions. She wanted to know how they kept classroom material up to date, how they recorded a child's progress, how they balanced the curriculum between different subjects and how they ensured that children who moved school were not handicapped by different curricula in different parts of the country. The circular was controversial, trespassing as it did on teacher autonomy. The National Union of Teachers registered a formal protest. The government remained unmoved and a subsequent departmental report based on the replies to the circular concluded that local authorities were lax. They lacked 'a clear view of the desirable structure of the school curriculum, especially its core elements'.[4] Whitehall was straining at the leash.

The Callaghan government had by now reached the end of its road. It gave way to the first education secretary ever to get to Number Ten, albeit a hesitant and unpopular one within the service – as she admitted in the chapter 'Teacher's Pest' in her memoirs.[5] Thatcher's new government was as timid on education as it was on health. A mild education secretary, Mark Carlisle, was soon followed by the ideologically non-interventionist Sir

Keith Joseph. In 1976 Joseph had set out his philosophy in clear terms: 'The blind, unplanned, unco-ordinated wisdom of the market ... is overwhelmingly superior to the well-researched, rational, systematic, well-meaning, co-operative, science-based, forward-looking, statistically respectable plans of governments'.[6] In a gloss on what this philosophy might mean for education, Stuart Maclure commented that 'Sir Keith Joseph was at heart a privatizer, but when he became Secretary of State for Education he was persuaded by his civil servants to adopt a more politically acceptable stance.'

In the early 1980s, politically acceptable meant avoiding trouble. Early legislation tinkered at the fringes of the education service, culminating in the Education (No.2) Act of 1986. New regulations covered matters such as school discipline, parents' rights, overseas student fees and staff dismissal. The law stopped councillors nominating majorities on school governing bodies. In general, Joseph was opposed to government imposing its will on education. Throughout Joseph's political life, intellectual radicalism struggled with inertia and indecision. In practice he was an apostle of live-and-let-live, perhaps a truer Tory than he was a radical Conservative.

This was not good enough for the Tory Right. By the mid-1980s a more strident activism was in the air, though not in any coherent direction. As in other areas of government policy, the free marketeers in the Tory think-tanks were in contention with the centralism of the Thatcher cabinet. Both sides drew strength from the growth of 'parent power' within local Conservative parties. Both saw education as the setting for a popular alternative to the 'producer-dominated' local councils. Education thus became an ideological battleground within the ruling party as well as with the Opposition. The Adam Smith Institute, the Hillgate Group, the Centre for Policy Studies, the Institute of Economic Affairs and the No Turning Back Group all produced pamphlets attacking left-wing councils and teachers. They found the political soil was fertile. Education authorities, Labour and Tory, were in contention with the teaching unions over pay and experienced strikes in 1985 and 1986. Yet Joseph seemed to have no response.

The Right wanted education vouchers and that will-o'-the-wisp of Tory education policy, 'wider parental choice'. A Tory adviser before the 1979 election, Stuart Sexton, carried the torch for vouchers through the first six years of the government. He was supported by politicians such as Baroness Cox, Angela Rumbold, Teddy Taylor and Rhodes Boyson, though never at the last ditch by the one politician who mattered. To this group, the state education service was riddled with left-wing poison. Parents had to be given market power to defeat or escape it. This power should be exercised in choice of school, in the running of the school and in what was taught in it. The curriculum had to be freed of socialist dogma. An Institute of Economic Affairs document said that 'the most effective national curriculum is that set by the market, by consumers . . . Attempts by government and by parliament to impose a curriculum, no matter how generally agreed they think it to be, are a poor second best . . . The government must trust market forces rather than some committee of the great and good.'[7] If such a programme required government to take power to ensure market diversity, so be it. The objective was diversity, not stronger government.

These libertarian sirens from the Right were soon silenced. Whitehall was as puzzled by the voucher concept as were most in the education world. The constraint on parental choice in the public sector was school capacity, not some formal bar to entry. Open enrolment was normal practice: but any child could get into an empty school, none into a full one. The issue was freedom for a school to expand or contract – and the resources to do so – and that was a matter not addressed at this stage in the debate. Vouchers were anathema to the Treasury because they would go to every parent, including those using private education, and would thus lead to a substantial rise in public expenditure.[8] Kenneth Baker recorded in his memoirs that departmental officials scuppered vouchers by 'first delaying, then proposing a super voucher which was so radical it frightened the cabinet and was rejected as unacceptable'.[9]

A ghost of the voucher concept survived in the Assisted Places Scheme for private schools. Assisted Places were public scholarships to up to 30,000 children to escape the state system into the private sector. They were to prove the salvation of many hardpressed private schools. With ending the requirement on local councils to introduce comprehensive secondary schools, this scheme had been the only mention of education in Thatcher's first Queen's Speech. With the advent of the national curriculum, opting out and the return of selection at eleven, it survived as an ideological appendix in Tory schools policy.

In 1986 the passive phase of Thatcher's policy came to an end with the departure of Joseph from the education department. In May that year Kenneth Baker arrived, hot-foot from his triumph in selling poll tax to his boss. His ambition undimmed by his time at environment, Baker was determined to overturn education policy, seeking a new battle in his campaign against the Left. He told Thatcher on his appointment that he intended to bring forward proposals for the 'fundamental reform of the education system'.[10] He caught her at the start of what was to prove her most creative period. He recalled her saying simply, 'Get on with it.' She warned him that officials at the Department of Education would give him constant trouble. 'The ethos of the DES was self-righteously socialist,' she wrote of her time at the department. 'It was soon clear to me I was not among friends.'[11] She did not warn Baker that she would cause him trouble too.

The Right now had to sit back and wonder what Baker, previously regarded as on the Left of the party, would do with his new licence from Thatcher. The first area for intervention was to be the curriculum. Baker was to treat professional control over classroom practice in schools with as little respect as the government was later to show to doctors. Joseph had already axed the old Schools Council, a curriculum advisory body composed of teaching professionals. In his 1986 Act he had tentatively requested that local authorities publish their syllabuses for each subject. He hoped that something approaching a national curriculum might be introduced by agreement. When in retirement in the Lords he was chided by a minister, Baroness Hooper, for having himself planned a compulsory curriculum. He denied any such intention. He had 'never thought of imposing mandatory requirements for any of those subjects. I spoke, Heaven help me, in terms of exhortation and example, not in terms of imposing the law.' The minister, in what was the motto of late Thatcherism, replied unkindly that Joseph's approach was 'part of the problem, because exhortation did not work'.[12]

Baker moved education to the top of the government's agenda. He was committed to curricular conservatism. Eight pages of the 1987 election manifesto were to be devoted to education, against just a few lines in 1979. The result was a plethora of cabinet suggestions. Norman Tebbit minuted the Prime Minister on a government 'contract' for each school, with the LEA being deprived of grant if the school under-performed. Nigel Lawson was more radical. He deplored Baker's arrival at education: 'It was hard to imagine that we would get from Kenneth the fundamental thinking about education reform that I was sure was needed.' He even set up a secret Treasury group to prepare a report on the future of the education service for the Prime Minister. He warned his officials 'that they were not to breathe a word to anyone at the Department of Education'.[13]

Lawson's plan, prepared by an official named John Anson, was to remove education altogether from 'so-called education authorities' and bring it directly under Whitehall. This, Lawson said, meant that 'the State would be able to lay down and enforce both a core curriculum and the standards of attainment required'.[14] It was a continuation of the approach mooted by Lawson during the poll tax debate. Thatcher herself was not prepared to be so radical. She agreed to a cabinet sub-committee on education reform, to keep a watching brief on Baker's activism and prepare for legislation after the 1987 election.

Baker shared Thatcher's reluctance to go straight for Lawson's centralization. He commented in his memoirs that 'fortunately the cabinet was not persuaded to go down that route'. He was backed by officials at his own department. The head of the schools branch at the time was Walter Ulrich, a stern civil servant who had served in both the Treasury and the Cabinet Office. Baker commented on Ulrich's 'formidable intellectual bullying', not least of his permanent secretary, Sir David Hancock. He felt Ulrich had held Joseph and his junior minister, Chris Patten, under the spell of his 'fine Wykehamist mind'. Both ministers had tended to 'concede the intellectual point rather than persist with the political argument'.[15] After the Treasury and the Foreign Office, the Department of Education had the strongest commitment to its own past policies, as Thatcher had herself discovered in 1970. Baker called this 'producer capture'. He saw many of his officials as conspiratorial allies of local authorities and especially the Inspectorate. 'I was determined not to be baulked as had my predecessors by official obstruction,' he said. 'If this meant forgoing the usual snail's pace at which reform in education was conducted, so be it.'

At least over the curriculum the department was prepared to collaborate with Baker's interventionism. Here at last was the 'favourable climate' presaged by Callaghan and the 1977 yellow book. Baker had no interest in vouchers or free markets. He might be guilty of what Lawson derided as 'PR-plus-money' politics, but he wanted to make an impact. He was frenetic. In his 1986 party conference speech he proposed to set up a completely new category of what were in effect government grammar schools. These would be known as City Technology Colleges, privately sponsored, centrally financed and with selective entry.

A little-noted feature of Thatcher's 'statecraft' was her ability to choose her moments to attack. She waited to confront the miners when coal stocks were high and the Labour party in disarray. She took on the GLC and local councils when they were in the grip of highly publicized left-wing factions. Baker was given his head to capitalize on the weakness of both local authorities and teaching unions in 1986 to assert his interventionism. The teachers' pay dispute of 1985–6 had seen unprecedented classroom strikes and left parents exasperated. The dispute culminated in a draconian Teachers' Pay and Conditions Act of 1987, winding up the independent arbitration machinery and imposing determination by the Secretary of State. Although teachers were employed by local authorities, their pay would in future be fixed by the Treasury as if they were civil servants.

Having established this salient, Baker now proceeded to exploit it. In a speech in Rotherham in January 1987, he denounced Britain's 'eccentric' decentralized approach to what was taught in schools. He praised the 'more or less standard national syllabuses' prevailing on the Continent and said it would be foolish to reject the idea of 'moving nearer to the curricular structure which obtains elsewhere in Western Europe . . . I am sure that we must so move.'[16] He rightly detected that his officials were happy to move in this direction: it was 'a policy for which they had a considerable degree of sympathy'.[17]

The curriculum for ages 5–16, known as key stages one to four, was published in July 1987. It tore up the tradition, delicately respected by Joseph, that what was taught in schools was the responsibility of teachers, guided by universities and monitored by professional inspectors. The sanctity of the secret garden was shattered. The curriculum was now a political football, kicked back and forth within cabinet. At its core were English, maths and science. These were surrounded with seven 'foundation' subjects: technology, history, geography, music, art, physical education and a modern language. Religious education was added as an afterthought. All would be compulsory to 16. In addition, attainment targets would be prepared, with national assessment at 7, 11, 14 and 16. Programmes of study – 'essential content which needs to be covered' – would also be published. Little was left to the discretion of teachers. The national curriculum would initially take up to 90 per cent of the teaching timetable. This was extraordinary, looking like political revenge against a calling once overwhelmingly Tory in persuasion. As Maurice Kogan pointed out, no other profession was subject to such central control over the content of its work.[18]

The new curriculum was deeply conservative and was the butt of much ridicule. Apart from the replacement of Latin with French, the subject bias was almost identical to that of the Secondary School Regulations drawn up by Whitehall in 1904, when state schools had last been subjected to central curricular authority. Baker characterized the new curriculum as 'balanced'. Critics pointed out that he could hardly talk about balance without specifying what was being balanced with what.[19] More substantive was the complaint that the 'back to basics' menu did little to confront children with the much-vaunted needs of 'international competitiveness'. There was no gesture towards new subjects such as economics and business studies, accounting, design and graphics, catering, health and hygiene. Nowhere did Baker relate his preferred subjects to 'the competitive skills they need for this new world'.[20] His was simply the traditional grammar school curriculum enforced on all secondary schools by law. There was no choice for parents, teachers, governors – or children.

The curriculum had to pass Parkinson's Law of Triviality. While nuclear defence might go through cabinet on the nod, teaching content was a topic on which every minister had a view. Should music and art be compulsory? What should be in a maths or English syllabus? How many hours should be left to teacher discretion? Thatcher appreciated the absurdity of much of this. She persistently complained in meetings with Baker that his curriculum was far too detailed and would become bureaucratic. 'I had no wish to put teachers in a straitjacket,' she recorded.[21] She had wanted just the core subjects to be prescribed by government. As so often, she was driven to defeat by the centralist logic of what she had unleashed. She finally admitted that 'the original simplicity of the scheme had been lost and the influence of HMI and the teachers' unions was manifest'. She accused Baker of being unable to stop his runaway train.[22] She had not set it in motion: Joseph had been content to leave well alone. As with poll tax two years earlier, Baker's self-confidence and positivism had carried her away.

The national curriculum was introduced in Baker's 1988 Education Reform Act, the biggest and most wide-ranging since the 1944 Act that it supplanted. Baker prefixed the title with the word 'great' and described the resulting bill as his 'gerbil'. It was a parliamentary monster, necessitating two guillotine motions and constant revision. Some 570 amendments were introduced in the House of Lords alone, later passing the Commons on three-line whips with just two days' debate. An article in the *Modern Law Review* hailed the bill as 'the highpoint of elective dictatorship', with a veritable fusillade of 'Henry VIII' clauses granting reserve powers to Whitehall.[23] Nationalizing the curriculum was just one small part of the Act. It also abolished the Inner London Education Authority (Ilea), which had survived GLC abolition in 1985 (see chapter eight). A national system of testing and assessment was also introduced. This was initially liberal in character and was welcomed by the teachers and education press. To Thatcher this fact alone was 'enough to confirm for me that its approach was suspect'.[24] With testing she feared she had made a mistake. She significantly referred to the national curriculum as her 'most important centralizing measure' but realized that the complexity of enforcing and testing meant that it 'soon ran into difficulties . . . by the time I left office I was convinced that there would have to be a new drive to simplify it'.[25]

As a result of this internal controversy, the curriculum was to be much amended as education secretaries came and went with bewildering speed – there were four in three years from 1989 to 1992. Both John MacGregor and Kenneth Clarke agreed with Thatcher on a less *dirigiste* line, but the concept of core and foundation subjects survived all change. Attempts by subject lobbies to make content and assessment more flexible were resisted by members of Whitehall's subject steering groups. Appointments to these groups were the source of fierce argument. Thatcher contrived both to oppose an over-centralized curriculum and yet insist on close vetting of the subject groups and their work. Of the history working group, she noted that one member was 'the author of a definitive work on the New History' and as such Not One of Us. As for the history group's report, 'I was appalled. It put the emphasis on interpretation and enquiry as against content and knowledge.'[26] Yet the greatest irony was that a curriculum justified on economic and vocational grounds should turn out so traditional and unvocational in content. Ministers, like parents, wanted schools to teach only what they had been taught.

The curriculum-testing regime ran into instant opposition from teachers, many of whom refused to touch it. This led to a shambles eventually resolved by Sir Ron Dearing, brought in by Clarke's successor John Patten, to cool tempers. Baker's curriculum was shortened and its preparation and assessment combined under one quango. But it remained awesomely centralized. It defied the Institute of Economic Affairs' belief that a curriculum left to parental choice would be 'far more responsive to children's needs and society's demands than any centrally imposed curriculum, no matter how well meant'.[27] As Bash and Coulby were to conclude after the passage of the 1988 Act, 'the imposition of the National Curriculum gives the lie to the prominence of libertarian conservatism. Indeed, it is this that has caused considerable unease on the Right ... Where is the freedom of the individual to pursue his or her own ends when the central state acts in an undeniably collectivist manner?'[28] Parents might be given a wider choice of schools but not a wider choice of what was taught in them. To the Right this was an alarming 'shift towards epistemological totalitarianism'. The department had even wanted to include the independent schools in the national curriculum. If the purpose was to improve the skills output of the education system as a whole, there was no sense in excluding an important 'leadership' sector. The schools lobbied successfully for their exclusion.

Curriculum was only half the Act. Its second substantive thrust was political, an extension of the Thatcher/Baker campaign against local government. The original cabinet committee that had prepared the 1988 Act had included strong Treasury representation. Lawson goes out of his way in his memoirs to praise his under-secretary, John Anson, who became a *bête noire* to education department officials. To Lawson, as noted earlier, 'wresting the schools from the so-called local education authorities would provide the essential basis for educational reform'.[29] To Thatcher this had proved too much: 'she was not prepared to take on the local authorities, who would greatly resent the loss of their responsibility for the schools.' Instead the committee proceeded, according to Lawson, 'in a way unlike any other on which I have served'. Anson and Brian Griffiths from the policy unit would present papers which Thatcher would use as 'Baker's marching orders'. Baker would come to the next meeting with revised proposals, 'get handbagged' and try again.

Thatcher eventually plumped for an uneasy compromise between centralism and localism. As a way of demonstrating no confidence in local government, she approved a new category of quasi-nationalized public-sector school (joining Assisted Places in public schools and City Technology Colleges), an opted-out one. She credits Griffiths with the idea.[30] Baker says it was his, discussed with Thatcher in 1986 as a way of preserving many grammar schools from comprehensivization.[31] Certainly the idea was current at the education department under Joseph. Either way, the intention was clear, to create a sanitized layer of secondary education between the private and local-authority sectors, roughly along the lines of the old grammar schools and perhaps embracing the church primary and secondary schools. Tory politicians would fiercely deny this, but it was obvious to head teachers and administrators.

School governors were to be re-empowered. They were to be encouraged to take all the pupils they could attract and, if a majority of parents so wished, they would be able to opt out of local-authority control altogether. They would then receive grant calculated by central government. What was termed the local management of schools initiative (LMS) was widely welcomed. Some councils, such as Cambridge and Ilea, were already practising versions of it. It gave all schools a more competitive edge. Since additional money would have to be directed from unpopular schools to popular ones, all had an incentive to improve their parental appeal. Although this gradually led to costly overcapacity in poorer schools, it injected more responsiveness to parental influence on school planning. That, at least, was as long as the school remained part of a local authority and the word planning retained any meaning.

The sting of the Act was 'opting out'. This meant that any school's governors or parents at odds with a council decision, for instance on accepting undesirable pupils or threatening it with closure, had an escape route. On the vote of a majority of parents, it could remove itself from local control and receive a grant direct from Whitehall. This was later termed 'grant-maintained status'. There was no doubt of the motive behind this innovation. As Thatcher declared in her post-election conference speech in 1987, 'hard-left education authorities and extremist teachers' were now in her sights as public enemy number one. The new Act, she said, would 'allow popular schools to take in as many children as space will permit. This will stop local authorities putting artificially low limits on entry to good schools . . . We will give parents and governors the right to take their children's school out of the hands of the local authority.' Her meaning was best captured by a speaker opposing it at the 1987 conference. David Muffet from Hereford and Worcester pleaded with the cabinet, 'Do not demolish the house just to get even with the Philistines. It didn't do Samson any good.'[32]

For local education authorities (LEAs), the Act presaged chaos. They were to be prevented by law from planning school capacity and thus investment. Any board of governors or parents who disagreed with a local plan could simply go it alone. This was curious since the government was pressing for greater efficiency throughout the public sector. The Audit Commission reported in 1988 that with declining school populations and increased mobility, the current rate of school closures would have to rise from fifty a year to over a hundred. What was not clear was how the government was to decide, as it was empowered to do, on the viable size for an opting-out school in this context. Of the first 340 schools, all secondary, granted the new 'grant-maintained' status, 63 had been under threat of closure.[33] Opting out sabotaged efficient school planning. As a result, the Treasury insisted that popular opted-out schools would not automatically be permitted capital to expand when there were empty places at adjacent schools. This clearly conflicted with the stated objective of the legislation. As with the hospital changes, the Treasury's concern for national efficiency flatly contradicted the professed ambition of Thatcherite reform, which was greater institutional or personal discretion.

The 1988 Act fractured the previous structure of local-authority schooling in Britain without putting any coherent structure in its place. It foresaw a patchwork of institutions, some still owned and controlled by the local council, others quasi-autonomous but under the protection and funding decisions of central government. Commentators found much of this baffling. The greater managerial freedom given to parents and governors under LMS could have been left to settle down before being overtaken by so drastic a measure. As Paul Meredith pointed out in his legal survey of the Act, 'Given that the enhancement of parental choice and of the responsibility of governors . . . [is] among the central purposes of open enrolment and delegated management, it is not easy to see the need for a further category of schools, where governors will be expected to assume full managerial responsibility independent of the LEA'.[34]

The hidden agenda to opting out was that adumbrated by Lawson and his Treasury officials back in 1986, and was subject to the limitations that they correctly forecast. There was an implicit assumption in the 1988 Act that merely giving parents and school governors more power would fail to achieve the goal of ridding education of local democracy. The subsequent fate of the 1988 Act − reinforcement by the 1993 Act − was proof of this pudding. If to local councils the 1988 Act seemed a political vendetta, to Whitehall it was the start down the road to a centralized school service. As Stuart Maclure said in his commentary on the Act, officials had 'for generations been on the receiving end of jibes about being the last practising exponents of the late Lord Lugard's colonial principle of indirect rule. Now after years of powerlessness and lack of executive authority . . . they sensed the prospect of real power and real management.'[35] Many officials were less enthusiastic about this extension of their power than they had been over the curriculum. As the Home Office was reluctant to run every police force – preferring remote control – so the education department feared the burden of administering every school. Yet this was the implication of the 1988 Act.

Under section 33 of the Act, the Secretary of State required local authorities to submit to him plans for the development of school government in their areas. If an authority failed to do so then the Secretary of State had reserve powers to make a plan of his own. There was much argument during the passage of the 1988 Act over the basis on which schools could vote to opt out. Ministers sought to make it as easy as possible. If a poll of parents failed to achieve a majority for grant-maintained status on a postal ballot of all parents, a second poll could be held requiring simply a majority of those voting. For good measure, once a school had opted out, the Secretary of State had reserve powers to appoint new governors if he felt the existing ones were 'failing in their responsibilities' (section 53.6). This was real belt and braces politics. Money to support such schools would come from local-authority budgets but on a formula decided by the Secretary of State and related to what other local schools would be getting on a per capita basis. In the early years this was enhanced by Whitehall as an inducement to opt out. Increasing the number of grant-maintained schools became a fixation of ministers. Voting to opt out was seen as tantamount to a vote of confidence in Thatcher's government.

Much of the criticism of the Act – which yielded an industry of legal interpretation – was directed at its alleged privatizing, fragmenting and divisive consequences. A diatribe against the Act by Whitty and Menter spoke of the 'atomizing of British education'.[36] Public money was being directed towards the successful, middle-class secondary schools. Grants to schools to opt out of local-authority control, greater rights for parents on governing bodies, the Assisted Places Scheme and the new grant-aided City Technology Colleges were destructive of a well-planned education system. The government's divisive intention was 'to reward schools which can demonstrate their capacity to compete successfully for individual clients in the market'.[37]

These developments, said the critics, presaged the privatization of British state education. The better-off schools (and pupils) would pass through the Purgatory of grant-maintained status in preparation for the Heaven of the private sector. Critics saw a residue of unpopular schools left with 'rump' education authorities: a scatter of Dotheboys Halls in working-class and ethnic ghettos. Even Maclure, no left-winger, concluded that the new Act was a complete repudiation of R. A. Butler's social reforming aims for the education system. 'Where he saw the object of educational reform as the creation of social harmony and social cohesion, the enterprise culture would substitute aims of self-reliance, competition and wealth creation. It would reward effort and punish idleness.'[38] The Act was educational Darwinism.

This impression of what Baker was doing accorded with the prejudices of his left-wing critics, and the hopes of some of his right-wing supporters. The former feared and the latter hoped that the British school system would be broken three ways: between private, grant-maintained and local-council institutions. There would be three tiers of school, and by association, three tiers of child. The bottom, local-government, tier would dwindle as brighter children were selected by examination or parental choice to go to 'better' schools, which would always be oversubscribed and thus reject less bright pupils. This was a far cry from the free-market voucher enthusiasm of 1979, but it was an echo of it. The state-school system was not to be smashed but recast in a more competitive mode, held together only by per capita grants and a centralized curriculum. Money would follow the parent. Maclure was right to use the word Darwinism.

Yet this ideology was not the dominant force behind education policy as the 1980s gave way to the 1990s. The corridors of

Whitehall have little time for Darwin. By the time Major appointed John Patten as his education secretary, any thought of atomizing the education service had vanished. As Coulby detected in 1989, 'the popular rhetoric of the day concealed the fact that the proclaimed denationalization of schools and colleges was actually a delocalization and a centralization – bluntly nationalization'.[39] In the first place, the opting-out strategy had not proved as successful as Baker had hoped. Thatcher declared after the 1987 election that 'most schools will opt out'.[40] But only 1,000 of the 24,000 state schools in England and Wales had opted out by 1995. Half of these were in just eight local education authority areas. Most were either former grammar schools eager to reassert their 'selective' status, or smaller city schools fearful that they might be closed.

Although Baker had promised that he would not permit opted-out comprehensive schools to use academic selection to restrict entry at 11, his successor Kenneth Clarke weakened that promise, supported by the Prime Minister. With the publication of school league tables, head teachers became understandably averse to respecting parental choice. They wanted pupils who would score highly on GCSE and A levels. This meant securing the brightest intake at 11. Nobody with knowledge of English secondary education could pretend otherwise: selection by ability at 11 was back on the school agenda after three decades of absence. Selection of pupils by schools, the essence of 'selection by ability', is not at all the same thing as selection of schools by parents. Nor did popular schools have any incentive to expand. Not only might this 'dilute' their intake and thus their league table position and institutional self-esteem, it was also banned by the Treasury if it left empty places elsewhere.

An important reason for the decline in opting out was that the government's other policy, giving school heads and governors more autonomy under LMS, was a success. This appeared to dismay ministers. Shortly before her fall, Thatcher considered new measures to stifle local education authorities once and for all, even if it needed another Act. She saw them as vampires, looming round her at every turn. She approved a paper from Griffiths' policy unit on 'unbundling' local-authority control and leaving councils with merely an advisory role, 'perhaps in the long term not even that'.[41] This, she said, would have 'eased the state still further out of education'. This belief, that local government was the state while central government was not, was Thatcherism at its most visceral.

Thatcher's departure did not dim this determination. Under John Major, John Patten took up the centralization policy with enthusiasm. In 1992, legislation passed through parliament, with little prior consultation and even less protest, stripping councils of their sixth-form and further education colleges. Some of these were based on ancient grammar schools or private technical colleges. They were brought under a new government Further Education Funding Council. The seizure of some of England's most ancient and distinctive academic institutions passed virtually without notice outside the education world. There was no concession to local opinion, no parental vote or request from governors. The colleges were simply nationalized by what amounted to government fiat.

The next step was a white paper with the euphemistic title *Choice and Diversity*. This declared the government's desire that by 1996, 'most of the 3,900 maintained secondary schools as well as a significant proportion of the 19,000 maintained primary schools [in England and Wales] could be grant-maintained'.[42] In the triumphalist words of the junior education minister, Eric Forth, this would 'mark the end of the long-standing local education authority monopoly of state school provision'.[43] After a hesitant start, Lawson's 1986 nationalization proposal was back in the running. Every effort would be made to prevent obstruction from local democracy.

New rules were introduced to make opting out easier than under the 1988 Act. It would be made illegal for local councils to lobby against opting out. In addition, the new Act set up a structure for administering grant-maintained (GM) schools under the authority of the Secretary of State. So far the 1,000

GM schools had enjoyed a period of relative autonomy, receiving grants without Whitehall strings. Mrs Thatcher had insisted on this, regarding them as 'independent state' schools, in effect a revival of the old direct grant institutions. She recorded her annoyance that the education department hated this concept and changed her speeches to call them 'grant-maintained'.[44] (They were later renamed again as 'self-governing institutions'.) Yet the idea that all state primary and secondary schools could opt out of any planning or investment framework was implausible. A school is an inflexible asset. If the 'money followed the parent' it would lead to large market imperfections, with gross undercapacity in some schools and overcrowding in others. It would be expensive and the Treasury would never tolerate it. Opting out of local planning and control implied opting in to something else. That something was Whitehall.

John Patten's Education Act was more gargantuan and certainly more centralist than Baker's 'Gerbil 1988'. Baker had 238 sections; the 1993 Education Act had 308 sections. An unprecedented 1,000 amendments were tabled during its passage and 55 new clauses added. Patten often declared his intention as being to set in place a new framework for primary and secondary schools that will endure well into the next century. His department now tore aside the veils shielding GM schools from its oversight. A new agency, to be called the Funding Agency for Schools (FAS), would be established for England (and later one for Wales), with members appointed directly by the Secretary of State. Its powers over the new GM schools were unconstrained. Governors could be appointed and sacked. The agency could expand or contract GM schools, set up new ones and close down old ones. It was given power by the Secretary of State to cripple competition from the surviving local-authority sector. The funding agency could prevent local authorities opening or even expanding new schools to compete with its own (as it did in Sutton in 1994). The local-council monopoly might be over, but there was no nonsense about a duopoly.

Under the Act, the FAS was in no sense 'quasi-autonomous'.

It was *de facto* and *de jure* under the Secretary of State's authority, indeed little more than a schools planning adjunct of the department. It must comply with directions contained in orders from the department (under sections 6 and 9). It must institute value-for-money studies of schools under its charge (under section 8). Under section 12, the Secretary of State could make an order giving it 'sole responsibility or joint responsibility with the LEA for ensuring the provision of sufficient school places in an area'. In particular, the agency would be put in a position to determine the 'character' of a school and thus its selection system. This meant that Whitehall could dictate whether or not a particular secondary school would be selective or comprehensive, a matter of some importance in the event of a change of government. This put MPs, and thus ministers, in the firing line for questions not just over the fate of individual schools but even over pupil admissions. Pupils rejected by GM schools found themselves in limbo if they had failed to apply to local-council schools in time. As with the trust hospitals, a measure of local competition had been instituted as a spur to efficiency. But resource allocation and planning were set on a centralized path.

The Act laid down that in any dispute between the funding agency and a surviving local education authority the Secretary of State, who is the agency's boss, would be the judge. This power of arbitration was similar to that enjoyed by the health department over NHS 'contracts'. In its commentary on the Act, Longman's *Education and the Law 1994* pointed out that 'it would be wrong to view the funding agency as an independent body acting at arm's length from the central government; rather it is the direct agent of the Secretary of State, amenable to centralized direction and control'.[45] The Act was seen as delivering a fatal blow to the local control of education.

Yet it had an Achilles heel. Whereas the further education and sixth-form colleges had been nationalized compulsorily, the 1993 Act retained the voluntary principle for secondary and primary schools. Opting out still involved opting, and by the mid-1990s this had come to a virtual halt. The vast majority of secondary schools (and almost all primary schools) had decided to stay with local authorities. Even where schools had opted out, they found themselves returning to use local-council services under contract. They purchased staff pensions and recruitment services, cleaning and maintenance, counselling, even pupil assessment and enrolment. This was much as envisaged under LMS. Councils had themselves been shocked by the 1988 Act into being more tolerant of institutional delegation. So successful had been that part of the Act that councils recovered the loyalty of the bulk of their schools and parents – and vitiated the Act's wider goal.

What the government appeared to have done was re-establish the old 'class-based' tiers of pre-1965 secondary schooling in a new guise. There would now in England and Wales be private schools, intermediate colleges and grammar schools, and council 'modern' schools. The difference was that the middle tier was run by government. In 1979 Whitehall controlled virtually no schools or colleges in Britain. Its support of public-sector education (mostly universities) cost taxpayers £800m, or roughly 8 per cent of total public spending on education. By 1995–6, following the nationalization of some schools and all colleges, the cost was £8.2 billion or just over 20 per cent of spending. This was a real-terms rise of more than 300 per cent.[46] Spending doubled in just two years between 1992 and 1994. Like the Home Office, the Department of Education had become a vastly more important player in the game of government.

Meanwhile intense efforts were being made by the education department to evolve what was called a 'common funding formula', whereby central and local government would determine a fixed sum that ought to be spent on each pupil nationwide. Given the capping of all local spending to a fixed assessment of needs, the end result of this would be to eliminate all variations in public spending on schools. In time, each state school in Britain should have a wholly standardized budget, any variations dependent on private fundraising (or fees). The effect of this would be to negate the devolution of GM and LMS school management to governors, as well as to undermine the discretion of elected education authorities. School budgets were not just statutory in status but subject to central formulae which in individual areas could well seem arbitrary. Governors and committee members found themselves in the same position as police authorities and health authorities: governors only in name, cheer-leaders in practice.

In 1995 the Treasury precipitated a crisis that tested the new regime to destruction. It allowed roughly 1 per cent more in cash for school budgets, but conceded a statutory 2.7 per cent pay rise to teachers. Although education committees had some small room for manoeuvre it was rarely enough to make up for this gap. Gillian Shephard, the new education secretary, faced the probable sacking of thousands of teachers and pleaded with the Treasury for relief, if not in extra grant at least from the rigours of capping. The Treasury refused both more money and so clear a breach of capping discipline. The governors of a GM school in Dursley in Gloucestershire invited Shephard to sack them and appoint replacements, as she would be obliged to do under the Act, as they refused to balance their budget. The governors of a GM school in Derbyshire (Newbold School, near Chesterfield) resigned *en bloc* rather than sack seventeen teachers, having sacked six the year before.

Later Shephard had to send her own governors to augment those at Stratford GM School in East London, after the school had failed an inspection. *The Times* reported that she had found to her embarrassment that she could not sack the existing governors, which she could in the case of council schools, because under the 1993 Act, 'ministers did not anticipate that grant-maintained schools would ever be judged as failing'.[47] She had to appoint a majority instead. Yet Shephard still declared that grant-maintained schools were 'completely independent of the government'.[48] This description seemed wholly at variance with reality. The Treasury was now running the state schools of England and Wales and the Chancellor, Kenneth Clarke, did not mind who knew it. Angry that opting out appeared to have failed, he was unconcerned at the punishment meted out to local-authority and government schools alike.

The centralist impact of the Thatcher/Major education acts was not unforeseen. Sir Peter Newsam, a former director of the Inner London Education Authority, warned before the passage of the 1988 Act that Britain was accepting 'direct ministerial control of the education service'. Though not of the government's political persuasion, Newsam bore the scars of political interference from the London left-wing militants. He asked, 'What if one day this country were to find itself with a Secretary of State possessed of a narrow vision of what education in a democracy should aspire to be, coupled with a degree of self-regard and intolerance . . . that caused him or her to seek to impose that vision on others?'[49] A Democrat education secretary in America gave one answer to that question: in 1994 a national history curriculum was written for American schools from which references to the British colonies and even George Washington were expunged as racist.

In 1988 Baker had promised the House of Commons that his bill was 'about devolution of authority and responsibility, not about enhancing central control'. This was eccentric. Both Baker and Patten protested that they had never meant to be centralizers. They believed that they were 'rolling back the frontiers of the state', in conformity to Thatcherite doctrine. Perhaps they did not realize what they were doing. As with the poll tax, both men combined ambition with the insecurity of being on the party's moderate wing. Like ailing sharks, they had to keep moving to breathe. 'Strike high and adventure dangerously,' was how Baker put it in a quote from Milton.[50]

The reforms undoubtedly began as a response to a widespread parental aversion to the educational innovations of the 1960s and 1970s. Thatcher could have moved in one of three ways: privatization (through vouchers), decentralization (through LMS and a revitalization of local democracy) or partial or total nationalization. The last was the least painful in the short term and most accorded with the Treasury's desire for control – despite education not being 'out of control' in the sense that spending on health and the police appeared to be. The Tory Right had begun the Thatcher era with its hopes high of a victory for libertarianism and diversity in education. Baker and Patten trumped them. They nationalized the grant-maintained schools and sought a common funding formula that would deliver a standard unit of schooling for every child irrespective of local democratic choice. Academic league tables, curriculum reform and rate-capping made all schools more uniform. The fragmentation of public secondary education stirred the ghost of 11-plus selection from its grave.

What is most astonishing in retrospect is that the paradox, of state selectivity and curricular diktat on the one hand and proclaimed parental choice on the other, occurred to so few Tories. Thatcher was only dimly aware of it. Not until the second volume of her memoirs did she come clean, in a stark passage. In defending grammar schools for clever children of different background, she wrote, 'we were defending a principle – namely that the state should select children by the simple criterion of ability and direct them to one of only two sorts of schools – that is far more consonant with socialism and collectivism than with the spontaneous social order associated with liberalism and conservatism. State selection by ability is, after all, a form of manpower planning.'[51] It was a consideration, she said, that she had 'only come to appreciate in recent years'. Instead, the Thatcher and Major governments centralized power over the content and organization of education in a way that seemed the antithesis of everything for which Conservatives traditionally stood. They behaved in precisely the way the wartime coalition had done in 1944 and Labour in 1965. They had imposed the will of government on a previously diverse system to make it more uniform. They had done so with draconian powers over the organization and content of education that a future government might use to further quite different ends from its own. This was the real irony. The best that can be said for this exercise in nationalization is that, by 1995, it had largely failed.

CHAPTER SEVEN

TAMING SHREWS

Where there is much desire to learn, there of necessity will be much arguing, much writing, many opinions – JOHN MILTON

Britain's universities completed the 1970s in good shape. They were regarded by the rest of the world as efficient and high-quality. Blessed with the English language and subsidized fees, they were second only to American ones for international desirability. It was said that there were as many good universities in Britain as in the whole of the USA, and more than in Germany or Japan. Not only had Oxford and Cambridge retained their scholastic pre-eminence alongside the American giants, so too had civic universities such as Manchester, Leeds, Edinburgh and the colleges of London University. Higher education was an urban growth centre and an 'invisible' export industry. It was also an expensive feature of public spending.

The writing on the wall for these institutions was clear from the start of Margaret Thatcher's administration. 'There is going to be in future a somewhat greater degree of direct intervention in the affairs of individual universities than has been customary or necessary in the past.' So said the new chairman of the University Grants Committee, Sir Edward Parkes, in October 1980 to the assembled committee of vice-chancellors. 'We want you to concentrate on your strengths and not support pallid growths.'[1] The reason, he implied, was that universities were about to be subject to an unprecedented assault on their

135

privileges. There was a risk that 'we shall cease to control our destiny, because . . . the greatest threat to the United Kingdom universities today is not a financial one'.[2] Those present shuddered. What could he mean?

British universities had always enjoyed protection from the more bitter disciplines of public-expenditure control. They were regarded as private institutions in receipt of public funds. Tradition dictated that scholarship should be independent of external pressure, be it from commerce, from party politics, or from the state. The university as a self-governing, self-disciplining and self-reliant institution dated back to the religious foundations of the Middle Ages. Oxford and Cambridge were able to weather some of the storms of the 1980s through recourse to historic endowments, and to a rediscovered aptitude for private fundraising. The scholar frequently stood over against the state, or prided himself on being a nuisance to it. Universities in England, Wales and Scotland based this independence on royal charters, as did the old boroughs. A charter was a guarantee of freedom from interference in institutional self-government. But charters come cheap. Independence is expensive. No charter was proof against Thatcherism.

The great civic universities, which began life in the nineteenth century, depended on income from student fees and on gifts from commerce and local benefactors. Even the Victorians realized that these sources of income were not enough to enable higher education to expand or attract poorer students. Although government had in the past bought services from some universities, it was in 1889 that the Treasury made its first direct grants to needy institutions. The first, of £15,000, saved the fledgling university of Sheffield (then still a university college) from bankruptcy. A later vice-chancellor of Sheffield was the historian, H. A. L. Fisher, whom Lloyd George brought into his cabinet during the First World War as President of the Board of Education. Fisher understood both the need of the economy for well-qualified graduates and the need of universities to have academic freedom in supplying them. Grants should be arm's-length and

assured over time, otherwise institutional planning was impossible. This particularly applied to the growth of scientific research,
boosted by the war economy.

At the end of the Great War the Treasury was still spending
relatively little on higher education, £150,000 in all. Fisher
proposed in 1919 that a separate body, the University Grants
Committee (UGC), be established to administer this money and
co-ordinate state research on science and medicine. Grants to the
poorer civic universities were specifically intended to free them
from the narrow vocational demands of local patrons and spon-
sors. The UGC's terms of reference were prepared by its first
chairman, Sir William McCormick, under Fisher's aegis. The
document was unique in the history of public finance. The
committee was to be answerable direct to the Treasury and not
to a spending department. Grants were to be assured over a
rolling five-year period, an extraordinary concession from a Treasury whose mind was, and is, bounded by a one-year horizon. (If
universities needed to plan five years ahead, why not schools or
railways or navies?) The UGC's membership was not political or
lay but academic, another unusual concession to the autonomy
of a profession in receipt of public money. The secretariat was
supplied by the Treasury.

The only other organization with a comparable deal was the
Arts Council, set up by Keynes after the Second World War and
modelled in part on Fisher's precedent. The willingness of the
Treasury to accept such departures from convention was probably cultural. Universities and the arts were subjects in which
Treasury officials had a personal interest. They liked them and
knew people who worked in them. They were thus happy to keep
them close, favoured jesters at the court of public finance. As
students of courtly life know, such positions can be lucrative. The
closer a recipient is to the source of its cash, the more reluctant
that source is to be stingy. The universities and the arts were
never better treated than when they were directly under the
Treasury. But such favouritism has its risk. Students of courtly
life also know that there is nobody less enviable than a courtier

down on his luck – and no patron more dangerous than one who no longer sees the joke.

The UGC's early history was benign. As its obituarist Michael Shattock has pointed out, 'The injection of state funding had the effect of removing an absolute dependence on pressures exerted by private donors. The constitution of the UGC offered a guarantee that the state itself would not seek to undermine institutional autonomy.'[3] Through most of its life the UGC was a model of the arm's-length principle. It comprised a part-time chairman and ten scholars. On their advocacy, public money to higher education rose over the inter-war period to cover almost a third of university spending. There was no hint of the Treasury or the UGC telling universities what to teach or what to research.

This detachment was too good to last. Even the longest arm's length cannot withstand the force of public money for ever. Pipers always end by calling tunes. After the Second World War the government moved steadily from the role of passive benefactor of higher education to that of active stimulant. A perceived economic need for graduates of all sorts, notably scientists and engineers, led to an expectation on the part of both donor and recipient that government money would have to increase. The UGC was given a planning as well as a financing role. This culminated in the Robbins report of 1963, advocating a big expansion in the university population. Robbins took it as read that the cost of this would be met by central government and also perceived the dangers that this dependency might involve. In a significant inversion of Fisher's case for state subsidy, Robbins remarked that there was still a place for the private benefactor, to give universities 'the enhanced sense of freedom and flexibility that comes from the possession of funds that are not dependent on government and not limited by official regulations'.[4] No longer was the state seen, as in 1919, as the guarantor of academic freedom against the private patron. Robbins saw that patron as a potential guarantor of academic freedom against an interventionist state.

By the time of Robbins, the pressure to expand the universities was overwhelming. The post-war teenage 'bulge' was approaching university age and in 1962 an Education Act formally laid down that local councils, reimbursed by the Treasury, should finance fees and residential grants to anybody with two A levels admitted to a university. The UGC accepted the inevitable and new universities followed thick and fast: Sussex, York, Essex, East Anglia, Lancaster, Kent, Warwick. Variously called the Shakespeare universities, the pink-brick universities (as opposed to civic red-brick) and the New Universities, they were commonly attributed to Robbins himself. All, with the exception of Stirling, were planned pre-Robbins.

Yet it was Robbins' emphasis on a close relationship between the university and economic growth that signalled the advent of a national university system and a 'policy' to back it up. For the time being, each university remained an independent, self-governing institution with a Privy Council charter, meeting student demand on its own terms. The block grant continued, and with it the implied respect for academic autonomy. The new universities adopted the costly Oxbridge residential tradition, as had the civic universities. British higher education was not just high-quality but expensive, catering for just 8 per cent of the age group. Quality not quantity was still the watchword. But after Robbins the concept of a wholly autonomous university sector, unresponsive to the demands of the economy, was vulnerable.

In 1964 the UGC was transferred from under the wing of the Treasury to the more down-to-earth sponsorship of the Department of Education and Science. It now began to deplore its own impotence, its lack of a more indicative role in university planning overall or in the case of individual institutions. The nearest to direction was a 'letter of guidance' to a vice-chancellor, usually followed by lunch at the Athenaeum. In 1968 the UGC reported, almost casually, the need 'for at least the outline of a central strategy'. On the one hand it bewailed its inability 'to control the flow of human material' through higher education,[5] on the other it saw its own independence dwindle as universities became more costly and the Treasury more protective of public money. In

1974 the Treasury ended the quinquennial grant system and universities had to come within the annual grant horizon of other public institutions.

The Treasury also refused to let university fees rise with inflation. Since these were paid automatically by local councils to any student gaining admission, and then reimbursed by the Treasury, the latter could see no point in letting them rise merely to transfer more money to universities via local authorities. Fees declined and direct grants through the UGC rose. But the effect was to reduce the income that a university could automatically increase by taking more students. It became more dependent on a (limitable) central grant. By throwing the burden of university subsidy on to grants, the Treasury was in a position to exert greater leverage on university finance than it would have had by allowing fee income to rise. As Shattock pointed out, this policy was a slap in the face for right-wing advocates of a voucher for higher education (which is what the old local-authority fee-plus-grant system had been *de facto*). 'One of the main grounds for government refusing to endorse the call of some of its supporters on the Right to raise fees ... to create a completely market-driven system, was that government would then lose control.'[6]

The crunch for the Thatcher government's higher-education policy came early, with the public-spending round of 1980–81. The Treasury demanded cuts in planned expenditure of 8 per cent against 1979–80, with cuts of 5 per cent in real terms over each of the next two years. This imposed an unprecedented strain on the UGC, with many academics telling its members to resign in protest. The committee decided to make the best of a difficult job, activating for the purpose its dormant role as a planning agency. Research was now graded according to output, a quantitative approach long deplored by English visitors to American campuses. Sir Keith Joseph attempted unsuccessfully to persuade universities to abandon protected tenure for academics. Universities regarded as poor performers, Bradford, Salford and Aston, had their grants cut by over 30 per cent. The grants were now cash-limited, which meant that whatever pay rises were negotiated for staff nationally had to be met within budgets that frequently made no allowance for them. (Previously supplementary grants had been payable to meet negotiated pay rises.) The Treasury further increased its financial leverage on universities by gratuitously halving domestic student fees and shifting yet more of their income on to cash-limited grants. It also told them to charge overseas students the full cost of their courses, to the rage of many in the universities as well as the Foreign Office.

This regime was devastating for some institutions. Aberdeen and University College London came close to bankruptcy and recovered only by such desperate measures as asking senior staff to take immediate early retirement. Salford seriously considered closure, eventually cutting its size by 40 per cent. The advocates of central planning now advanced through the 'cuts' salient. Whether to expand a particular physics laboratory or shut down a classics department became a matter for the UGC, not a university academic board. The old letters of guidance on course structure became emphatic recommendations. In 1982 the UGC sought to restore some morale by offering 250 'new posts' over each of three years, for which universities would have to bid. They were privately advised not to bid for 'social science' ones. Bidding to a government agency for lecturerships was an innovation. The only bulwark against complete capitulation to Whitehall was that the UGC remained a body composed of professional academics. It remained a strong advocate of its autonomy over policy. It vigorously resisted pressure to cut unit costs per student, regarding this as the tell-tale of quality, even if this meant stalling any further university expansion.

For a brief moment, the education secretary of the day, Keith Joseph, appeared ready to respect this autonomy. In 1981 he wrote to Lord Croham, then investigating university finances, promising not to curtail the UGC's 'responsibility and freedom of action'. Despite the growing furore over cuts, his junior minister, William Waldegrave, told a constituent that the government had been right to stand back from professional decisions made by the UGC. This had been a 'demonstration of good sense on the part of successive governments'.[7] Joseph's non-interventionism was sustained throughout his time at the Department of Education. As in so many areas, Thatcherism hesitated before taking the centralist plunge.

That plunge came with Joseph's departure and the arrival of Kenneth Baker in 1986. The change was total, from what Joseph described as exhortation to what Baker denied was centralist rule. Within a year Baker's views on higher education, and those of his officials, were set out in a white paper called *Meeting the Challenge*.[8] This was to form higher education's contribution to the 1988 Education Reform Act. It was a devastating document with a deliberately double-edged title. Baker was angered by university antagonism towards the government following the cuts of 1981–3, playing to his leader's similar fury. Thatcher spoke of some universities 'pushing out poison' to the students and resented giving them one penny to do so.

There was no denying that the cuts had deeply offended institutions whose independence had long been assured by government. Equally Thatcher struck a chord with many supporters by questioning why academics should have tenure for life, while being shielded from spending cuts and relieved of accountability for their output. The universities gave no quarter. In 1981 364 economists had written to *The Times* savaging Thatcher's economic policy. Oxford subsequently denied Thatcher the honorary degree customarily given to prime-ministerial alumni. Nigel Lawson said that he afterwards tore up all requests for money from that university.[9] It was war, and one in which it was unlikely that Thatcher would take prisoners. By the mid-1980s a junior lecturer was earning less than a policeman or a qualified nurse.

The Baker white paper was not aimed at limiting public expenditure. The UGC had shown during the 1981 cuts crisis that it could do that. These were not uncontrollable hospitals run by millionaire consultants. The government wanted higher education brought to heel. The white paper was unequivocal and political: 'The government considers student demand alone to be an insufficient basis for the planning of higher education. A major determinant must also be the demands for highly qualified manpower, stimulated in part by the success of the Government's own economic and social policies.' Those policies required that the government and its 'central funding agencies' would do all they could to 'bring higher education institutions closer to the world of business'. The world of business was seen by ministers, few of whom had any experience of it, in a golden haze: it was a vague amalgam of the free market, hostility to unions and sympathy to the Tory party. Yet what this world of business wanted from the universities was left unresolved. The education department assumed, on the basis of no evidence, that it wanted more scientists and technologists. Equally unresolved was how demand and supply might be brought into equilibrium. The answer did not lie with student choice, nor with the preferences of employers expressed in industrial sponsorship or in graduate pay scales. Nor was this a matter to be left to universities and polytechnics themselves. So where was Adam Smith's invisible hand?

The answer given by the white paper was bald. In future Whitehall would decide what were the requirements of industry, commerce and the public services. It would do so 'bearing in mind also employers' requirements for recruits with lower levels of educational qualification'. This puzzling addendum hinted at one response to the cuts of 1981. Government might wish to stifle demand for higher education lest industry find young people over-qualified for its 'lower level' needs. 'If evidence of student or employer demand suggests subsequently that graduate output will not be in line with the economy's needs,' said the white paper, 'Government will consider whether the planning framework should be adjusted.'

That a supposedly free-market cabinet could put its imprimatur on such phraseology is extraordinary. Yet it passed cabinet on the nod. Baker was purporting to implement the 1987 Croham report on university finance. This had certainly advocated indicative planning of university capacity, but it also recommended that the block grant system stay, and with it the implied respect for academic freedom. Baker and his officials rejected this. They abruptly abolished the UGC and substituted a new Universities Funding Council (UFC). Instead of being composed of academics the new council had fifteen members, of whom only seven could be academics. Such was the paranoia of Thatcherism at this time that 'the enemy' must never be in a majority on any quango. The chairman, Lord Chilver, of Cranfield Institute of Technology, held strong views on higher education's obligations to industry. The new UFC overturned Robbins' dictum that such agencies should be a 'device for interposing between government and institutions persons selected for their knowledge and standing'. But soon even Chilver had trouble squaring his free-market beliefs with the *dirigisme* of Thatcher's Whitehall.

In place of the block grant, the education department introduced a concept borrowed from the new managerialism, that of the internal contract. The contract was to give a veneer of autonomy to university planning. Sir Peter Swinnerton-Dyer, chief executive of the new funding agency, spoke of 'buying certain services from universities . . . The government will use the power which the situation gives it to press for higher quality and greater efficiency, just like Marks and Spencer.'[10] Yet a contract implies choice. The universities had none. The contract process was draconian and short-term. The Croham report had recommended that universities receive money for three years forward as against the then current one year. This was rejected by the Treasury, and by Baker at its bidding. Not only would money be given annually, but it would be subject to an annual planning cycle, to enable 'detailed reviews of particular aspects of universities' work, by subject or otherwise, to be conducted continuously'.

This response was a major external intrusion on academic autonomy. It was also regarded as unfair. A university department which was 'under-performing' might need time to improve. The calibre of students and staff will vary over time and be inflexible in the short term. Yet the white paper crisply stated

144

that money for the next year would be withdrawn if 'the funding body after discussion with the institution involved is satisfied that the provision contracted for cannot be delivered, or only partially or inefficiently delivered'. In future money should be supplied for courses 'on general criteria which are applied systematically across all universities'. This was centralist planning with a vengeance, but also planning of the most short-term nature of an 'industry' whose quality is essentially long-term.

In a ferocious assault on the white paper, the professor of administrative law at London University, John Griffith, commented that it was 'impossible to find any parallel for this provision, which empowers a minister to fine a public authority without any recourse to a court or independent arbitrator. Even a district auditor has no such power over spending by local authorities or their members.'[11] Academic performance would in future be assessed centrally, by subject sub-committees of the new UFC. As was predictable, quality proved hard to define. To a crude teaching indicator such as hours taught had to be added some value criterion, such as popularity with students as portrayed in surveys. Research output was even harder to quantify. Universities were already plagued with publication mania. 'Score points' for publication now became a matter of life and death, since it was taken by the UFC as the prime output of scholarship. This was no free-market contract. The government was the monopoly purchaser of university services and judge of their quality. It was dictating its terms. Whitehall soon abandoned the word contract.

The UFC was emphatically not the old UGC reborn. It was a wholly centralist body, intended as a conduit for policies and money from the Department of Education. It was encircled with Baker's much-loved 'Henry VIII' reserve powers. Under its terms of reference, the council would receive 'guidance and information offered regularly by the Department of Education on funding provisions and prospects, the nation's needs as regards the size and broad balance of the university system and specific policy developments'.[12] What the last phrase meant was unclear.

The terminology of the 1940s still echoed down the corridors of Whitehall. In addition, a Treasury memorandum would be prepared 'codifying the arrangements for and requirements concerning the payment of grant to the UFC and its transmission to universities'. Anything less like competitive contract tendering is hard to imagine.

As if this was not enough punishment for academic freedom, Baker decided on a *coup de grâce*. He ended scholastic tenure for life for newly appointed staff and for existing staff gaining promotion, a measure at which Joseph had merely nibbled. This was intended to help universities, now struggling to perform 'to contract', to get rid of staff who were poor at teaching or were unproductive researchers. Tenure had to go if drastic reorganization of departments was to yield any efficiency dividend. The proposal, from a government whose antagonism to the universities was palpable, caused as much controversy as the ending of autonomy. A tight professional restrictive practice was being challenged, with covert support from many university administrators. Lecturers and professors were to become as vulnerable to redundancy as any salaried employee. Tenure might have underpinned the concept of scholarship since Erasmus. That was too bad. It sat athwart the government's desire to curb 'underperforming' departments.

When *Meeting the Challenge* passed into law as part of the 1988 Education Reform Act Baker refused to insert into it even the blandest references to scholastic freedom. As Graham Zellick pointed out in a legal commentary on the Act, 'The government maintained throughout that scholars of high quality and excellence would not be vulnerable, but this is entirely unrealistic. Faced with budgetary problems ... staff even of the highest quality may be a luxury which cannot be afforded.'[13] Not until the bill reached the House of Lords, where the tenure clauses were threatened with defeat, did Baker concede an amendment by Lord Jenkins of Hillhead. This stated that university contracts should 'ensure that academic staff have freedom within the law to question and test received wisdom and to put forward new ideas and controversial or unpopular opinions, without placing themselves in jeopardy of losing their jobs or privileges'.[14] It is remarkable that a modern liberal government should have found this so unpalatable a clause.

To John Griffith this was 'not so much an invasion of the relative and modest amount of autonomy presently enjoyed by universities and their academic staff. It is an almost total usurpation, a dissolution of the university system comparable to the dissolution of the monasteries.'[15] The same parallel was drawn by Maurice Kogan. The universities 'have been treated like religious houses in the early sixteenth century, full of libidinous abbots and corrupt nuns and most in need of reform'.[16] Kogan wrote that the essence of a scholarly community is not the performance of commercial objectives. 'It is barely appropriate to talk of objectives other than in terms of the inner psyche because the motive force is not that of pre-stated social considerations but of the disinterested and often serendipitous pursuit of truth.'[17]

To these critics, the basis on which a university should be run was collegial rather than managerial, with disciplines shared rather than imposed hierarchically. This was perhaps an archaic Oxbridge view, and few of the critics were without their vested interests. But the tension between the Treasury's reasonable search for 'value for money' and the sustenance of professional autonomy ran through all Thatcher's reforms. In *Meeting the Challenge*, the battle was one-sided. The proposed changes seemed not so much a shift of emphasis, more a punishment for past slights. In 1985 the Jarratt report on university administration had been sold to universities as solely concerned with their management and not their academic work. But as income fell and supervision rose, the two became inseparable. As 'self-governing' schools were to find, if a government cuts your income each year without cutting its expectations, you not only run out of money, you run out of autonomy.

The white paper was clearly intent on reordering these expectations. This required intervention in academic planning, which in turn required value judgements to be made on the worth of individuals and institutions. The Jarratt committee was plainly shocked at the inadequacy of most university management, and took refuge in jargon: 'We stress that in our view universities are first and foremost corporate enterprises to which subsidiary units and individual academics are responsible and accountable.' It suggested that each university set up 'a formal planning process with effective management information monitoring and evaluation systems and should structure their use'.[18]

To this the universities had no real response. Few could deny that their administration was often lax and their use of costly resources wasteful. Public money was at stake, on which the welfare state was making increasing calls. Everyone else had to prove value for money. Why not universities? Kogan and Griffith might dismiss Jarratt as the Sir Thomas Cromwell of the universities and Baker as Henry VIII. But this did not answer the question. How should university money be allocated, whether by a UGC or a government agency? By their inability to answer the question university apologists were ineffective in stopping the collateral damage that the 1988 Act did to their autonomy. They were unable to fix limits to government intrusion on their scholarly freedom, or even to defend the old UGC.

What is most strange about Thatcher's higher-education reforms is how little headway was made by the Right. University finance in 1979 still bore all the marks of a voucher system: of autonomous institutions competing for students who carried with them a government fee-plus-grant. Because these institutions were predominantly anti-Thatcherite they never defended themselves in these terms, nor did the Right come to their defence on the same basis. As a result, the cabinet could find itself signing up to a white paper that put universities at the service of 'the Government's own economic and social policies'. The 1988 Act ran directly counter to the concept of a free-market university sector.[19] Indeed Thatcher barely mentions university reform in her memoirs. She was happy to let Baker mete out whatever punishment these turbulent priests had coming to them. As if despairing of a coherent Thatcherite university sector, she ardently supported the new 'Free University' of Buckingham, founded with private money beyond the tentacles of state intervention. She became its chancellor after she left office. A publicly financed university, in other words, could not avoid being just another government department. If it wished to avoid interference, it should go its own way.

There was other unfinished business for the 1988 Act to clear up. In 1979 roughly 40 per cent of British higher education was under the auspices of local authorities: that is, degree course work at polytechnics and other local colleges of higher education. By 1987, with restrictions on university expansion, this proportion had risen to half. These colleges were the other side of the 'binary' structure put forward by Tony Crosland in 1965. The polytechnics represented the vocational, work-oriented strand in higher education, the universities the more cerebral, academic strand. The policy sat incongruously alongside the 'comprehensive' philosophy being applied to secondary education at the same time. Crosland was later to repudiate what he saw as an artificial and divisive bias in his higher-education policy, but none of his Labour successors bothered to change the structure he instituted.

The polytechnic sector had already seen some of its more prestigious institutions become universities, including Aston and Salford. This was in itself an acknowledgement that university status was something which a college might aspire to, rather than rival. Under the binary system, the polytechnics received central-government money under a 'pooling arrangement' roughly similar to the old UGC, via a National Advisory Board. But they remained owned and governed by local authorities. Under the 1988 Act, local authorities were stripped of this ownership. As with local further education and sixth-form colleges, this was not to be 'voluntary' opting-out. It was compulsory seizure. The NAB was wound up and the colleges given a new Polytechnic and Colleges Funding Council (PCFC) of their own, under a similar Whitehall regime to the UFC. In a word, they were nationalized from local-council ownership as universities had been nationalized from UGC-protected autonomy.

The relevant sections of the white paper hardly bothered to explain this rejection of all that local councils and their ratepayers had given to generations of non-university students. The appearance was of a tidying up of what seemed from Whitehall to be a bureaucratic inconsistency. Kenneth Baker's proclamation read like the edict of a commissar: 'To reflect their national role, give scope for better management and permit greater responsiveness to management needs, major institutions of higher education under local-authority control will be transferred to a new sector.'[20]

The essence of the polytechnics had been that they did not have this 'national role'. They were local. They prided themselves on being distinct from the universities, on offering low-cost courses, many of them tailored to the local jobs market. Colleges such as Brighton and Oxford were lively institutions, preferred by some students for lacking the airs and graces of formal universities yet granting 'proper' degrees. True, they lacked the independence of a university charter, but they honoured the government's requirement to link higher education with industry and commerce in the community. They were closer to the fabled 'world of business' than most universities. In terms of the government's own strategy, the colleges offered the government a separate group of sub-contractors for higher-education services. They offered the nation's students a genuine choice.

The government rejected this view and asserted the opposite. Every institution of higher education should now be regarded as national. The polytechnics were freed from the embrace of local government and local politics – a move welcomed by most college principals, who saw 'nationalization' as a boost in status. Yet Baker's takeover of the local-authority colleges remained what a tabloid headline might call a 'state power grab'. It swept up an extraordinary range of diverse institutions, many of them traditionally autonomous, and brought them under state control. These included religious teacher and clerical training colleges, who were shocked to find that their traditional character and intake were at risk from central directives. The 1988 Act was dismissive of their concern. The new PCFC members were told to listen to the complaints of such colleges in the following terms: to 'have regard (so far as they think it appropriate to do so, in the light of any other relevant considerations) to the desirability of maintaining what appears to them to be for the time being an appropriate balance in their support of activities as between institutions . . .'[21] This meant that the PCFC, and through it the government, could do what it liked, including stripping the colleges of their religious character.

One thing the 1988 Act did not initially do was abolish the polytechnic category or the distinctive character they felt they possessed. 'Binary' was at least reflected in Whitehall's twin funding councils, the UFC and the PCFC. This did not last for long. What happened next astonished even those hardened to Whitehall's centralist instincts. The dualism was too much for the education department. Within four years, the PCFC was disbanded and merged with the UFC under yet another quango, the Higher Education Funding Council (HEFC). Binary was abandoned and the colleges were told they could call themselves anything they liked, including full universities. Britain was suddenly dotted with such new universities as Oxford Brookes, John Moores (Liverpool), de Montfort (Leicester), Westminster and Nottingham Trent. Gone was any pretence that a bifurcated pattern of higher education might offer government and students a choice. Nothing better symbolized the standardization of British higher education than this uniform application of the word 'university'.

The reason for this decision appears to have been twofold: to double Britain's 'university' population at a stroke, and to bring all teaching and research under a single planning aegis. The end of the polytechnic appeared a clear victory for the university as the monopoly supplier of higher education in Britain. Yet in my view it was not the university but the polytechnic that triumphed. The constitutional status of the British university had been shattered. In its place was Baker's concept of a work-oriented, vocational, commercial institution, run more like an externally accountable public corporation than a collegium of scholars. This concept was essentially that of the polytechnic. The local-authority sector may have lost the war, but it won the argument. The polytechnics had not become universities. The universities had become polytechnics.

Like many of the pluralist institutions discussed in this book, British universities had by the late 1970s laid themselves open to easy criticism. Their relaxed lifestyle, limited teaching time and often mediocre standards were the butt of satire. Yet British universities were more efficient than comparable institutions abroad. Entry requirements were tougher, courses were shorter and teaching was more personal. A European survey published in 1989 rated British higher education as the best in Europe on almost every score.[22] The more glaring inefficiencies, such as the duplication of scientific research, were being tackled by the UGC in the early 1980s. The government quite reasonably sought a rise in academic productivity. It is hard to believe this could not have been achieved without the capital punishment of 1988. As Joseph had accepted, the UGC in its final years honoured its role as strategic planner, and did so while remaining a buffer between ministers and academics. It had defended academic autonomy with its budget cut three years in a row.

Perhaps the UGC idea of arm's-length rule was simply out of date in an era of big government and rising public spending. It had been based on the 1919 gentlemen's agreement and the domain it inhabited had been described by Shattock as the 'relatively small, enclosed world of government, the universities and the scientific establishment . . . This world had for the most part been overtaken by the pressures of politics, demography and financial stringency in the 1980s and 1990s.'[23] Having lost the Treasury as honoured patron, the UGC fell victim to its scorn. Universities were to be no different from any other part of the public sector (though their capital was eccentrically regarded as private to keep it out of public borrowing). If a university was not up to scratch, the government's job was to see it improve. In 1994 the new Higher Education Funding Council began to spawn its own quangos, with a Higher Education Quality Council, advertising for part-time 'quality auditors'. For these posts 'management experience in relation to education is preferred but not considered essential'.[24] Academics, like surgeons, would in future be judged not by their peers, but by that high priest of Thatcherism-in-government, the management consultant.

A revealing interview was given in 1984 to the BBC by the university expenditure official at the Treasury, Nick Snallnow-Smith. Making a general point, he remarked that 'we have a role in trying to achieve value for money and in encouraging departments to look for that . . . We're interested not only in whether it costs x million pounds, but what that x million pounds is intended to do. You can't have a sensible discussion about a proposal unless you do that'.[25] Just as 'maintaining the Queen's peace' justified Victorian governments in global intervention, so 'propriety in the spending of public money' justified their modern successors in equally enthusiastic domestic intervention.

Michael Power, who moved from accountancy to academia, concluded of one of the wilder exercises in bureaucratic centralism: 'The Research Assessment Exercises conducted by the higher-education authorities in the UK have contributed to a climate in which quantity takes precedence over the quality of publications, because mechanisms of research output measurement enable an audit of research performance to be conducted.'[26] In other words, as long as audit demanded quantity, quantity it would get, even of the inherently unquantifiable. Departments spawned 'income generating units' (or IGUs) whose task was simply to squeeze words out of academic staff to boost the research formula performance. Journalists with a high book output were inundated with requests to become 'visiting professors', to enable a university to claim their books as part of its output.

Higher education was another Thatcher policy heavily conditioned not by her positivism but by her aversion, in this case to

153

left-wing academics and left-wing local authorities. Yet her changes were eagerly seized on by the Treasury to effect what was to prove a remarkable reversal of all that the UGC had fought so hard to defend in the early 1980s, in particular the identification of quality with cost per student. Real expenditure per student was to fall by 25 per cent between 1990 and 1995, as student numbers rose by an equivalent percentage. A new government quango, the Student Loans Company, set up to administer a state student loan scheme rather than leave this to the private banking sector, was in 1995 near to collapse. Of £751m lent since 1990 just £20m had been recouped by 1995, and the chief executive had been dismissed.[27] The company did not prove the happiest of Thatcherism's ventures in nationalization.

Thatcher was not wholly unconscious of what she had done to the universities during her term of office. In a rare moment of self-doubt, her memoirs refer to the 'unintended' centralization of her higher-education policy. She listed the severe constraints under which she had placed the universities: 'By exerting financial pressure we have increased administrative efficiency and provoked overdue rationalization.'[28] This had led to criticism that she had infringed 'the future autonomy and academic integrity of universities'. Some of this criticism, she said, had weight: 'Many distinguished academics thought that Thatcherism in education meant a philistine subordination of scholarship to the immediate requirements of vocational training. That was no part of my kind of Thatcherism.' She appeared to feel it had all been an accident, rather than a grand design. This is probably half true. But it is hard to believe that Thatcher was led reluctantly to the trough of centralism, least of all by Kenneth Baker.

Before she was toppled, Thatcher showed a glimpse of remorse. She asked Brian Griffiths of her policy unit to examine ways of allowing universities to recover more independence, 'to opt out of Treasury financial rules and raise and keep capital'. She thought such a measure would achieve 'a radical decentralization of the whole system'.[29] He did not have time. All centralizers proclaim their decentralist intentions, during and certainly after their time in power. The trouble is that they never get round to carrying them out.

CHAPTER EIGHT

LANCING BOILS

And the cities hostile and the towns unfriendly
And the villages dirty.

— T. S. ELIOT

Standing on the stairs at Conservative Central Office on the night of her 1987 election victory, Margaret Thatcher said something strange and out of character. She remarked that 'we must do something about those inner cities'. Nobody knew quite what she meant. She had already done something about most of them. She had decided to run them, though none had offered any gratitude for this at the polling booth. Urban Britain had voted Labour as never before, and it was this to which Thatcher was referring. Thatcher subsequently asked her industry secretary, Lord Young, whom he would like as his inner-cities minister. The dapper Young replied without hesitation, 'Kenneth Clarke.' When asked why he replied, 'because he looks like he lives in one'.[1]

The great industrial cities of Britain had by Thatcher's third term become resentful colonies and she felt the time had come to give them the attention of a minister of their own. Clarke seemed well cut out as the Coriolanus of the saloon bar, with his scruffy suits and straight talk. By then the government had passed some fifty acts of parliament altering the structure and curbing the discretion of local government (the tally after fourteen years was to be one hundred and forty-four.[2] She had treated British urban government in the manner she most deplored in Brussels' treat-

156

ment of her. Local sovereignty had been infringed, meddling regulations imposed and democratic assemblies by-passed. Town halls were deluged with Whitehall paper and visitations by government regulators and inspectors. After the 1987 election Thatcher visited a derelict site in the Lower Don Valley, walking alone across the scorched wilderness for dozens of photographers. She duly declared 'Action for Cities'. It was a reprise of her election night remark.

British local democracy is subsidiary to national democracy, and no constitution should be custodian of stagnation. After 1979, central government took the view that subsidiary democracy had failed to offer British cities efficient administration and effective leadership. Narrow and politically partisan groups had become an obstacle to enterprise and renewal. During the 1970s, virtually the only development that had taken place in the big provincial cities was of council housing and government offices built with public money. Any observer of the decayed centres of Manchester, Glasgow, Liverpool, Leeds, Sheffield, Newcastle, Cardiff and the East End of London could hardly quarrel with the Tory diagnosis. These cities might be victims of economic history. But their leaders plainly could not measure up to the challenge of rebirth. American, German and French cities had lost their industrial base yet recovered. Hamburg, Essen, Lille, Bordeaux, Pittsburgh, San Antonio had discovered a new way. Britain had not. As Mrs Thatcher's first environment secretary, Michael Heseltine, replied to all who criticized his interventionism, 'But nothing is happening!' The debate about local democracy under Thatcher must acknowledge this baseline.

Thatcher's concern was belated. In her first two years of office, Heseltine had been a solitary custodian of urban policy. He battered his colleagues with papers and the Treasury for money. Only after riots in Brixton and Toxteth in 1981 did he get his message through, giving a cabinet paper the ironic title, 'It took a riot'. Within six months of taking office in 1979, Heseltine had announced urban development corporations (UDCs) for the docks areas of London and Liverpool. These were followed by nine more – in Cardiff, Manchester, Tyneside, Teesside, West Midlands, Bristol, Leeds, Sheffield and a second in Manchester. Scotland was covered by the Scottish Development Authority. The new UDCs were enshrined in a Local Government, Planning and Land Act of 1980 which took its cue from the Attlee government's New Towns Act of 1946. This had set up new towns in the Home Counties round London and formed the constitutional basis for the second- and third-generation new towns (such as Cumbernauld, Peterlee and Milton Keynes). They were run by Whitehall corporations and were kept apart from the local councils in whose areas they were located, though they would be handed over when fully established.

Like Attlee's 1946 Act, Heseltine's Act declared no confidence in existing local government to promote development. Ministerial appointees would have authority, answerable only to the environment secretary in London. Their powers included planning control, compulsory purchase of land, the freedom to build roads and houses, even permission to demolish historic buildings. Most important, the corporations could appropriate, and thus 'unfreeze', the land of other public bodies. These powers were intended to rule out interference by elected councils. Heseltine was explicit: 'We took their powers away from them because they were making such a mess of it. They are the people who have got it all wrong. They had advisory committees, planning committees, inter-relating committees and even discussion committees – but nothing happened.'[3] The UDCs were 'free from the inevitable delays of the democratic process'. Years of attempting to get East London boroughs to agree on planning Docklands had failed. Reviving the cities was apparently beyond the capacity of local democracy in Britain, if not in other countries abroad.

The government expanded on this theme in evidence to a House of Lords select committee. It said that elected councils 'look too much to the past and too exclusively to the aspirations of the existing population'.[4] Like the children of bad parents, cities would do better by being in government care. Not only were the children taken into care, the parents were denied access. In retrospect the Act reads like a colonial edict for imposing emergency rule on a defeated tribe. All contact with local democracy was ignored and accountability disregarded. The Act deliberately placed no obligations on the boards for local participation, consultation or even publicity. The House of Lords felt this went too far and secured a last-minute insertion of a Code of Consultation. This insisted that the UDCs at least liaise with local councils and issue press releases. The environment department had resisted even this suggestion. In any case, having consulted, the corporations were under no obligation to take notice of what they heard.

Where the corporations made decisions that cut across local-council plans, a council could object to Whitehall, but Whitehall would decide who was right. Since the UDCs were its creature, the councils were likely to get short shrift. Accountability was to be up, not down or out. As Nigel Broackes, first chairman of the London Docklands Development Corporation (LDDC), pointed out, his was 'not a welfare association but a property-based organization offering good value'.[5] This was a curiously limited definition of an omnicompetent authority for the most bruised of Britain's urban communities. Yet some Tories began talking of extending the UDC concept to areas such as Toxteth in Liverpool or Tottenham in London, where the existing local authorities were (rightly) felt to be unsympathetic to the government's outlook.

As a prelude to the establishment of the UDCs the Chancellor of the Exchequer, Sir Geoffrey Howe, declared six experimental 'enterprise zones' in which development would be permitted free of regulation, training levies and local rates. Companies would also receive 100 per cent tax allowances on any investment. The most prominent was on the Isle of Dogs in East London, where Howe had a visionary dream of a new Hong Kong.[6] By attaching to these zones the word enterprise, Howe concealed what was a new regional subsidy, of the sort the government was determined to abolish elsewhere. For all the speculative spirit which surrounded London's Docklands, its new roads, railways and tax breaks consumed far more public money than Whitehall had ever given local government in the area before.

Lawson described this aspect of urban policy as 'rolling back the frontiers of the state and improving the functioning of the market economy'.[7] This was not true. All that was abandoned was planning control, with disastrous visual and commercial consequences: the sites were grossly overdeveloped and many swiftly went bankrupt. The enterprise zones were industrial policy by a different name. At Canary Wharf the Reichman brothers went into *de facto* receivership, still gobbling up subsidies. The zone induced an oversupply of office blocks in East London in the same way that the 1964 Labour government's hotel subsidy induced a rash of ugly hotels in West London. Thatcher realized this from the start. As Geoffrey Howe records, she originally censored his enterprise-zone idea from the 1979 manifesto, remarking that 'it smacked too much of regional policy by another name'.[8] When Howe was Chancellor she was less inclined to oppose his favourite scheme. For Howe and Heseltine alike, urban renewal was not only too important for local democracy, it was too important for the free flow of market forces. It needed the helping hand of the taxpayer. The enterprise zone, like the urban development corporation, was Attlee-ism reborn.

Nor was this all. Heseltine galvanized a little-known power in the 1971 Planning Act permitting him to make special development orders (SDOs) over the heads of local authorities. Previously used in National Parks, where the government might wish to override a development approved by a local council, the SDO was now to be used for the opposite purpose, to push through office development where local councils were reluctant. An SDO would be used, said Heseltine, 'to stimulate development in acceptable locations and speed up the planning process'. In particular it would avoid any need for a public inquiry. The new procedure disregarded local objections to large buildings along the Thames at Vauxhall and Hays Wharf. In the latter case the order reversed the outcome of a previous public inquiry and inspector's recommendation. The SDO procedure undoubtedly reflected exasperation at Britain's dilatory planning regime. It also showed how constitutional checks could be circumvented by central goverment when it chose. There was no 'national interest' at stake in the cases to which the new power was applied. Later secretaries of state avoided SDOs, perhaps embarrassed at their potential power. In the case of the London SDOs, the resulting offices either remained empty or, at Vauxhall, were salvaged by that last resort of the London speculator down the ages, a central-government tenant. They became the headquarters for MI6.

The UDCs were bloodily and expensively successful. Almost all were opposed by the democratic authorities in whose territory they had been established. The East London councils declared war on the LDDC. In Liverpool and Manchester local politicians would have nothing to do with their corporations. In other areas, such as the West Midlands, only the subsidies made available to the UDCs by the government induced a measure of collaboration. I once asked Newcastle council to help restore railway property on Tyneside. The council leader, Jeremy Beecham, pointed me down the hill to the UDC offices: 'That's the only place in this city with money these days.' But the money was spent, sites were cleared, roads and services put in, new buildings constructed. As Heseltine said, 'UDCs do things.' They injected new executive talent into areas which had not seen it for years. Ideas were at a premium. In Liverpool, the Mersey shore was revitalized, as was the Tyne bank in Newcastle. Whatever the cost of the LDDC, huge investment was drawn to London's East End that had ignored it before.[9]

Over time, a change in the composition of city Labour groups and a growth of *realpolitik* on all sides led to more collaboration between councillors and UDC members. The cities realized that they had to co-operate or be forever marginalized by government. Visiting UDC areas in the mid-1990s I found a new spirit of partnership. Most councillors realized they had to take urban-corporation officials into their thinking, if their own plans were not to be worthless. The corporations settled into the fabric of local politics and became, for the most part, wealthy propagandists for their areas. Their officers had found that their neglect of local leaders left them lonely. They felt their lack of accountability and sought new vehicles for local consent. Partnership may not have been *de jure*, but it was *de facto*, and it was invigorated by Heseltine's innovation of the City Challenge concept in 1989. This demanded that local leaders get together to bid for central grants, or lose them altogether.

Whether urban renewal in Britain required the renaissance of Attlee's non-elective.corporatism is moot. Certainly local democracy had atrophied in the 1970s, leaving city leadership far behind that in other developed countries. Whatever the diagnosis, the government in the early 1980s had no doubt as to the cure: centralization. The antagonism towards local government of Thatcher and her ministers, already noted in the chapters on poll tax, education and the police, was now extended beyond urban renewal. When Kenneth Clarke visited America in 1988 after taking on his new portfolio, he was impressed at how cities there had persuaded large developers to invest in renewal. He failed to notice that elected city leaders were invariably the initiators of such progress. Heroic mayors and go-getting city fathers were central to success, from Boston to Philadelphia, Baltimore, Cincinnati and Chicago. (In a few British cities, such as Glasgow and Birmingham, the same had been true.) Yet Clarke's biographer states baldly that on his return his 'aim was to get more private finance into the inner cities without giving the cash to the detested city councils'.[10]

With enterprise zones and UDCs up and running, Thatcher decided not to revive city government but drastically to reduce its scope and power. City democracy in Britain is deep-rooted. The original prosperity of Birmingham, Manchester, Leeds and Newcastle was built on strong local leadership. To most historians, the growth of cities lay not in the standardization of Dickensian commissioners, but in a civic spirit made accountable in some way to local citizens and interests. It was this that infused Victorian enterprise. Thatcher believed such enterprise could be tapped again, but through central patronage rather than election. In doing so she rejected all evidence from the past and from abroad. City governments in Europe and America were basing renewal on dynamic civic boosterism, rooted in the local political base. Hamburg, Geneva, Milan, New York, Tokyo all looked to the future with high-profile elected mayors and city councils, most of them enjoying discretion over large budgets. British cities, and especially London, are unique among democracies in the paucity of citizen participation.

In his 1994 pamphlet *Fear of Voting*, Jerry White pointed out that in the 1890s Londoners elected 12,000 citizens to serve on councils, boards and committees. These ran the capital's health, education, welfare and transport. The biggest cull of these urban democrats took place under Attlee's nationalization programme in 1945–8. As White comments, '1946–48 represented the most important reduction in local government functions in history and an unparalleled centralization of government power.'[11] Health, electricity, gas and social security were all removed from local government at that time. The second biggest cull was under Thatcher. Today roughly 12,000 Londoners still sit on boards administering local services in the capital. The difference is that just 1,914 are elected. The vast majority are appointed, mostly by central government.[12]

Heseltine had been content to sidestep local democracy in his haste to revive Britain's cities. His successors at the environment department (and at the Welsh and Scottish offices) wanted to go further. The six great industrial cities of England after London were covered not just by city councils with district-council powers but by wider conurbation authorities. Their areas were uncomfortably called West Midlands, Greater Manchester, Merseyside, South Yorkshire, West Yorkshire and Tyne and Wear. All were seen by the government not just as the enemies of renewal but as the enemies of Toryism. The latter was true; all were Labour. In 1983, after Heseltine's departure from the environment

163

department, a cabinet committee had been set up under Willie Whitelaw to consider the reform of local government. This committee (its appellation, Misc 79, conveying an aura of a conspiracy) reported that it could see no purpose in the metropolitan county councils that had been set up in 1965 for London and in 1974 for the conurbations based on the other cities. Without consultation or further ado it decided to abolish them. Only their lord-lieutenants and postal designation would remain. Functions should be delegated to subordinate districts, to joint boards or to central government. This proposal was put into the 1983 manifesto and outlined in a 1984 white paper with the loaded title, *Streamlining the Cities*.

The white paper was a political sensation. The government proposed to eliminate as useless seven democratic entities that had been in existence for just a decade, or two decades in the case of London. A quarter of the electorate was to be stripped of one of its votes. The justification for this was cursory. 'The hopes of the last reorganization have been disappointed,' said the white paper.[13] The government was determined to 'attack the national overhead' and the metropolitan councils were standing in the way. 'Priorities are now more practical and less theoretical' than in the old days and what was termed 'a certain fashion for strategic planning' had proved exaggerated. In addition, the councils were perpetually warring with their subordinate districts. They were extravagant. The provincial six had increased their spending since 1979 by 12 per cent in real terms, excluding police (whose even greater increases were ordered by ministers). GLC spending had risen by a half. Other local councils had not increased spending at all.

The white paper led to an uproar in London, though hardly a peep elsewhere. The provincial metropolitan counties had been in existence for only ten years. They were being replaced, at least at their cores, by the old city corporations: Birmingham, Manchester, Liverpool, Leeds, Sheffield, Newcastle. In London, by contrast, an elected government had existed in one form or another since the birth of the London County Council in 1889 and was now to be replaced by no London-wide body. The GLC at its dissolution owned many housing estates in both the inner and outer boroughs. It administered the Thames barrier, the fire brigade, waste disposal, grants to the arts and charities and the Royal Festival Hall. Nor was there any doubt that it would have survived had it not been in Labour hands. The political motive for its abolition was blatant. It was a left-wing thorn in the side of the government. The GLC stuck its tongue out at Westminster from County Hall, directly across the Thames from the Houses of Parliament. Political banners festooned its façade, accusing ministers of the collapse of London's economy. (Ministers should have replied in kind from the defence ministry opposite.) Norman Tebbit was unequivocal. The GLC had to go because it was 'left-wing, high-spending and at odds with the government's view of the world'.[14]

In the debate that took place between the white paper and the passage of the Local Government Act 1985, ministers were drawn into diverse defences of GLC abolition. Thatcher claimed abolition was popular, simply because it was in the 1983 election manifesto and she had won: a crude recourse to Hayek's 'plebiscitarian dictatorship'. The most substantive argument was that the GLC was extravagant and wasteful, while its 'strategic' rationale had become superfluous. The former was incontrovertible; even the council's last leader, Ken Livingstone, admitted as much.[15] Whether structural reform could have achieved the same savings we cannot know and the government was in no mind to try. It was already proposing to cap local-government rates, which included the GLC. This was not enough. It wanted to wipe Ken Livingstone, as one minister said, off the television screens for good. In a civil servant's phrase that reflects most of Thatcher's reforms, 'the present government does not proceed from analysis to conclusion but from commitment to action'.[16] It was a blatantly partisan reason for tampering with the democratic constitution.

The denial of any strategic rationale for city-and-suburban government was implausible. The white paper had stated that

165

the search for a strategic role for the big cities 'may have little basis in real needs'. This was mendacious, as subsequent events showed. The mix between railway and road spending, the location of big office development, transport interchanges, new tunnels and bridges all called for city-wide planning and executive authority, certainly in London. The GLC and the metropolitan counties may not have been strategically effective, but that did not invalidate the idea of strategy. Nor was urban policy made more coherent by the continued proliferation of Whitehall initiatives and ministers, usually in response to short-term crises, of which ethnic disturbances always proved the most potent. The initiatives seemed virtually interchangeable: Business in the Community (BIC), the Financial Investment Group (FIG), Urban Development Grant (UDG), Inner City Enterprises (ICE), sixteen Task Forces, five City Action Teams (CATs), the Urban Programme (UP), the Urban Programme Management Initiative (UPM), City Challenge, City Pride. These schemes emerged from Whitehall in a continuous dribble from the 1980s into the 1990s, mostly shifting the same ring-fenced central grants round in politically attractive patterns.

The true purpose of *Streamlining the Cities* was to move conurbation planning to Whitehall. The government did not abolish strategic planning; it centralized it. The Secretary of State, Patrick Jenkin, later contradicted his own white paper and declared his intention to perform the strategic role himself. He told the House of Commons that 'there will remain the need for an overview of land-use planning issues in the metropolitan areas. To meet this I shall where necessary give planning guidance ... to the boroughs and districts.'[17] He explained that London now extended to the M25, with an impact that covered the entire south-east. Similar factors governed the other conurbations. He and his successors, or at least their officials, would in future act as chief planners for the seven biggest cities in England. (In a centralist's pastiche, ministers were appointed to care for portfolios of cities: in 1995 it was Lord Astor for Bristol, John Bowis for Nottingham, Derby and Leicester, Ann Widdecombe

166

for Sheffield and Hull, John Watts for Wolverhampton, David Curry for Leeds and 'East Thames'. There were many others, few of whom ever went near their charges.) They were like the colonial sinecures or plural benefices of the eighteenth century. Districts and boroughs might draw up their own plans, but these must 'have regard' to the 'strategic advice' that Whitehall issued. Jenkin gave himself reserve powers to write his own district or borough plans if he so chose. In London, a London Planning Advisory Committee was set up, with much emphasis on the word advisory. Its advice went to Whitehall, not to any London representative body. A 'London Plan' published by the government in 1989 disregarded almost all the committee's advice, notably on transport investment.

All this was denied by ministers during the passage of the 1985 Act. They protested that abolition was, as elsewhere, really about decentralization. The white paper had made the bizarre pledge that the only GLC activities not being devolved to the boroughs would be 'flood protection in the London area and a few minor aspects of other functions'. In a debate on the Act a transport minister, Roger Freeman, was put up to say that the government believed in the non-planning of transport, 'where the passenger not a bureaucrat or a politician makes the decision'.[18] Shortly afterwards, his department told London Transport to move a Jubilee Line extension from bottom to top of its investment priorities, and stopped British Rail's southern approach tunnel into King's Cross. One was a personal effort by Thatcher to forestall the Reichmans' imminent bankruptcy at Canary Wharf. The other arose from Heseltine's desire to boost the economy of the East End. These were both strategic planning decisions with the same political motives that Tories used to excoriate in Labour governments. It is hard to believe that Freeman understood what he was reading.

Some London functions did transfer to the boroughs. These included derelict land reclamation and most non-trunk roads, the GLC housing estates and, after 1990, inner London's schools. Housing and schools were already under threat of nationalization and were meant to disappear from the local-government realm in time. But the boroughs were undoubtedly happy to have the 'metropolitan' tier removed from over their heads. What irked them was to be made statutorily answerable to central government's 'reserve and default powers'. Under the Act, the Secretary of State required the boroughs to give him information about their staff numbers and the purposes for which they were employed. This was gratuitous even by the standards of Thatcher's Whitehall and was motivated by a desire to prevent the upsurge in spending that usually accompanies administrative reform.

The shift in power from London democracy to central government was almost complete. By 1985 Whitehall controlled London Transport, London's Docklands, London's land use planning, main roads, museums and galleries and suburban transport. It had also nationalized the South Bank arts centre. This was on top of its control of London's police, hospitals, gas, electricity and water (not at that stage proposed for privatization). The Secretary of State also took under his wing the supervision of waste disposal, establishing a London Waste Regulation Authority. The only other city with a remotely comparable degree of centralization was Paris, where it was shortly to be dismantled under a forceful mayor, Jacques Chirac. The centralization passed largely unnoticed at the time, though some Tories did take up the cudgels against Jenkin's reserve powers. The former Prime Minister and London MP, Edward Heath, said that the Act 'would put an extraordinary accretion of powers into the hands of the Secretary of State'. His former environment secretary, Geoffrey Rippon, said the powers were 'intolerably far-reaching and unacceptable'.[19] He threw Hayek back in Thatcher's face, accusing her of committing what Hayek had called the 'deadly blight of centralization'. Thatcher was unmoved.

In a memorandum on metropolitan county abolition, the government claimed it would yield a saving of £100m a year. The accountants Coopers and Lybrand later estimated a very different outcome: a range from a saving of £4m to an additional cost of £70m. No figure has since been validated or audited, though Manpower Watch and other researchers generally take the view that abolition outside and inside London has led to no appreciable change in service cost or efficiency.[20] The reason was simple. Beneath the surface, most of these bodies did work that had to be done. Somebody needed to run police and fire services, plan buses and trains, build airports and organize, or disorganize, traffic. In the six metropolitan counties, the former city councils took on these tasks. In London there was no core authority. The result was a galaxy of government quangos, statutory joint boards and voluntary joint committees of the boroughs.[21] The alphabet soup ran to some fifty bodies, including the LFCDA, LBGC, LPAC, LRC, LWRA, LCAT, LRT, LTB. The South Bank centre found itself with a board appointed entirely from White-hall. The GLC's historic buildings unit passed to English Heritage. No London politician was appointed to the London Regional Transport board. Twelve 'lead boroughs' took on a ragbag of metropolitan functions: Havering for planning, Westminster for the Coliseum opera house and the City of London for Hampstead Heath. Even then a mass of properties and powers were 'left over', to be administered until disposal by a new London Residuary Body (LRB).

This final liquidator lasted four years under its chairman, Sir Godfrey Taylor.[22] Its existence was extended when in 1988 the government decided to abolish the Inner London Education Authority. This final London 'abolition' had been rejected as unnecessary in 1985. Ilea had been kept in being as a rare instance of a directly elected *ad hoc* authority in British local government. It proved less stridently left-wing than it had as a GLC committee, attracting some members specifically committed to education in the capital. Its fate was sealed when inner Londoners voted it a Labour majority in 1986, for Thatcher a vote too far. London's schools passed to the boroughs and London colleges passed direct to central government. The decentralization of schools to the boroughs, much welcomed by them, was swiftly followed by Kenneth Baker and then John Patten appealing to every London school to opt out of borough control and come under the government's new Funding Agency (see chapter six). Devolution was intended to be short-lived.

The GLC had lost many friends with the lunacies that surrounded its departure. Its staff grew to 20,000, spending at the end apparently without limit. The patronage of causes such as Media Workers' Crèches and Babies against the Bomb left it open to easy ridicule. Ken Livingstone admitted in a Commons debate in 1991 that 'from the beginning the GLC was flawed'. It had been born of a desire by the 1959 Conservative government to create a body not dominated by Labour. Indeed its creation was bitterly opposed by Labour. Livingstone correctly identified the central weakness: 'The GLC was caught between being a strategic authority without the powers to perform that function and a body which overlapped and conflicted with the boroughs in the provision of personal services. That was a recipe for conflict . . . It was also nonsense to create an authority that had such a vast housing stock.'[23] Whatever the future might hold for London, as the chroniclers of the abolition concluded, 'Nobody wanted to see a return of Gargantua.'[24]

The wider verdict on Thatcher's abolition of the metropolitan counties and the GLC is an acquittal in the former case but an open verdict on the latter. There had been no great cry for the creation of a democratic body for the West Midlands or South Yorkshire back in 1974. London, on the other hand, had enjoyed such a body since the nineteenth century. London politics had a vigour to it that was wholly lacking elsewhere. In the years after abolition this was partly anaesthetized. The new, labyrinthine joint committees settled down. Few Londoners missed accountability for waste disposal or the Royal Festival Hall. The transfer of functions to boroughs went smoothly. 'The sky did not fall . . . Cassandra was confounded,' remarked one London government official.[25] A reason for this was the unsung heroes of abolition, the local and central officials who bore the burden of the reform. I recall speaking to a French official at the time who professed amazement that any bureaucracy could have coped with the extent of change imposed by ministers in the 1980s. The strength of the British administrative tradition is best seen at such times. Officials who strongly opposed such reforms as poll tax and GLC abolition struggled to make them work, often out of loyalty to no more than their own professionalism. Bureaucracy seeks an equilibrium, even amid chaos.

An otherwise partisan publication, *The Crisis of London*, remarked that despite the widening democratic deficit, 'taking London as a whole, the boroughs and the City have proved a workable and stable polycentric system: the past five years have seen a tangible growth of civic pride in the borough centres that is curiously at odds with this book's message of a capital in crisis'.[26] As a result, a new revisionism began to emerge, that London did not really need democratic government. Its problems were too vast, too expensive and too intractable to be left to any body other than central government. *The Economist* pointed out that, despite being deprived of a strategic authority of its own, London worked better than most big cities.[27] Indeed in some respects the Balkanization had yielded unexpected benefits. One was an increase in local innovation. Westminster and Wandsworth became leaders in municipal privatization. Camden and Islington took more trouble over their appearance. Pedestrian and traffic-management schemes mushroomed over the capital. Jenkin's reserve powers remained, for the time being, in reserve.

Yet Banquo's ghost refused to leave the feast. Thatcher had stripped London of the one form of accountability that could not be replaced by any minister or joint board: some democratic embodiment of its shared identity and lobby for its shared interests. A 1991 survey for the Rowntree Foundation found public responses to the absence of a GLC were specific. There were few complaints about the boroughs. There were many about the lack of any strategic transport and infrastructure authority for London as a whole.[28] While no government was likely to delegate transport investment in the capital to local government and local taxation, the public felt the lack of a politically potent London voice as enjoyed by New York, Paris or Tokyo to lobby in Brussels as well as in Whitehall. The heated debate that surrounded the Greater London Development Plan in the mid-1970s was absent from the 'London Pride' document[29] published in January 1995 by a coalition of London interests, chaired by Lord Sheppard of GrandMet. With the co-operation of the boroughs but no democratic basis or forum for debate, the document sank without a trace. Its imaginative proposal, accepted by the business community, for a London transport investment levy was dismissed by the Treasury.[30] At a February cabinet committee meeting it was not so much rejected as laughed out of court.

At no point did London's eighty-five MPs perform as a team or lobby for the capital. There was a standing cabinet committee for London, a transport minister and a shifting stage army of other ministers allocated to 'look after' different parts of the capital. As the sagas of the Jubilee Line and Channel Tunnel rail link showed, London's interests were forcibly subordinated to the politics of Westminster and Whitehall. Some 450 civil servants were scattered round different departments 'running' London, including 150 in the environment department alone.[31] In 1994 the government appointed an official, Robin Young, to co-ordinate them. Under the new Integrated Regional Office and Single Regeneration Budget initiatives, he would enjoy the imperial title of 'Regional Director of the Government Office for London'. His status was indicated in the press release of his appointment. It said he would 'make arrangements to visit and meet colleagues in the London world as soon as possible'. He might have arrived at a distant colony. Small wonder the Rowntree study concluded that 'there is a widespread perception that the arrangements for London government are defective and that further reform is inevitable'.[32] Yet the Labour party, strongly committed to giving London back a strategic authority, was still unable to specify what this might mean in practice. Labour was aware that the (mostly Labour) boroughs would guard their new powers, notably over education, jealously.

Ever since GLC abolition, environment secretaries have seemed sensitive to the wounds they inflicted on London democracy. Even Kenneth Baker acknowledged during the abolition campaign that the one objection he found hard to answer was 'that London needed a voice, since every other capital city had an elected authority to run it'.[33] The gazetteer of world cities could not come up with any that had no elected city-wide government.[34] Whenever they were polled, Londoners demanded the restoration of an elected body of some sort to 'govern London'. At the time of abolition in 1985, 74 per cent of Londoners wanted this. Ten years later the British Market Research Bureau found the figure remained the same, including Tory as well as Labour voters. There appeared to be an instinctive bond between the inhabitants of a city and the democratic process. So strong was this feeling that the City's Lord Mayor and Corporation were even suggested to fill the vacuum, with the boroughs sending members to sit on an expanded Court of Common Council.[35]

New 'voices' for the capital were duly conjured out of quangoland. They were given catchy names such as London Forum, London First, London Pride and even 'London: Making the Best Better'. Each was tested for political correctness – the presence of 'businessmen' and the absence of local councillors – and showered with the blessings of Whitehall. Bodies tainted by past GLC or present Labour associations, such as the London Planning Advisory Committee and the Association of London Authorities, were suspect. This was the 'new magistracy' triumphant, shadowy figures moving between consultants' offices, university seminars and hotel suites. The government of London did not disappear, it diffused in a fog of bureaucracy and lobbying. Its participants shared only one thing in common. Nobody had ever voted for them.

One ghost loomed over the scene. The most prominent GLC asset for which the London Residuary Body had been unable to find a new use was County Hall. The building sat empty and gloomy on the South Bank opposite Westminster. The spirit of the GLC cursed each potential buyer, be it a university or a hotel or a conference centre or a Japanese corporation, its most recent suitor. None could find a use for it. The great Edwardian portico seemed to guard the corridors and chambers within, waiting for renaissance. County Hall was a temple to London's lost accountability.

CHAPTER NINE

TORY SOCIAL ENGINEERING

The first duty of a State is to see that every child born therein shall be well housed ... To effect this the Government must have an authority over the people of which we now do not so much as dream – JOHN RUSKIN

In the summer of 1974 Margaret Thatcher was briefly the Tory housing spokesman. At the time I had written a series of articles on London housing estates and she asked if I might show her round some. We began in the tea room of the House of Commons but got no further. 'I want you to show me these terrible council estates,' she commanded. I explained that there were both good and bad estates in London, there were successes and failures. 'No,' she said, 'there are just bad ones.' I was given a cup of tea and placed politely beyond the pale. Twenty years later she was still scathing about council houses: 'The state in the form of local authorities has frequently proved an insensitive, incompetent and corrupt landlord.'[1] In approaching government she set out to break this corruption in unquestionably her most radical pledge. She would enforce a tenant's 'right to buy' any property owned by a local council. It was a pledge to which she committed herself personally.

True privatization is about surrendering not just ownership but power. It is about withdrawing government and permitting markets to regulate demand and supply unaided. We have seen how hard Thatcher's ministers found this detachment. To achieve reform they felt obliged to take more power rather than less. But in selling council houses Thatcher made a determined bid for withdrawal. The houses were political villains on every count. They were mostly owned by Labour councils and occupied by Labour voters. In 1983, owner-occupiers voted 3:1 Tory, council tenants 2.5:1 Labour.[2] They consumed subsidy. Such occupancy was devoid of possession, pride or incentive for improvement. It symbolized the enslavement of the individual to the state. Council housing was a challenge to Thatcher's belief in a home-owning democracy built on private savings and initiative. It should go.

Housing is one area of Thatcherism to which other commentators than myself regularly apply the word nationalization.[3] The primary reason is that Thatcher did not own the council houses she wanted to sell; councils did. She had to acquire sovereignty over them to force their disposal. This involved legislation and costly intervention by government. But council-house sales were just a part of Thatcher's housing policy. She believed in housing as a tool of social policy, and defended mortgage interest tax relief on that basis. To her, such tax expenditures were justified social engineering to counter, as she put it, the social engineering of the Left. Even when selling council houses, she rejected market pricing and insisted on discounts of up to 60 per cent, denying the public sector billions of pounds of revenue in the process.

Thatcher shared Bevan's enthusiasm for 'that lovely feature of English and Welsh villages, where the doctor, the grocer, the butcher and the farm labourer all lived in the same street'.[4] Her route to this social paradise was the same as Bevan's, through subsidy: subsidized council-house sales, subsidized mortgages and eventually a rented sector heavily supported by housing benefit. 'The state must continue to provide mortgage tax relief in order to encourage home ownership, which was socially desirable,' she wrote.[5] As to who should determine social desirability she had no doubt. 'I did not believe that local authorities should be the main agents for [social] improvement ... I wanted to get local authorities out of managing and owning.'[6] Like Bevan she needed to control what she wished to reform.

The building and letting of homes stood alongside education

176

as one of the twin towers of local autonomy in Britain. They were symbols of the community's role in determining the character of its neighbourhood and the welfare of its citizens. Most local councils saw their housing stock as the property not of any one tenant but of the community, and it was on behalf of that community that they met their statutory obligation to house those homeless or in need. With resources for new building severely curtailed under the Tories, right-to-buy further limited their ability to honour this responsibility. Housing the homeless increasingly took the form of using private 'bed and breakfast' hotels.

Thatcher saw the housing stock quite differently. She treated it as a past public investment, much abused, to be sold off at will to any tenant lucky enough to be in possession and able to buy. Discounts were intended to boost the policy, though there was little political or commercial rationale for them. It was possible that selling council houses with vacant possession on to the open market might force down local house prices. Selling cheap to elderly sitting tenants who had no intention of moving had no impact on any market. It did not relieve housing distress. A more coherent Thatcherite welfare policy would have gone in an opposite direction. It would have compelled councils to evict any tenant wealthy enough to buy in the free market and let the house to somebody in real need. At very least it would have forced councils to use receipts from selling their more desirable properties to renovate their undesirable blocks of flats.

Right-to-buy was a political crusade. As with school opting-out, Thatcher was unconcerned at the planning or investment consequences of her policy. She simply wanted council houses sold and no more council houses built. To most Tories, the procedure was simple. Somebody should fix the tenant up with a mortgage, hand him the keys and say good luck. In practice it was not that simple. Right-to-buy meant the central government breaking a local contract between landlord and tenant, and turning the landlord into a forced seller. The 1980 Housing Act, followed by a housing act almost every year for a decade, asserted central power over local-authority housing sales. If an individual tenant had difficulty persuading a council to sell, or even found it dilatory in selling, section 23 of the Act gave Whitehall the right to take over the transaction.[7]

This power was not idle. Many councils were outraged by compulsory right-to-buy (most had been selling houses voluntarily over the years). Greenwich and Rochdale invited the government to send commissioners to run the policy. Two hundred other housing authorities experienced similar intervention. Norwich went to the High Court after being ordered to give what the council felt was fast-track status to right-to-buy applicants. In his judgment Lord Denning remarked that section 23 of the Act was 'a most coercive power ... that enables central government to interfere with a high hand over local authorities'. Yet he could not quarrel with it being the law.[8] MPs protested at the 'dictatorial' powers that the government was taking. One Tory backbencher remarked, 'It is all very well making the Secretary of State the gauleiter of housing, but on these benches we should remember that the next gauleiter could be a commissar.'[9] For good measure, the government was no more deferential to the rich. At the same time, the great West London estates were being forced to sell freeholds on demand to long leaseholders. The government thus secured a bizarre alliance of Liverpool City Council and the Duke of Westminster in opposition to its housing policy.

Right-to-buy proved a piecemeal success. By the late 1980s one and a quarter million houses (but very few flats) had been transferred to their occupants, almost all in England. This was a fifth of the total council housing stock. The pace slowed towards the end of the decade as the supply of popular semi-detached dwellings dried up. 237,000 were sold in 1982, but only 83,000 in 1991. Few wanted flats in tower blocks. Over the Thatcher period local government's share of housing in England alone declined from 31 per cent to 23 per cent. But the impact on either the public sector or the private sector was marginal.

Sitting tenants rarely sold on and sales were more a discounted capitalization of future rents.

One by-product of right-to-buy was large cash balances piling up in council bank accounts. This revenue amounted to £18 billion over the 1980s, more than was raised in any other single privatization and comprising 43 per cent of total privatization receipts. Council housebuilding had previously been subject to government control through loan sanction. Now local authorities had cash of their own, which many wanted to channel back into relieving homelessness or restoring rundown estates, on which spending had been curtailed. Nigel Lawson as Chancellor was appalled at this. He had never envisaged that right-to-buy should offer councils 'an almost untrammelled ability on their part to spend the entire proceeds'[10] of this enforced privatization. Various complicated means were introduced to stop such spending and use the receipts to reduce overall public borrowing. Lawson insisted the receipts be 'spread' over a number of years through a variety of controls. Part of the balances had to be devoted to paying off a council's past debt. Only part could be spent for housing. In 1984, this part was fixed at 50 per cent, in 1985 at 40 per cent and in 1986 at 20 per cent. Controls were constantly varied, but the effect was to emphasize that while local government might propose what to do with their balances it was for the Treasury to dispose.

The Treasury's attitude to these receipts was duplicitous. Central government's receipts from privatization were 'negative public expenditure'. Though separately accounted, they stood against overall borrowing and thus balanced cuts in taxes or rises in public spending (see chapter two). However, local councils were not permitted to treat receipts in this way. The government thus forced councils to dispose of assets but was not prepared to permit them to benefit in any short-term sense from the sale, either within their housing accounts or more generally. This not only demunicipalized the houses, it centralized control over the value realized thereby. In 1987 the Chancellor boasted a £1 billion undershoot on his public borrowing total. This was due in part to an unexpected surge of over £2 billion in council-house sales. As we saw in chapter three, the mid-1980s was a time when central-government spending was running ahead of inflation. The 'raid' on local assets to reduce public borrowing was as crude as the attempted raid on nationalized industry revenues described in chapter two. Small wonder many councils were unenthusiastic about disposing of probably the only part of their estates that had market value, the easy-to-sell cottages and inter-war semi-detached houses. Most tower and slab block estates had nil or negative value, as councils found when they later sought to hand them over to housing associations.

The true character of the government's housing policy becomes more apparent when we examine policy in the round. Thatcher did not seek merely to sell council houses. She used public policy aggressively to achieve specific social objectives. She approached housing as had the Labour party since 1945, as an integral part of a political programme. She ended the *laissez-faire* relationship between the centre and local government because she disliked its consequences, regarding council-house estates as little short of the enslavement of the people. Government had to take powers to buy the slaves and set them free, while further enslavement had to cease. Nothing better illustrates this point than the expenditure figures. Central support for council housing saw the biggest cut in any single programme in the early years of the government. Council rents were forced upwards. New estate building and renovation were devastated. Local authorities built or restored 70,000 houses in 1979; by 1989 the total was down to 13,000. Since this total had been running at 2–300,000 a year in previous decades, a chapter in the history of the welfare state had emphatically come to an end.

Yet the public impression of Tory housing policy – of council-house sales and a halt to new building – is far from the whole story. Previously, rents had been subsidized in two ways: through benefits in cash and through cheap rents. Roughly half the rents in the public sector (and many in the private sector) had been relieved through cash benefit to poor tenants. This relief was paid by local councils but 100 per cent reimbursed by central government, not as housing policy but as social-security policy. The incoming government in 1979 was determined to end the additional subsidy from central and local government that held down council rents; it duly cut revenue subsidies to local councils to achieve this end. Consequently, these rents rose, and more tenants were induced to draw housing benefit, the burden of which was borne by central government. Throughout the 1970s, the proportion of council tenants receiving housing benefit of some sort was 40 per cent. Under Thatcher it rose swiftly to over 65 per cent. Central subsidies to council revenue accounts to hold down rents fell by two-thirds in real terms over the decade. Yet at the same time central-government spending on housing benefit doubled. What was happening was extraordinary. A form of welfare that had been at least half paid for out of local taxes – that is, subsidies to hold down rents – was replaced by a subsidy, admittedly more targeted on the needy tenant, entirely paid out of central taxes.

While housing benefit was means-tested and directed to the poor, the same was clearly not true of government help to the private and voluntary sector. One of the most remarkable facets of public finance in the Thatcher years was the robustness of her generosity to private buyers. What she persistently termed 'socially desirable' subsidies to mortgage tax relief rose over the decade by roughly 200 per cent in real terms, standing at £7 billion in cash in 1990. In that year over £2 billion was also being spent on discounts to council-house purchasers. This was over three times as large as all other items of housing expenditure.

These mortgage subsidies were Thatcher's personal bounty. The Treasury fought them tooth and nail for ten years. Thatcher's belief in the virtue of home ownership defied all attempts by Howe and Lawson to reduce the cost to the Exchequer. The subsidy was the most glaring instance of her belief in the dominance of politics over economics and of social policy over the free play of market forces. Howe wrote that the tax relief was 'a glaring anomaly, distorting the housing market almost as much as rent control, unbalancing the investment market . . . and unjustly favouring the better off and the south rather than the north'.[11] His junior minister, Nicholas Ridley, was no less caustic and went with Howe in 1983 on an abortive visit to Number Ten to persuade Thatcher to abandon, or at least reduce the value of, the relief. Lawson was equally adamant. He wrote that each attempt to end the relief 'ran up against the brick wall of Margaret's passionate devotion to the maximum possible amount of mortgage interest relief'.[12]

The overall effect of these changes can best be seen in a chart produced by Hills and Mullings, whose book should be consulted for the best discussion of the tortuous statistics of the operation.[13] Real net current spending on council housing, mostly subsidized council rents, fell over the decade from £3.5 to £1.4 billion, but this was matched by housing benefit over the same period rising from £1.8 to £3.6 billion (all at 1987–8 prices). On the capital account, support for council and housing-association capital spending fell from £5.3 to £1.3 billion, but this was matched by mortgage tax relief to owner-occupiers rising from £2.6 to £5.2 billion. The parallelism is uncanny. The shift of both current and capital spending out of the local-authority sector almost exactly balanced the additional burden assumed by central subsidy and tax relief. Tories supposedly did not believe in housing subsidies. Yet taking them all into account, Thatcher was devoting more public money, including tax relief, to housing in real terms when she left office than in 1981.

Nor did the government abandon all public-sector housebuild-ing during Thatcher's campaign against local councils. It merely sought agencies detached from the dread institutions of local democracy. On the principal that 'my enemy's enemy must be my friend' Thatcher lighted on the charitable housing-association movement and showered favours on it. The more conflict-ridden were her relations with local government the more cosy they became with this alternative sector. A 1987 white paper lavished praise on a movement which, in substance, was doing the same as local councils, supplying publicly subsidized housing for rent. The associations were described as 'vitally important . . . independent sector . . . key role . . . new style of management'.[14]

Some associations were co-ownership companies operating in suburban and rural areas, scarcely distinguishable from private developers. But most were charities formed to build or renovate houses and flats for rent in the larger cities. Many of the latter were virtually alternative council housing departments, their staffs no less committed to 'social housing' than those of the councils. They were spirited suppliers of housing with strong local roots. Almost half their activity was in the London area and the top hundred associations (out of some 5,000) controlled two-thirds of the stock. In general the associations tended to be smaller and more responsive to tenants' needs than council housing departments, though the latter would add that associations did not have to look after decrepit high-rise housing blocks.

Some 90 per cent of housing-association finance came from a quango directly financed by central government, the Housing Corporation. This was to be Thatcher's own, preferably her only, housing agency and it took pride of place in the environment department's annual housing reports. It would challenge the local councils in housebuilding as the Funding Agency for Schools would challenge them in education. When the Tories came to power, the Corporation had 100 staff and a budget of £50m. By 1990 it had 700 staff and a budget of over £1 billion. Two years later it was building 35,000 new units at a time when government was permitting just 6,000 new starts to local councils. While councils were having their powers curtailed at every turn, the Corporation was encouraged to step into their shoes, with powers to build and run new estates and even operate hostels and shelters.

The associations responsible to the Corporation had no accountability except to audit and their own charitable terms of reference. They were run by their professional staff, mostly under self-appointed trusts. In a new Act in 1988, the government reformed their finances, giving the associations a freer managerial rein but a tighter political one. In particular their rents were no longer to be related to 'fair' rents or to other public-sector formulae. They had to recoup development costs. They were to receive fixed grants and be encouraged to seek partners in the private development sector. They were to become, in effect, co-operatives which happened to enjoy access to government as well as private finance. If they chose to exercise a 'social' rather than merely a 'not-for-profit' function, that was up to them. Beyond an initial down-payment of grant, there would be no further state help (except through housing benefit).

This 'pseudo-privatization', as it was called,[15] of the housing-association movement helped the Treasury more effectively to relate subsidy to what were termed housing outputs. Advances for building projects were 'up front'. They were no longer tied, as they had been before, to the eventual cost of a project but to its initial estimate. This gave a direct incentive to cost control. The Housing Corporation became not so much an agency of the welfare state, more a nationalized state bank to the rented sector. (Its tenants had no right to buy.) Housing associations were 'providers' to the Corporation as 'purchaser'. The formula worked well as planned. Housing starts increased fourfold between 1988 and 1994. The associations could set their own rents and, where appropriate, collect the rent not from the tenant but the housing-benefit office. Public money determined both their initial capital expenditure and often their return on that capital through rents. In return, the government insisted on stringent performance controls, viability tests and competitive tendering for subsidy. Small wonder the private rented sector continued to languish under the Tories.

At the time of the passage of the 1988 Act, Mike Langstaff commented that housing associations had become deliverers of central-government housing policy in a way that local authorities never had. They provided exactly what ministers wanted to purchase, low-cost housing for the deserving poor – or outside the cities often the not so poor. To him, Whitehall monitoring had 'moved past checking legal and fiduciary propriety ... and progressively eroded the autonomous, self-governing nature of housing associations, turning them into hired agents of central government'.[16] Yet the houses were built. The local authorities were left with a separate problem, struggling with the poor in the 'sink' high-rise and inner-city estates as they were intended to struggle with the 'sink' schools that did not opt to come under government's funding regime. By the start of the 1990s, the associations were the lead agents of social housebuilding in Britain.

Before 1979, central government saw its task in housing as doing no more than to exhort and encourage local councils to 'meet housing need'. Government supplied money and monitored building standards, boasting only of how many houses 'we have built'. That 'we' was a vague amalgam of local action and central encouragement and financial assistance. Under Thatcher this hands-off approach was abandoned. Prior to 1987, government policy remained largely concerned with the channelling of money, shifting the focus, as we have seen, from the locality to the centre. After the 1987 election, the government took a more active interest in such subjects as the condition of estates and the rise in the numbers of homeless young. The latter were increasingly noticeable on the streets of London's West End. They were, said Thatcher, 'the most disturbing political issue in housing at this time'.[17] Official indices of homelessness and of numbers taken into bed-and-breakfast and hostel accommodation rose throughout the 1980s. The former tripled between 1978 and 1991.[18]

What was clear was that government housing policy and local housing need were growing increasingly detached from each other. The result was spasdomic but embarrassing pressure on ministers. The 1987 manifesto nervously accepted that 'more now needs to be done'. The response was that familiar sign of guilt in British government, a rising tempo of random initiatives: Inner City Policy, the Comprehensive Community Programme, the Urban Housing Renewal Unit and the Priority Estates Project gave way in the late 1980s to more snappy titles such as Estate Action, City Grant, Tenants' Choice and Rough Sleeper.

185

Most of these initiatives by-passed local authorities. They took the form of ring-fenced central programmes, many from the fertile brain of the government's long-standing housing minister, Sir George Young. They mirrored exercises by the environment department for urban renewal (see last chapter). Government policy had not only demunicipalized public housing but overtaken its role as innovator.

Under the 1988 Housing Act, the government made a despairing last effort to remove hard-to-sell council housing from local-authority hands. Rather than privatize individual units, it encouraged councils to transfer property direct to housing associations and even private landlords. If councils would not transfer, then tenants could vote to force them to do so. For the worst estates the environment secretary, Nicholas Ridley, introduced Housing Action Trusts (HATs). These promised the residents of down-at-heel estates up to £100m per estate if they became a self-governing housing association. Proposed without consultation and requiring a majority of residents to vote against council ownership, they were a surprising failure given the sums on offer (three were set up after Thatcher left office). Thatcher blamed the environment department, and responded with yet another initiative of her own, Community Housing Trusts, backed by what she called 'a new quango at arm's length from the DoE and not in collusion with the local authorities'. This idea disappeared with Thatcher herself. Her last words on her housing revolution were grim: 'The inertia of the DoE had won in the end.'[19]

In many respects, Thatcher's housing policy was both too radical and not radical enough. She lacked the courage to nationalize the entire council stock and modernize it for outright sale. (This policy was, however, considered by John Major in 1995.) As a result estates deteriorated even when there were local resources to maintain them. This added to the vicious circle of inner-city poverty. Public money was spent instead on the sector that needed it least, on private ownership and what the Victorians called the deserving poor. Thatcher herself appeared to have no objection to public-sector housing or to housing subsidy, only to the limited category of council housing. Lawson was wrong when he wrote that public housing 'would have been cut back as much, if not more, if it had been a central government rather than a local government responsibility'.[20] Central-government spending on housing rose rather than fell throughout the 1980s, injecting tax money into the market, inflating rents and encouraging many young people to take on unrealistic mortgages. This left them with negative equity when the market turned down in the early 1990s.

A belated attempt in 1987 to assist the private rented sector other than via housing benefit was for the most part a failure. This was despite new tax reliefs and a pukka policy initiative called the 'right to rent'. The sector continued to shrink, falling by a half during the 1980s as owners of rented or rentable property continued to convert for sale. Peter Kemp has concluded that government policy actually 'de-privatized' the rented sector.[21] Certainly, by 1990, the ratio of private to public within the rented sector had shifted in the direction of the latter. Much of this can be put down to the English preference for home ownership over renting, but it was a preference Thatcher did everything to encourage. Her mortgage policy offered young people what they most craved, tax relief on their incomes and an incentive to save through home ownership. Not surprisingly they did all they could to avoid 'wasting' money on rent.

Local councils were widely recognized as bad managers of the housing estates they had so imperiously constructed in the previous quarter-century. What was curious was that Thatcher did not stop to make them better landlords. Nor did she merely shift control from local to central government. She shifted it to a form of central subsidy that was immune to cash limits: subsidy in cash on demand to housing benefit and mortgage tax relief. The Treasury's resistance to demand-led spending was never more vociferous than over housing. By the end of the 1990s it was not local-authority housing that was 'out of control', but Thatcher's own preferred subsidies. For once, she had defeated the Treasury on an area of policy where, prior to taking office, her party had anticipated making the greatest savings.

Tory policy in the 1980s redefined public intervention in the housing market. Thatcher appears to have abandoned the traditional welfare basis for housing subsidy, which is that it should relieve need, a basis on which the Right would probably agree with the Left. In its place she substituted what amounted to a voucher, available to all with the means to buy their own shelter. Every citizen, she thought, should be entitled to help with his home, means-tested only for those claiming it in the form of housing benefit. Thatcher saw housing policy as crucial to encouraging savings, boosting the family and promoting self-sufficiency and choice. In 1986 the cabinet made this objective explicit. The 'leading housing policy aim', it said in its annual spending white paper, was 'to encourage home ownership'.[22] There was no mention of need. This was to be relieved through social security and other benefit payments. Thatcher had not only moved the burden of public spending on housing away from local government. She had sought to end housing's central role in the welfare state, yet elevate it as an engine of middle-class thrift. Despite the impact of this on public spending, she had brought housing policy firmly under central control. This was her most emphatic exercise in social engineering.

CHAPTER TEN

FORMING A JUDGEMENT

And I, my lords, embody the law – W. S. GILBERT

Margaret Thatcher passed more legislation affecting the private lives of British citizens than any other peacetime prime minister. She did this not because she was inclined to do so, but because she was in government and passing legislation is the business of government. Some of her laws were, she felt, needed to promote civilized values and to discipline a society that seemed alarmingly out of control. Others emerged from a growing middle-class demand for greater *ad hoc* regulation.

New controls on strikes, pickets and restrictive trade practices were justified as anti-monopolistic. Extensions to the 'Nanny State' were more controversial. The Thatcher and Major governments introduced laws on subjects as diverse as dangerous dogs, crash helmets, seat belts, drink-driving, noise abatement, video nasties, foreign wives, gay rights, historic buildings, late-night parties, rural trespass, contract tendering and health and safety at work. Each involved limiting personal or corporate freedoms. Each increased the discretionary power of courts and government. Under John Major the growth of what was termed family policy empowered civil servants to search out fathers of broken families and impose maintenance awards overturning previous court settlements. Home secretaries took powers to increase as well as reduce sentences and to fix the length of time anyone convicted of murder should stay in gaol. Every now and then a hapless minister would also be appointed to make 'a bonfire of regulations'. It was like putting a match to an iceberg.

In the absence of a Bill of Rights or other restraint, a British government is under no obligation to state the limits to its power. Every Tory manifesto professed an intention to move power from the government to the individual. Ministers in their party conference speeches were eloquent of the need for this. But the pledge was never honoured in terms that could be proved or codified. In most areas, government did the opposite and nobody could do anything about it. There was never a white paper on liberty. Some measures were the result of Britain's membership of the European Community. Some followed intensive lobbying by special interests, not least from environmental, safety and minority-rights groups. Many of the petty meddlings criticized by the media were the result of the public demanding more protection from risk, more conservation, better design, less pollution, less danger of disease or accident.

Libertarianism was one part of Hayek's prospectus Thatcher had never espoused. She was all for personal responsibility, but not for the withdrawal of external nannying that many might say was the concomitant of that responsibility. She wanted 'Victorian virtues' without the Victorian value of non-intervention by government. In her memoirs she was naïve on this. To those who said that family life should be private, Thatcher replied, 'Only the most myopic libertarian would regard it as outside the purview of the state: for my part, I felt that over the years the state had done so much harm that the opportunity to do some remedial work was not to be missed.'[1] Once again the need to undo the evils of past socialism was called in aid to justify intervention by present Thatcherism.

Top of the agenda was crime. The subject was intractable. Thatcher had made law and order her political preserve, yet to the public she had no policy. Each year she promised improvement yet each year she had to admit failure. As we saw in chapter five, she honoured her explicit pledge, 'Never, ever have you heard me say we shall economize on law and order.'[2] She increased police pay and resources throughout her term of office. There were six criminal justice acts in Britain between 1925 and 1985. The Tories then passed one every eighteen months, each more controversial than the last. Thatcher's Home Office was like a signal box with its wires cut. Operators pulled levers frantically, yet the trains kept crashing.

Crime was unfortunately an area of public policy which had measurable inputs but no sensible measures of output. Failures of policing, like failures of national defence, are all too easy to publicize, successes never so. Throughout the 1980s the number of crimes recorded by the police moved steadily upwards. Whether this reflected actual crime or some complex statistical bias is a matter of controversy.[3] Either way the government was compelled to extend the reach of the criminal law in an attempt to allay public concern. The irony was that by legislating to make ever more misdemeanours 'criminal', and then recruiting more police to record them, the government ensured that the crime rate was likely to keep moving upwards.

Penal policy under both Thatcher and Major gyrated between liberal and tough stances. But throughout there was a drift of judicial power and discretion from courts, judges and prisons towards ministers and civil servants. At the start of the 1980s, the tough approach was in the ascendant. The Criminal Justice Act 1982 brought back a favourite institution of Tory activists, 'military-style' detention centres for young offenders. They were to prove more effective in quieting Tory conferences than in reducing the reoffending rate among young criminals. The Act did, however, seek a specific executive aim, a reduction in the costly prison population. It reduced the power of courts to award custodial sentences except where custody was 'strictly necessary', and was successful in cutting the numbers in gaol.

The mid-1980s saw an attempt to re-establish a 'liberal' consensus on crime and punishment. Led by Leon Brittan and Douglas Hurd, the Home Office turned its attention away from prison and towards punishment in the community. A Leeds Castle seminar in 1987 led to the 1990 white paper, *Crime, Justice and Protecting the Public*. This was the culmination of the 'anti-prison' penal policy of the preceding decade. Prison should be only a last resort for violent and disturbed criminals, said the paper. Punishment 'in the community' was the new catchphrase. This ran parallel with an emphasis on Neighbourhood Watch, community policing and the greater use of cautioning. The late 1980s also saw the first mild slackening in the crime rate, though, as statisticians are careful to point out, this could have had as much to do with economic recovery or a change in police recording practice as with an actual decline in crime. The resulting 1991 Criminal Justice Act was generally seen as fine-tuning the criminal justice acts that had gone before. Custodial sentences in Britain actually fell during the 1980s.

The 1991 Act ran immediately into trouble. Its 'unit fines', a centralized scale of payments yielding nationwide consistency and reflecting ability to pay, were widely ridiculed. One wealthy offender was charged £1,000 for dropping a crisp wrapper. Kenneth Clarke had to back down. His successor, Michael Howard, proved hostile to the liberal inclinations of his predecessors. He introduced yet another criminal justice bill, putting the clock firmly back to the early 1980s. Prison returned to fashion, including 'short, sharp shock' institutions for young offenders. The right to silence and the availability of bail were restricted, as were common-law rights involving pop concerts and hunt sabotage. In a sharp U-turn, Howard proclaimed an enthusiasm for prisons in all his public pronouncements. It sent a shudder down the Treasury's spine. The judiciary responded to political direction and drove thousands of convicts back into the gaols. These U-turns had a chaotic impact on the penal system in the early 1990s.[4]

Criminal justice acts were now tumbling out of the Home Office. Howard was remarkable among Home Secretaries in his view of the extent of his remit. Not only did he believe that 'prison works', he agreed with Thatcher that politicians, not judges, should determine the nature and length of the more severe punishments. A stream of instructions passed from the

Home Office to the prison service on matters as diverse as telephone privileges, visiting hours, strip and search and whether or not staff should shop for prisoners. The Home Secretary was most particular about the treatment of 'special category' prisoners, such as IRA terrorists. This made a mockery of the status of the prison service as a semi-autonomous agency. The Home Office found itself drawn into detailed rules of prison discipline and protection, yet had to find ways of shifting accountability on to the prison service and prison governors when security broke down (as at Parkhurst in 1995).

More controversial was the interpretation put by ministers on the Criminal Justice Act of 1988. This stipulated that ministers could not only recommend a royal prerogative of 'mercy' to shorten sentences but could lengthen them as well. 'I took the greatest satisfaction in this,' recorded Thatcher.[5] The Act laid down that murder convictions should invariably carry a 'life' sentence, and the tariff system, whereby judges recommended maximum sentences for murder, was ended. In the view of the government, murder was such a serious crime that the length of punishment could not be left to judges (a view supported by Howard in a BBC interview in February 1995).[6] The majority of the appeal court judges, perhaps naturally, opposed this centralization of sentencing. In the same BBC interview, Lord Donaldson criticized the usurping by a political executive of a crucial component of judicial independence, the sentencing of convicts. The refusal to consider parole for the murderer, Myra Hindley, showed that ministers dared not act against public opinion. Lord Donaldson suggested that the politicization of sentencing might even constitute 'cruel and extraordinary punishment' and be against European law. Certainly its constitutionality was suspect.

If the Home Office felt politically strong enough to pursue this vigorously centralist course, the Lord Chancellor's department was not to be outdone. The surprise appointment of a Scots advocate, Lord Mackay, as Lord Chancellor in 1987 brought a new area of law into focus. Mackay was not part of the London judicial establishment but of the quite separate Scots one. It was as if a foreigner had been appointed a cabinet minister. Thatcher, then at her most radical, gave Mackay his head. Encouraged by the Treasury, he threw himself at the reform of the courts and the legal system. Already in 1985 the government had dipped its toe into this most jealous of professions. The Administration of Justice Act had ended the solicitors' monopoly on property conveyancing but had dodged the question of solicitors appearing in courts of law, traditional realm of barristers. With the government now extending its deregulatory philosophy from trade unions to the professions, it was unlikely that the courts would be immune for long.

Mackay announced in October 1988 that he would be publishing green papers on this subject. Michael Zander's account of their gestation indicates a similar process to that already seen in the case of education, health and poll tax.[7] Proposals emanated not from an independent body or any open deliberative process: they were produced by an interdepartmental committee, chaired by an official from the Lord Chancellor's department and with representation from the Treasury and the Department of Trade. When the papers appeared in January 1989, the legal profession erupted. They advocated an end to the Bar's monopoly on rights of audience in court. 'The government is not prepared to leave it to the legal profession to settle the principles which these codes [of court practice] should adopt, because they will be of such great importance both to the administration of justice and to the public.'[8] The government would decide who could license advocates to appear in court and which training would be appropriate. It would be advised by a Legal Affairs Commission which it would itself appoint.

Zander remarked that it was 'doubtful whether any single event in the long history of the English legal profession ever provoked so fierce and so broadly based a negative reaction'. Most opposition was, predictably, to the ending of the restrictive practices themselves. But equal fury was directed at the extension of executive power over the courts. The dependence on government of the proposed Legal Affairs Commission drew scorn from barristers and solicitors alike. The law lords abandoned all pretence of constitutional independence and attacked their most senior judge, the Lord Chancellor, without reserve. The most astonishing attack was from the Lord Chief Justice, Lord Lane, who called the green paper 'one of the most sinister documents ever to emanate from government'.[9] Lord Devlin said the government was 'treating judges like civil servants'.[10] By 1990, the force of professional opposition had dented the determination even of Mackay and Thatcher to press ahead with the changes. The lawyers, unlike the miners, had too many friends in high places for a frontal assault. The Courts and Legal Services Act of that year effectively put deregulation back into consultation, though it was not abandoned.

The bruising experience appeared to reinforce Mackay's enthusiasm for other reforms of the courts. Already in 1985 the Prosecution of Offences Act had dismantled the localized structure of police prosecution. The Act was rare among Thatcher's reforms in being based on a Royal Commission report (albeit one set up by Labour, reporting in 1981). This recommended the replacement of local police prosecuting solicitors by a nationalized Crown Prosecution Service (CPS). The Royal Commission had rejected the old 'police solicitor' system as outdated. It was based on the Victorian tradition that the police were *de jure* private citizens bringing malefactors before the local magistrate, advised in this by a local solicitor. The method of getting this advice varied widely round the country: 'Some [police solicitors] report to a county council, some to a police authority; some control their budgets and staffing, others do not; funding arrangements differ.'[11] The inability of the Director of Public Prosecutions (DPP) to issue directions on prosecution policy left wide discretion to local forces, and much scope for inconsistency in prosecuting practice. This was bound to seem troublesome to a centralist government.

Diversity was a natural consequence of a service that had always been both localized and privatized. The Royal Commission had been keen to retain at least this local character. It proposed that the police hand over prosecuting decisions to a new service under the professional direction of the DPP but responsible to the local police authority. The commission was specific as to how this new service should be constituted. It rejected nationalization, saying that it would 'involve a large bureaucracy and tend to lead to slow and remote decision-taking'.[12] The new service should be locally based and account-able to the same democratic body as the police. Police authorities should in future be renamed Police and Prosecuting Authorities and the local Crown Prosecutor would sit alongside the Chief Constable.

The government would not hear of this idea. Its view was that such local accountability would open the new service to 'improper local interference'.[13] Instead a centralized model was constructed with no sideways accountability to any local authority. Police solicitors moved overnight to become government civil servants in what amounted to a completely new nationalized industry. Whatever accountability might previously have existed via the police to the police authority – which the Royal Commission planned to enhance – now evaporated. The new CPS was accountable only through the Attorney-General to parliament. Crown prosecution had been a 'privatized', or at least sub-con-tracted, local service, which, in the interest of standardization and eventually of cost control, was now brought fully into the public sector.

Most advocates of penal reform approved of the CPS concept as distancing the police from the process of bringing an accused person to trial. Yet within eight years of its establishment, it was being criticized as susceptible to 'politically inspired policies introduced by a particular Home Secretary'.[14] Changes to the CPS code on prosecuting practice towards young offenders bore 'the unmistakable stamp of the Home Secretary's latest policy'. In the same issue of the *Criminal Law Review* a spokesman admitted that 'the code has to take account of the environment in which the criminal justice process works'. He did not say who should be the judge of that environment, or whether it should be national rather than local. This was precisely the centralist bind that the Royal Commission proposal for a strictly local service meant to avoid.

Meanwhile government was struggling to assert control over the cost of the courts themselves. The cost to the Exchequer rose an extraordinary fourfold in real terms over the 1980s. To the Treasury this was unacceptable, a new branch of non-cash-limited spending, which had to be nipped in the bud. Yet the British courts were entrenched in history, some would say entrenched in the constitution. The most junior tier, run by local magistrates and covering 95 per cent of criminal cases, had long been a key institution of local autonomy. Selection of magistrates was a responsibility of lord-lieutenants through their appointments committees, a custom dating back to the fourteenth century. The magistracy was also an occupation of many local Tories and their spouses, a much-bruised breed in the early 1990s. Ministers would only move into this territory with great care.

The magistrates courts were seen as expensive and inefficient, unmanaged by Whitehall yet a direct charge on central government through the Home Office. In December 1991 it was announced that as of the following April, responsibility for them would be transferred to the Lord Chancellor's department and brought within the overall management of the court service. Lord Mackay told the House of Lords, 'It is an important principle for me . . . to have as homogeneous a magistrates courts committee and area as we can.'[15] Local diversity was out of date. The subsequent 1994 Police and Magistrates Court Act was intended, according to Michael Howard, 'to yield improvements in the efficiency and effectiveness of the service, secure maximum co-operation in the management of the service with other parts of the criminal justice system, and improve the accountability of the service both locally and to parliament'.[16] Accountability to parliament would theoretically increase by bringing administration more directly under Treasury control. How the intention to improve local accountability was to be realized was a mystery.

Under section 69 of the Act the Lord Chancellor would in future be able to amalgamate magistracy areas and their committees at will, rather than depending, as in the past, on local agreement. 'We have,' said Howard, speaking for the Lord Chancellor, 'a duty to consider the best interests of the service as a whole.' It was announced that the one hundred and five magistrates committees in England and Wales would be cut to between fifty and sixty. Magistrates court committees would be 'restructured so that they can better fulfil their task of providing strategic direction'. Committee membership 'would no longer be primarily representative . . . members would be chosen for their particular experience or skills.' The local justices' clerks would, for the first time, be placed on a statutory footing and be subject to the discretion of the Lord Chancellor to 'issue standards of performance that he expects the magistrates courts service to achieve'.[17] A new magistrates courts inspectorate would be set up to enforce these standards and a uniform computer system installed.

To the magistrates this appeared to be an intrusion of central and possibly partisan government into the administration of local justice, which had long been free of this taint. So fierce was the opposition to combining magistrates committees – ostensibly a sensible reform – that by 1995 only one amalgamation had actually occurred. A tension had been established between what were seen as uncontrollable local costs and a need for central budgetary accountability. The government's method of resolving it, by taking power not just over money but also over the agencies of administration, was seen as so draconian as to produce an equal and opposite local resistance. Such was the confusion that Labour could not decide during the debate whether this was a 'centralizing' measure (Tony Blair) or a 'privatizing' one (Paul Boateng).[18]

In April 1995, the engine of reform rumbled on to reach the Crown and county courts and the High Court. Like the magistracy, they were steeped in history, autonomy and costs. In the 1970s, the Beeching Commission had recommended the abolition of the medieval assizes and quarter sessions and instituted the Crown courts. They were regarded as costly and dilatory (though far less so than most others in Europe) and were duly hived off into a new agency, the Courts Service Agency. This was intended to be self-financing through the charging of full costs. A chief executive was appointed, answerable directly to the Lord Chancellor, with some 10,000 court staff in England and Wales under his command. The new agency started work in April 1995 with an initial objective of reducing by at least fifty the number of civil courts in use, to cut down delay and improve an inefficient sphere of public administration. In the government's view, courts should no longer be under suspicion of being organized for the convenience of judges – any more than hospitals were for consultants or universities for academics. That suspicion was best allayed by their being organized by the Lord Chancellor's department, under an agency appointed by and responsible directly to him. Britain watched another nationalized industry in the making.

A large component of the cost of these courts was legal aid. Granting such aid was, like health care, an open-ended government commitment which appeared to rise exponentially with economic growth. Between 1990 and 1995 alone, the cost of legal aid doubled to £1.3 billion (cash). In 1981 the total was just £180m. There was no formal control on the total, and all the government could do was tighten eligibility. The outlays were becoming increasingly chaotic and unfair, with many solicitors being so badly paid as to abandon the work altogether, while fifty criminal barristers and a hundred civil barristers each received more than £100,000 a year from the legal aid fund. In January 1995 Lord Mackay told the legal profession that enough was enough. His corner of the welfare state had to be cash-limited. He proposed to give budgets to regional legal aid offices and then franchise out work to approved law firms. There would be various tiers of advice and help, but ultimately the rationing would be delegated to local solicitors. Although the parallel was anathema, legal aid solicitors would be like fund-holding doctors. They would have an obligation both to advise on what form of

199

litigation or arbitration was appropriate and, if necessary, do the work themselves. If their allocation ran out before the end of the year, too bad on them and their clients.

The new 'franchise' holders would expect to be doing as much as 90 per cent of their work for the regional legal aid boards. A thousand such offices were designated by the central Legal Aid Board. They were expected both to show a 'proven commitment to legal aid work', said Lord Mackay, and to operate to what he called 'a predetermined quality', a concept as yet unspecified.[19] Like the former police solicitors, now state Crown Prosecutors, lawyers appearing for the defence were being drawn closer into the public sector under the umbrella of cost standardization and control. Many solicitors saw themselves becoming the 'Crown Defenders', mirroring the Crown Prosecutors of the CPS. In the course of 1995 those proposing to take up franchises were asked to subscribe to Whitehall employment codes of practice. They were in receipt of a cash-limited Treasury block grant, rather than being paid what was a personal entitlement of a client. They were on the way to becoming another state service, 'providers' to the government's purchasers.

The changes instituted by Lord Mackay in 1988 were aimed at a public service long recognized as out of budgetary control and in urgent need of reform. Early Thatcherism had not dared touch the law. Lawyers were mostly Tories and their professional privileges were, to many cabinet ministers, a domestic concern. They would return to the law should they lose office. Unlike the academics, the teachers and the doctors, protecting the autonomy of lawyers was a 'moral issue', as the former Lord Chancellor, Lord Havers, called it on television at the time of the Mackay reforms. Caution was therefore all. Yet by the early 1990s the cost of legal services allied to the determination of a radical minister forced legal reform to the top of the Treasury and thus the cabinet agenda. Once again the catalyst to radicalism was the need to control spending: reform riding on the Treasury's coat-tails. Once again the price paid for reform was centraliza-tion. The outcome was halting, staccato change; but change there was. It undermined the semi-autonomous status of professional and constitutional bodies which had been targeted as culprits of budgetary indiscipline. For what it saw as the very best of motives, the centre marched in to take control. The Crown Prosecution Service, the Courts Service Agency, the reformed magistracy and the cash-limited legal aid fund all testified to a new era of centralized justice.

CHAPTER ELEVEN

MR MAJOR'S POODLES

They threatened its life with a railway-share;
They charmed it with smiles and soap.
— LEWIS CARROLL

Thatcher's fall in November 1990 did not spell the end of Thatcherism – if anything the opposite. The momentum of her last three years of hyperactivity drove the programme forward, often at reckless speed. The Major government remained true to the faith but with less instinctive caution, as if seeking to prove itself more Catholic than the pope. It struggled to privatize industries from which Thatcher had shied away, notably coal mines and the Post Office. It stepped up the pace of centralization in schools, universities, hospitals and the police. Major might seem a milder and more accommodating leader than Thatcher, but he was also less inclined to curb the radical ambitions of his colleagues or apply to them an overlay of political judgement. There was none of Thatcher's cross-examination of the minutiae of each step forward. The handbrake of Number Ten worked less well and the steering wheel had to perform more damaging U-turns.

By the end of the 1980s the concept of the purchaser/provider split was ingrained in Whitehall and cabinet thinking. It had enabled government to disentangle policy from management and public spending from service delivery. It offered a form of privatization under contract but without government losing control. The Major government soon turned its attention to two industries

202

from which Thatcher had averted her gaze and applied purchaser/provider to them with gusto. One was an existing monopoly, the railways; the other was a new one specially created to meet a political need, a state lottery. The former had been under an arm's-length public corporation, British Rail, itself fashioned from one of the great ventures of nineteenth-century capitalism, the railway network. The latter took what had been a straightforward private industry, gambling, and nationalized a substantial chunk of it in order to raise public revenue.

British Rail trains were not council houses, but to Thatcher they had much in common. They were popular, ate subsidy and were run by somebody else. As every minister since Huskisson (the first person to be run down by a train) was aware, trains rarely leave politicians in one piece. Thatcher knew this. Her position on British Rail was clear. She disliked trains and avoided travelling in them. She regarded them as a dirty and inefficient corner of the public sector, yet one for which the electorate had a perverse affection. Privatization would be technically difficult and unpopular. As a result she shut her mind to it. Her most loyal and long-serving transport secretary, Nicholas Ridley, wisely decided never to discuss railways with her and does not mention them at all in his memoirs. When her last two ministers, Paul Channon and Cecil Parkinson, pressed to be allowed to go for privatization, she warned them off. Her sole interest was in selling the railways' 'non-core' assets to keep down the subsidy. She wanted to cut the cost without frightening the natives.

Britain's railways in 1979 shared many characteristics with the National Health Service. Despite the ambitions of the Attlee government they had not been truly nationalized after the war. The relationship between Whitehall and the British Transport Executive set up in 1948 was customarily described as one of 'thankfully giving money and thankfully receiving it'. The relationship between the Executive and the old railway regions was much the same. The private-sector companies that had been grouped in the 1921 Act were now in public ownership, but this merely altered the reporting line of their general managers. They were big men, who answered to their professional staff and the traditions of their region. They remained barons in a railway confederacy. Government paid for them but neither planned them nor controlled them. Not until the Beeching reforms of the 1960s and the abolition of steam was a national approach to rail investment begun, but even then it still used the regions as agents. The government continued to pay a straight subsidy to the railway board on what amounted to a 'fund and forget' basis. There were intermittent attempts to relate subsidy to loss-making lines (known in the 1970s as the 'Cooper Bros formula') but these were unsuccessful. BR went its own costly way and responsibility was firmly devolved.

The story of the 1980s was of the centralization of this disparate industry, under the now familiar public-sector banners of cost control and value for money. First under Sir Peter Parker as chairman, then under the first Sir Robert Reid, war was declared on the regional general managers and their 'cost citadels'. With the support of the transport department, they were crushed and their vast appetite for subsidy checked. To visit them in the early 1980s was to witness the outposts of a liberal empire in its final years of decline. Managers still had their pride. London and North Eastern crews changed at St Neot's, as in pre-grouping days. Western region engineers still used Brunel's drawings on their tours of inspection. At Paddington and Swindon, the spirit of God's Wonderful Railway lived on.

Reid's restructuring, first as chief executive then as chairman, took ten years and was painful. Such was the internal animosity that few regional managers after the early 1980s ever won promotion to the main board. Not until 1990 were the regions finally wiped out, replaced by business sectors and 'sub-sectors' for InterCity, London commuter lines, local services, freight and parcels. These cut across regional boundaries, their executives owing loyalty to the chief executive and board in London. The new business sectors were given their own logos, uniforms and even train liveries. At the Department of Transport in Marsham

Street the railway directorate divided itself into divisions marking those in BR headquarters. Financial targets for each business were drawn up by government. When the second Sir Bob Reid arrived from Shell to take over as chairman in 1990 he was able to command what was at last a truly 'nationalized' industry.

Thatcher was happy to leave this well alone. She had already sold BR's holdings of hotels, ferries, hovercraft and property, relieving the board's call on central borrowing (and making privatization much harder by stripping the industry of market-able assets). Ministers saw these sales as ideologically sound, but a few would ask the board tentatively if 'more might be done'. There were studies of selling the London, Tilbury and Southend line and a line from Windsor to Slough. Private operators crept on to the network, such as Foster Yeoman's aggregates business and the Orient Express. British Rail catering was split up and put out to tender, as was British Rail Engineering. But BR remained the statutory monopoly for railways in Britain. The rail unions were exclusive suppliers of labour. There was a complex statutory procedure for the closure of any service; chang-ing it required legislation. Nobody was keen to send the privatiza-tion bull into this politically delicate china shop.

As over health and education, the Right kept nagging. The Centre for Policy Studies and the Institute of Economic Affairs regularly put out pamphlets debating different routes to privatiza-tion.[1] The former held seminars, including one in October 1988 at which the new Secretary of State, Paul Channon, was invited to speak. Channon was the first minister avidly to champion BR privatization. He declared that 'we do not believe that the best protection of the consumer is secured by keeping the industry in public ownership'.[2] He wanted an option, he said, that would 'free the railway from unnecessary public control', but he stressed that subsidy would continue even if the state divested itself of ownership. The familiar options – a unitary industry or one divided horizontally or vertically – were rehearsed but the minis-ter was careful not to register any preference.

A report on this conference prepared by the future cabinet

minister, John Redwood, was less cautious. He was dismissive of vertical separation of the railway between operating companies and a track authority: 'The objections to it are hard to meet.' Redwood pointed out the importance of internal cross-subsidy to any future for the railway. 'Property improvement is one of the most attractive business opportunities within the railway and will become one of the main ways of supplementing revenues from fares, to finance other necessary transport activities.'[3] Similar conclusions were being reached by the consultants, Coopers and Lybrand, for the BR board. They too examined break-up options, albeit in cursory form. Knowing the board's enthusiasm for a unitary railway, their conclusions were strongly biased in that direction. The Coopers report was considered by the board in April 1989. It was agnostic but was, like the Channon conference, dismissive of a track authority.

Rail experts disliked the segregation of train companies from the management of stations, signals and track for two reasons. First it was complicated and therefore bureaucratic, more so even than hospital contracts. Every train movement would require a series of bargains to be struck between an operator and separate entities owning track, stations, and even rolling stock. Since most of these relationships were monopolistic, they all needed strong regulation. The 'rent book' for the 'use' of Paddington station under the Railway Act of 1993 was reputedly the size of a telephone directory. Second, the biggest scope for cost-cutting on BR was in track and signalling. Although a squeeze was to be imposed on costs by putting maintenance out to tender, the provider of infrastructure would remain a single, initially a state, monopoly. The 1980s reorganization had suggested that the key to railway efficiency lay in giving train operators the greatest possible control over both costs and revenues, especially over how much they needed to spend on their track. If BR was to be split up, this argument went, then 'operators must own costs'. A railway company must feel in control of its assets and answerable to its customers, not to a regulator or a contract target.

The story of how the 'worst option' for the railway became

Whitehall's preference in the course of 1990–92 mirrors the rise of poll tax seven years before. At the start was another instance of a prime minister with her eye off the ball. As late as October 1990, Thatcher was telling her last transport secretary, Cecil Parkinson, not to mention privatizing BR in his party conference speech. In her memoirs she writes that she had consented only to an interdepartmental working party to 'study and report back'.[4] With the advent of John Major, this working party went active. Its membership included the Treasury's railway expert Steve Robson, Nicholas Blackwell from the Downing Street policy unit and officials from the transport and industry departments. BR was not represented, nor did the group include anybody with direct railway knowledge – again a repeat of the poll tax débâcle. Transport officials kept up a desultory battle for a unitary corporation, or at least a holding company with business subsidiaries. This was the option preferred by BR and was scorned as such by the Treasury. Scarred by the experience of the gas industry, both the Treasury and Blackwell from Downing Street were insistent that the railway be broken up. Yet they found little support from BR or the transport department for the simplest and most viable method, division into regional and local companies. They were also desperate to inject some form of service competition into the system. The Prime Minister's preference for a regional break-up appears to have carried no weight with the committee. His views did not send an electric current through Whitehall as had his predecessor's.

The involvement of politicians in the fate of BR was cursory. In October 1991 the new Secretary of State, Malcolm Rifkind, asked BR to consider letting outside operators use its track, in line with a recent European Community directive on 'open access'. In January 1992 he appointed Coopers and Lybrand once again to examine options. A senior partner in Coopers was Sir Christopher Foster, his enthusiasm for more Thatcherite reform undimmed by his close involvement in the poll tax and power privatization sagas. He managed to combine careers as academic, ministerial adviser, quango member and bidder for government consultancy contracts (not all at the same time) with agility. Rifkind was insistent that 'choice, competition and open access' would dominate the railway of the future. Yet at no point was he able to explain what form this might take, nor was the interdepartmental committee able to help him. By the time of the 1992 manifesto, the most that anybody could suggest was some 'franchising' of services to private companies by a rail regulator, while BR would 'continue to be responsible for all track and infrastructure'.[5] Major's own enthusiasm was reflected in the manifesto's desire to 'recapture the spirit of the old regional companies'.

July 1992 saw the publication of a short white paper in which these ideas became only a little more specific. To a rail regulator was now added a separate franchising authority. Its aim was to promote private operation wherever possible, but track, signalling and unfranchised services would remain with BR. There was still a curious confusion over terms, with talk of offering customers 'a choice' of services,[6] a choice incomprehensible to any railwayman. The government appeared to envisage franchising competitive 'pathways' to different companies down a particular stretch of track. This was not the privatization of the railway. It was the sub-contracting of individual services on an *ad hoc* basis to run over public-sector tracks to a predetermined timetable and level of subsidy. It was using the private sector to help deliver a public service. The policy at least had the virtue of modest simplicity.

Over the next months it became less modest and less simple. The 1992 white paper was received with bafflement by the railway industry. The government felt it had an election mandate for proceeding with a franchising authority and the Whitehall group moved into legislative mode. The result was the Railway Act 1993, introduced in a rowdy second-reading debate by yet another new transport secretary, John MacGregor. The relevant Hansard reads like a bad-tempered London commuters' rally. MacGregor did not pretend that the railway was being privatized. His purpose, he said, was merely to 'get as much private-sector involvement, attitudes, objectives and management into our railway system as we possibly can'.[7] Above all he sought 'private-sector capital to supplement the existing sources of BR finance'. This was the weakest possible definition of privatization.

John Major's new railway emerged from the Commons as, at this stage, a new nationalized industry owning and managing all BR's fixed assets of track and stations. Twenty-five passenger franchise operators would be selected by the so-called franchising director (with the acronym Opraf). He would invite either positive or negative bids to run trains over Railtrack to a time-table and a price supervised by another individual, the rail regula-tor (Ofrail). Trains would be owned by three new rolling-stock companies, dubbed Roscos. There would also be three freight companies.

The original competitive franchising model was thus converted into a purchaser/provider model. Railtrack became a monopolis-tic island of tracks, stations and signals surrounded by an ocean of British industry's most complex price and contract regulation. Railtrack had been envisaged as free-standing: 'truly independ-ent, commercially driven,' said MacGregor. It was later proposed for privatization as a monopoly. Any subsidy would pass from the Treasury via the franchising director to the train operators. None would go to Railtrack for passenger services. There was, however, an intriguing provision in the Act for subsidy to Rail-track to take 'socially desirable' freight traffic. The Secretary of State was empowered to give grants on the same basis as he did for roads, if a 'satisfactory cost/benefit' could be shown. This was a far more generous basis for investment subsidy than had been allowed to BR, which had to forecast a commercial profit on any investment. While the provision was not immediately used, its appearance symbolized a government wishing to give itself free-dom to subsidize a 'privatized' service that it had rigorously denied when the service was nationalized.

The rail regulator, John Swift, soon found himself drawn into the same political rows that began to dog his energy utility colleagues. How many stations should offer through ticketing? How much should a company be charged to use a station? The

Tory MP Robert Adley had christened the proposed structure 'poll tax on wheels'. Few ministers appeared aware of the full implications of the Act as it passed into implementation. In private conversation they seemed bemused, assuring themselves and others that all was under control. Yet by 1994 the charges levied by Railtrack on BR's as yet unprivatized divisions were proving too costly for the franchising director, who was hoping to sell them soon. John Swift duly fulfilled his obligation to 'listen to the views of the Secretary of State' and cut the charges.[8] He thus boosted the franchise programme but damaged Railtrack's market value and the government's plans to sell it in the market. Then in May 1995 the government announced that most rail fares in the new franchising system would be capped, initially at RPI and long-term at RPI minus 1 per cent.

What was now clear was that the key to the profitability of all these services was in the hands of the regulators and the terms imposed on them by ministers. This applied whether the services were publicly or privately owned. Either way they were monopolies under contract to the state. The new train operators would be besieged by regulation. The franchising director was to allocate franchises for which, at first, the government forbade BR to bid, a slur that did nothing for railway morale. This was then reversed. The new companies would run trains rented from Roscos but have no control over up to 70 per cent of their outgoings. They would have little control over their prices. Even discounted and Supersaver fares were to be capped. One manager told me, 'My room for management manoeuvre is confined to a paint pot and a travel brochure.' His profit would depend not on his own enterprise or productivity but on the various deals he had to negotiate from time to time with regulators.

The franchising director would not only decide on who should be granted a franchise but also on how much premium or, more likely, subsidy would go with it. This meant deciding which services and indeed which lines should stay open or should close. Yet whatever decision he made on subsidy could be overridden by Whitehall under reserve powers in the 1993 Act. The Secretary of State could make an *ex gratia* payment to an operator to keep a line open should closure seem imminent. This offered unlimited scope for operators to blackmail not so much the franchising director as ministers and the Treasury. The delicate politics of line closure, which ministers had in the past delegated to BR, would come thundering into the House of Commons with all the noise of Bevan's famous bedpans. The outgoing chairman of BR, Sir Bob Reid, told the then Secretary of State, Brian Mawhinney, on leaving office in 1995 that in future he, the minister, would be chairman of British Rail. The rail regulator and the franchising director were, jointly with the Secretary of State, now the proxies for the old BR board. An industry whose commercial decisions had previously been made at arm's length from Whitehall now found them subject to Whitehall overrule.[9]

The 1993 Act had one additional twist in its tail. The Treasury inserted in the Act an unnoticed innovation requiring that any premiums flowing to the franchising director in bids for profitable lines would not be his to reallocate. They would go to the Treasury. In this respect the railway was similar to commercial television companies, the Post Office and hospital trusts. In the past, BR had decided whether profit in one part of the network should be ploughed back as investment or cross-subsidy for other lines. A surplus on the London-to-Brighton line could be used to rebuild Victoria station or keep open the service to Lewes. Under the 1993 Act, neither an operator nor the franchising director had this power. The Department of Transport and Treasury would receive any premiums and dispense them as subsidies as and when they, not the railway, felt a loss-making line should be kept open as a social service. The railway industry would no longer redistribute its own surpluses. That function passed to central government.

The planning and allocation of internal surpluses is the litmus test of industrial sovereignty. The 1993 Railway Act converted the railway into a patchwork of heavily regulated local providers to a state monopoly purchaser/planner. The Act did not privatize the railway service. It sold off its assets and transferred control of them to a bureaucratic framework of complex internal contracts. The transport economist, Stephen Glaister, no particular friend of nationalization, pointed out in a pamphlet (written with Tony Travers) that 'previous privatizations were deliberately designed to place industries beyond the immediate reach of government. In the case of the railway, the industry may end up under *more* direct control than at present.' The old British Rail did, by virtue of its size and scope, enjoy a large measure of independence of government. The new subsidy arrangements would lead to ministers being 'unable to resist political pressures to intervene ... undermining the achievements and improvements which privatization could bring'.[10] The form of arm's-length nationalization initiated in 1948 was not completed until the final reorganization of BR in 1990, ironically the year of Thatcher's fall. The Major government promptly undid this particular corporatist achievement and put another form of corporatism in its place. Control of what had been a unitary but devolved industry was brought under close Whitehall oversight, both as to subsidy and as to regulation. The 1993 Act threw the railway up in the air and ensured that it fell straight into the Treasury's lap.

The same destination awaited Major's second candidate for nationalization, the lottery. The British do not give liberally to charity. Since the founding of the welfare state they have expected the government to relieve them of that responsibility. They pay taxes to support the welfare state and are reluctant to top up that spending by giving to charity from their taxed income. Nor has the Treasury been keen to relieve such gifts of tax. It is subsidizing one welfare state and is understandably chary of subsidizing a second one through tax relief. If private citizens feel they have identified a need not already covered by government, that is their business, not that of the Exchequer.

Such a Scrooge-like approach underpinned decades of Treasury opposition towards tax relief for charitable giving. The only concessions had, in the past, been to relieve charities themselves of tax and to permit individuals to 'covenant' money over five years or more. In the latter case charities could reclaim the tax assumed to have been paid on that covenant. This involves a different psychology from that of American tax-deductible giving. In America a charity receives the gift untaxed, while the donor feels he has been rewarded by the state for his generosity. In Britain, the charity receives the gift taxed and must go to the state for a refund. The donor never sees this refund and (with recent exceptions) must give out of his taxed income. Although covenanting has grown rapidly in recent decades it is in itself little incentive to private giving.

Largely as a result, Americans give roughly six times more per head to 'not-for-profit' causes than do the British. Thatcher's enthusiasm for the voluntary sector led many in the charity movement to expect her to encourage welfare voluntarism through the tax system.[11] Each year the lobbyists would gather at the Treasury to plead for one version or another of the American approach. Not until 1986 was a timid 'payroll giving' scheme introduced by Nigel Lawson. This was deductible only for those with pay-as-you-earn tax codes and donating up to £100 a head via a corporate donor. They were able to suggest a choice of recipient, but the decision rested with the corporate charity committee. Not surprisingly this was not a great success. The Exchequer cost of the concession was registered in the 1991 public-spending Blue Book (table D1) as 'negligible'. Later the Treasury partially relented and limited sums could be claimed directly on the tax form.

The Treasury position on charities is understandable. The not-for-profit movement in America is, in the view of many experts, an uncontrollable leakage from the tax base. Provided an organization does not declare a profit and can show its aim as the public good, it can excuse itself and its backers from taxes. Schools, universities, churches, lobbyists all benefit. Orchestras found devices to enable their members to write their tickets, drinks, even (in one famous case) their pizzas against tax. Professionals could pay themselves any size of fees but their organizations were free of tax provided they declared no 'profit'. This threw an ever heavier burden on those who still paid tax.

The British Treasury in the 1980s faced demand-led expenditures that were rising exponentially in areas such as social security, housing benefit, legal aid and mortgage interest tax relief. These could not be cash-limited or otherwise curtailed in the short term as most were statutory entitlements. The Treasury already gave grants to many of the lobbyists for wider tax relief, through the Arts and Sports Councils and through direct grants to charities. If they found themselves forced to subsidize any public service, Treasury officials always preferred fixed and cash-limitable grants rather than open-ended or demand-led ones. Widespread tax deductibility for charitable donations would be a voyage into the fiscal unknown. Yet each year pressure to concede further relief to this politically potent sector increased.

At the end of the decade an extraordinary *deus ex machina* arrived on the public-expenditure scene. Lotteries had been considered a tawdry form of state fund-raising, normally associated with banana republics. They had flourished from the sixteenth to the early nineteenth century, paying for anything from the repair of the Cinque Ports to building London's water supply, ransoming slaves, relieving maimed soldiers, constructing Westminster Bridge and even creating the British Museum. The last public lottery in Britain had been in 1826, when the idea was abandoned as undignified. Central and local taxation existed to support deserving causes. To fiscal conservatives, lotteries were as uncertain in their revenue as tax reliefs were uncertain in their cost. Private lotteries were limited by law to small-scale tombolas. Other forms of gambling were regulated and taxed, though for no clear reason football pools were permitted to give away huge prizes and reap huge rewards in return.

The idea of reviving a national lottery had been mooted in the 1980s by arts lobbyists. A 1987 report on gambling by Lord Rothschild had suggested a national lottery. In the same year a freelance musician named Denis Vaughan wrote to Thatcher with a similar proposal. The idea was taken up by the Labour peer, Lord Birkett, in the House of Lords in May 1988. Meetings were held in the Houses of Parliament and cross-party support obtained. In 1990 a lottery promotion company was formed. It would set up a lottery independent of government to aid sports and arts charities, should the government change the law to permit it. Directors included Lord Gibson, former chairman of the National Trust, the former arts minister Richard Luce, the Earl of Harewood and Labour, Liberal and Conservative MPs. Vaughan was its driving force.

At this point the chief potential loser from a lottery, the pools industry, took fright and sought to cover its flank. Gambling turnover in Britain, mostly on horses and football, was rising fast, reaching £13 billion in 1990. Money on this scale had long attracted political – and Inland Revenue – attention. Like oil, banking and property, gambling was victim to periodic Treasury super-levies. As a sport-loving Chancellor under Thatcher, John Major had been lobbied by the pools promoters to consider a scheme to divert some of the government's gambling levy to cover the cost of improving British soccer grounds after a series of stadium accidents. The Treasury had conceded this diversion. In 1991 Major as Prime Minister approved a Sports and Arts Foundation as a vehicle for this cross-subsidy, its £60m annual fund offset against gambling levy. The quid pro quo from the pools lobby was explicit: the government would not set up a state lottery. The scheme was kept secret in the Treasury pending announcement in the 1991 budget.

Unaware of this the then Home Secretary, Kenneth Baker, was being swayed by the grander concept of the Lottery Promotion Company. Baker knew from overseas experience that a lottery could raise hundreds of millions of pounds, and his officials prepared a paper on this basis. In early 1991 Whitehall was therefore working on two rival schemes for channelling gambling money into charities. The Treasury/pools scheme involved a straight cut of 5 per cent in pools levy, in return for twice that amount put by the pools promoters into the Sports and Arts Foundation. This cost public revenue, but was predictable and cheap. The Chancellor, Norman Lamont, duly announced the scheme with much fanfare in his 1991 budget, having previously kept it secret even within Whitehall. Baker was furious. He recorded, 'This was a remarkable example of how budget secrecy does not help the good administration of the country or the cohesion of government policy.'[12] To him the Treasury had been victim of a crude political ploy by the pools industry to head off his lottery.

The Treasury disliked a state lottery. It risked diverting large and unpredictable sums from other gambling, and thus from other taxed expenditure. It could cost tens of millions in lost revenue. Baker was undaunted. His own office, he says, warned him not to take on the Treasury, concerned that if defeated the Treasury might seek revenge by trying to cut the Home Office's budget. 'However, I thought it absurd that Norman Lamont and the Treasury should have been bought off for as little as £60m.'[13] Baker now did what he was best at, glad-handing his way round cabinet colleagues with a plausible scheme that would look good in the upcoming election manifesto. He encouraged a private member's bill, sponsored by the Tory MP Ivan Lawrence, and by January 1992 he had persuaded Downing Street to let him proceed with a white paper. The Treasury was now faced with not one but two charity benefit schemes, its own and the Home Office's.

'It was typical of the Treasury,' Baker recalled, 'that having lost this particular battle they now wanted to profit from it. I had to insist on a cast-iron assurance, enshrined in the White Paper, that money from the lottery would be additional funding for public-sector projects and not a substitute.'[14] The Treasury had wanted to leave open this question of 'additionality'. Its argument was that a statutory lottery was in some sense state revenue, since it had been raised under statute and was handled through government-appointed bodies and audit. Treasury officials were equally keen to keep the spending away from the planning total, where it would soon seep into ordinary public spending and appear to increase it. A compromise was sought. The lottery revenue would be private and therefore taxable, to make up for any tax lost elsewhere. Twelve per cent would go straight to the Exchequer. But a further 26 per cent would be taken for spending on good causes, and this would be treated as public spending but 'ring-fenced' so as not to leak into other expenditure programmes. Baker accepted this as second best to independence. 'Some Treasury officials needed a stake through their hearts before policies are safe from their clutches.'[15]

The Treasury conceded the ring-fencing but in the most cursory way. The lottery revenues were firmly labelled general government expenditure and their separation from other programmes was covered by no more than a statement by the heritage minister during the passage of the bill. Peter Brooke promised, 'The government does not intend that the money provided for the lottery should substitute for that provided in other ways ... the government will not make a case-by-case reduction in conventional expenditure programmes to take account of awards from lottery proceeds.'[16] He declined to enshrine additionality in legislation. He appeared to trust a Treasury statement 'of intent'.

In December 1992 the private-sector lottery company campaigners had proposed a charitable foundation similar to that set up under the original Treasury/pools scheme, to disburse the lottery proceeds independent of government. That is what had already been established for the pools' £60m Sports and Arts Foundation. But such independence was unthinkable for the £1 billion or more a year that a state lottery might bring in. Norman Lamont insisted that the lottery concept could not be left either to voluntary charities or to the free flow of market forces. Clause 24 of the new Act gave the government powers to direct the distributing bodies in what Mr Brooke called 'the broadest terms on how the money can be used, for example mainly capital or partnership funding, and how it should be accounted'.[17] It was public money and it should be 'properly used'. There were no surprises as to who would be defining the word properly. The state lottery had to be a nationalized industry, and it duly was.

The Treasury now moved to protect its new baby. It banned any competitors. Private fund-raisers using tombolas or lotteries were stopped from offering more than £25,000 in a single prize, or from raising more than £1 million in total. This meant that potential beneficiaries such as the British Museum or Covent Garden Opera were prevented from having limited lotteries among their own supporters for development programmes. They were forced to go cap in hand to a government-appointed 'good cause' distributor. These distributors were, in the case of the arts, heritage and sport, the existing Arts Council, National Heritage Memorial Fund and Sports Council. In the long term it would clearly be impossible to keep lottery revenue 'ring-fenced' from other claims on public spending passing through these same bodies. Additionality could not last. An area of private spending (gambling) had been nationalized, and an area of public spending (arts, charities and sport) been given what would briefly be its discrete source of revenue. As with National Insurance and the Road Fund, such sources soon merge into the generality of state revenues. While arts spending was held for the first year of the lottery, it was planned to be cut for the years after 1995.

The new National Lottery was subcontracted to the private sector in what was the most generous private monopoly that the Tories were to establish. The 1993 Act set up a regulator, Peter Davis (of Oflot), who was to choose a single company to run the lottery for five years. In return it could take 5 per cent of whatever it could raise. A proposal from the entrepreneur Richard Branson to run the lottery at cost was rejected. The contract was variously estimated to be worth a profit of £50–150m a year over costs of roughly the same to the bid winner, Camelot. This was tax farming worthy of a Balkan monarch, and attracted much criticism. But while the Treasury was happy to subcontract tax gathering in this way, it was unwilling to subcontract expenditure. The 'good cause' money would be distributed through five agencies, all appointed by the government. In addition to those for arts, heritage and sport, new ones were set up for grants to charities and to celebrate the Millennium. They were appointed as normal quangos, vetted by the Tory whips' office.

Detailed financial directives, prepared by the heritage department and the Home Office 'with the approval of the Treasury', covered both 'broad policy directions . . . and financial directions which must be complied with to secure the proper management and control of money'.[18] Section 26 of the Act contained the familiar 'Henry VIII' clauses. Any distributor body, far from being independent, would have to 'comply with any directions given to it by the Secretary of State as to the matters to be taken into account in determining the persons to whom, the purposes for which and the conditions subject to which the body distributes any money'.[19] A convoluted subsection well illustrated the Treasury's paranoia over the lottery: 'The directions . . . may require a body to obtain the consent of the Secretary of State before doing anything specified in the directions.'

The hijacking of the lottery and a proportion of the gambling industry by the government angered its original promoters. It also infuriated the pools lobby, whom the Treasury had promised to protect from a lottery when they set up their £60m Sports and Arts Foundation. The foundation took a dive in receipts. The pools company, Vernons, saw a swift fall of 15 per cent in revenue. It laid off 20 per cent of its staff and stopped its entire £8m contribution to the foundation. In a sardonic comment during the second-reading debate, the Labour MP Bryan Davies remarked that he could not wholeheartedly oppose the bill: 'I do not shrink from nationalizing a part of the nation's gambling industry. As some of my colleagues have pointed out, the government are in an odd position in that they are involved in a nationalization measure. I rejoice in that.'[20] The Opposition spokesman, Ann Clwyd, found herself having to defend the interests of private-sector workers in the pools industry, whose livelihoods the government was jeopardizing in what she called 'the unacceptable face of nationalization'.[21] In a Commons debate later that year, Ivan Lawrence protested that the government had merely 'introduced a nationalized state lottery . . . We will rue the day that we were not more dedicated in setting up a charitable foundation.'[22]

The first year of the National Lottery realized roughly one billion pounds for this additional 'general government expenditure'. A new state monopoly had been fashioned from what had been one of Britain's most lucrative – and most private – industries, that of gambling. Private charities saw a sudden fall in casual donations as money was diverted into Camelot scratchcards. The potential of raising money for good causes through private lotteries was stifled by government statute. Of all Tory nationalizations this was the most blatant and bizarre.

CHAPTER TWELVE

The Magpies' Nest

Now you shall feel the strength of Tamburlaine,
And, by the state of his supremacy,
Approve the difference 'twixt himself and you.
— CHRISTOPHER MARLOWE

Thatcherism took office, in the judgement of history, in 1976. The arrival in London of IMF loan monitors was a moment of truth both for the Labour party and for post-war economic policy generally. The Chancellor, Denis Healey, had to turn back at the airport for fear of endangering sterling by his absence. His Prime Minister summoned him to the Labour party conference to steady his party's nerves. For the only time since the war, Whitehall was forced to tear up spending programmes overnight and make immediate real-terms cuts, and do so at a time of high unemployment. Ministers seemed gripped by panic. Sir Leo Pliatsky, a Treasury official at the time, recorded an unprecedented mismatch between 'what was required . . . and what was considered feasible and negotiable in cabinet'.[1] The Treasury was split between the heavy cutters and those inclined to defy the IMF. Healey wrote of his imperturbable permanent secretary, 'I had the impression that Douglas Wass himself was often worried that he might not be able to keep his own department under control.'[2] The end of 1976 was, said Healey, 'the worst four months of my life'.

Much of the statistical information that fed the crisis of 1976 was later known to have been incorrect, but that was immaterial at the time.[3] The Labour government had believed,

221

with Crosland, that public spending could be the spur to economic growth as well as its principal beneficiary. The period from 1974 to 1976 tested that belief to destruction. In his history of those years, Andrew Likierman told of fears that the Treasury had lost any ability to hold back departments intent on boosting spending under the cover of rising prices. 'The government could no longer control the relationship between planned and actual expenditure ... cost increases could simply be passed on and help to feed inflationary pressures.'[4] In 1976 every lever had to be thrown into reverse. Public spending was now a resource that had first to be earned by private-sector growth. James Callaghan's intellectual U-turn was spectacular: 'We used to think that you could spend your way out of a recession and increase employment by cutting taxes and boosting government spending. I tell you in all candour that this option no longer exists.'[5] Far from acting as a stimulus to economic development, as Wilson had intended for his Department of Economic Affairs, public spending appeared to 'crowd out' private investment and undermine investor confidence. Labour began its long *rapprochement* with the private sector, which reached its culmination in Tony Blair's first conference speech as leader in 1994.

To the Treasury the crisis had two consequences. The first was organizational: the urgent search for new tools to limit public spending. The second was psychological: a determination never to see the Chancellor suffer such humiliation again. A new regime of cash limits and cash planning totals crafted by the doyen of expenditure theory, Leo Pliatsky, was gradually introduced. The psychological shock was less easily rectified. It recurs as an afterthought in conversation with officials and ministers, including both Lord Howe and Lord Lawson, and in my view explains much of the Treasury behaviour described in this book. Even those not in Whitehall at the time refer with a shudder to the time when a Chancellor dared not leave the country and his officials were thought unfit to run the proverbial whelk-stall.

In 1983 the Treasury admitted a team from the BBC to glimpse its work and interview its staff.[6] The resulting book offered a rare insight into a usually secretive institution. The Treasury under its then permanent secretary, Douglas Wass, appeared as nice-but-nervous bank managers recovering from a trauma. They knew their power, as senior partners in the corporate state, but also their responsibility. Officials bore on their shoulders the Great Conundrum: how to persuade a democracy that two plus two equals four and will do so under all governments, however many Chancellors are hounded from office. 'A system of financial control in any institution is essentially one of tension,' said David Hancock, 'and the effect of that on the people inside is rather like people in a siege: it develops a sort of fellow-feeling . . . Self-confidence comes from that.'[7]

This isolation led to a cast of mind shared only with the Foreign Office in the corridors of Whitehall. The Treasury asserts that, like every department, it exists to serve its ministers; that the Chancellor of the Exchequer is, after the Prime Minister, the most important figure in the cabinet and he is therefore naturally *secundus inter pares*; but that the power of the Treasury is only as great as the political status of the Chancellor or the political will of the cabinet. This assertion is only partly true. Most departments are in business to implement legislation that is more or less transient. The Treasury sees itself as the guardian of lasting verities. It is accountant to the nation. The buck always stops at the Treasury. It stands for the need to keep down inflation and contain public spending, usually against the pressures of democracy. Indeed the more irresponsible a cabinet, the more stern must be the Treasury. An official in the public-expenditure division once told the 250 civil servants in her group to show constant vigilance since they were 'surrogates for the thirty million taxpayers'.[8] The books must balance in the long term, whatever politicians may ordain. The Treasury is the Day of Judgement institutionalized.

For this the Treasury must have control. The story of the 1980s – and of this book – is of a ceaseless search for that control.

223

Many in the Treasury thought that a Thatcher government would help in this search. As the head of the civil service at the time, Lord Bancroft, told Peter Hennessy, 'in exchange for the debilitating experience [of a hung parliament], to have a government coming in with a thumping majority and a strong reforming manifesto was welcomed by civil servants'.[9] The Tory manifesto commitment on public expenditure read like a Treasury mission statement. Without restraint, the goal of reducing direct taxes and public borrowing could not be reached. Thatcher stated that she would judge her ministers not by how well they defended their budgets but by how much they cut them.

We have seen that much of this idealism on public spending did not survive the new government taking office in 1979. The Callaghan government had already lapsed from the austerity of 1976–7. Spending was moving ahead in 1978, despite the Social Contract and pay restraint, under pressure from the impending election. That election cast its shadow over the Tories as well. Thatcher pre-ordained what was to be her post-election spending boom by promising in advance to honour the generous Clegg awards to public-sector workers. She also committed herself to spend more on defence, the police, the health service and pensioners. This undermined her bid to take £4 billion out of planned expenditure for 1980. She won just £2 billion. The following year saw the 'wet' rebellion over public spending, and its nemesis in Geoffrey Howe's ruthlessly deflationary 1981 budget.

Thatcher's enemies presented that budget as the first breach of the post-war welfare state settlement, but there is no evidence for this charge in the spending totals. Ministers found themselves trapped not by some Thatcherite innovation but by the opposite, the tyranny of expenditure continuity. They were surrounded by cows that were as sacred to Thatcher as to Labour: home-owners, pensioners, NHS patients, farmers, students and, above all, public expectation of fair treatment to the rising number of unemployed.[10] Little was heard in these areas of pushing back the frontiers of the state. On the Treasury's own definition, spending rose from 44 per cent of GDP in 1979–80 to 47.5 per cent in 1982–3.[11] Apologists explain that this increase was either 'demand-led' spending caused by recession or the result of specific manifesto commitments, for instance on defence and law and order.[12] Yet these were in large part political choices. They were interventions by the cabinet to boost planned public spending for electoral (or philanthropic) reasons.

This put the Treasury in a familiar quandary. The government had ordered it to reduce public spending in general but increase it in one particular after another. The new government's first spending review was introduced in the 1980 white paper with the ringing declaration: 'The government intend to reduce public expenditure progressively in volume [real] terms over the next few years.'[13] The commitment was expressly to reduce public borrowing, cut interest rates and cut direct taxes. In addition, the Treasury was to find more money for the army, the police, pensions and the NHS. The cabinet remit to the Treasury's public-expenditure division could not have been clearer – or more inconsistent. The only specific cuts mentioned in the manifesto were waste in local government and the ending of 'extravagance' in nationalized industries and land acquisition, though the Treasury ministerial team had identified many more candidates privately. These sums did not add up. Howe was later reduced to pleading that he had had no chance to 'see the books' in advance of taking office.

A year later the 1981 white paper admitted this failure. 'The outturns now estimated for 1980–1 are ... higher than the government would wish in the light of their financial and economic objectives. The government regard this development as one which requires the most serious attention.'[14] Gone was ringing declaration and in its place was 'serious attention'. The 1980s and 1990s were to see the steady abandonment of Thatcher's public-spending pledges. First she wanted to cut spending in real terms. Then she wanted merely to hold it steady, then she wanted at least to reduce its share of GDP. Howe watched her struggling against the political waves, allowing 'her heart to overrule her head (which was on my side)'.[15] After her fall,

John Major abandoned even the GDP target. With the 1990 recession, demand-led spending was rising fast and borrowing had to rise to meet it. Britain ran up its heaviest ever public borrowing requirement, of £45.4 billion, in 1993–4, a year after expenditure had risen above Thatcher's start line to top 44 per cent of GDP.[16]

Labour's 1976 bind was thus inverted. Labour had wanted to increase spending and found itself cutting; the Tories wanted to cut spending but found themselves forced to increase it. Spending ministers defied Thatcher's admonition and fought for every penny. Thatcher was herself an arch culprit. As head of the civil service she conceded pay rises to her favoured groups (soldiers, police and nurses). She was notoriously susceptible to defence lobbying, demanded more money to hold down local rates and refused to allow cuts in subsidies to home-owners. When Hugo Young suggested to Douglas Wass that he surely preferred a government, such as Margaret Thatcher's, that 'knew what it wanted', Wass's guard briefly dropped: 'Is there such a government? I don't know that there is.'[17]

The Treasury resolved this dilemma by reverting to its cultural roots. It had been told to proceed to point A (restrained public spending) at the same time as proceeding in an opposite direction to point B (extra spending commitments). Unlike ministers, it had to make a clear choice. It had been at point B in 1976 and the experience was traumatic. Point A was home base. After 1981 the Treasury's control of public spending evolved from tough to tougher. The concept of annual cash limits introduced by Healey was extended to cover forward plans. All planned spending had to be expressed in cash terms from 1982, with no automatic uplift for inflation. A 'star chamber' was set up, chaired by a senior minister, to adjudicate on recalcitrant departments, an innovation that was at least effective in upholding collective responsibility.[18] This committee was later institutionalized in the cabinet's EDX committee, a group of senior ministers and officials keeping departmental plans under rolling review.

The forms of control became ever more sophisticated. Despite much press comment on its declining prestige,[19] the Treasury's public-expenditure division came through the 1980s much strengthened. In a study of its work, Colin Thain and Maurice Wright concluded that, by the end of the decade, it had recovered from 'the disaster of the loss of control in the mid-1970s . . . The changed attitudes and objectives of both Labour and Conservative governments provided the opportunity, the stimulus and the legitimacy for the restoration of those traditional values represented in its historic mission.'[20] After 1982 and the political defeat of the cabinet 'wets', Tory cabinets were collectively well-disposed towards meeting the annual expenditure target. Individual ministers might fight for a bigger share and recessionary pressure might cause the target to be breached. But a 'control culture' was instilled both in Whitehall and in the cabinet.

This culture was aided by the Treasury's role at the heart of the government patronage network. Few ministers reached cabinet without having served in the Treasury. For politicians such as Margaret Thatcher, Geoffrey Howe, Nigel Lawson and John Major, government was conducted between three Georgian houses in Downing Street. They were homes to the Prime Minister, the Chancellor and the Chief Whip, with the famous green baize door to the adjacent Cabinet Office on Whitehall. Seen from these modest citadels, the spending departments of state were distant colonies. They were unruly outposts, headed by ambitious ministers in league with pressure groups and avaricious for money. Thatcherites regarded spending departments as suspect, and their long-serving chiefs such as Michael Heseltine, Douglas Hurd, Kenneth Baker and Kenneth Clarke as no less so. They were the big spenders of the Thatcher years, outside the Treasury loop. Until the appointment of Clarke in 1993, no Tory Chancellor for a quarter of a century had been a cabinet spending minister and, saving Thatcher's stint at education, no prime minister either. The gulf between the 'Downing Street culture' and the 'spending department culture' is one of the biggest in British politics. Yet it seldom attracts parliamentary, press or public attention or debate.

The same career centralism affected the lives of civil servants. Throughout this period, the Cabinet Secretary was chosen from the ranks of the Treasury (Lord Hunt, Lord Armstrong, Sir Robin Butler), as were senior administrators in the Cabinet Office and Downing Street. Until the 1980s it was customary for a departmental head to have risen up the ranks of his (or her) own ministry. Under Thatcher most permanent secretaries had Treasury experience. In November 1981 she abolished the Civil Service Department and put control over civil-service pay into the Treasury. Appointments then went to a new Management and Personnel branch of the Cabinet Office. In 1987, this too was disbanded and all public-sector 'pay and rations' were brought under the Treasury, though it was devolved again in 1995 to the Office of Public Services and Science. To be 'unsound at Great George Street' (the Treasury building overlooking Parliament Square) was anathema to officials, whose careers would span many governments. By the 1990s the analysis of the American academics Hugh Heclo and Aaron Wildavsky was vindicated. Expenditure control had become the central ethos of Whitehall, dominated by a 'private political/administrative community' of officials, all of whom knew each other and regularly exchanged jobs.[21]

For all the thrills and spills of Thatcher's relations with her Chancellors, she knew she was chained and shackled to the Treasury. She never doubted the centrality of the finance function in her government. There was no 'kitchen cabinet' of close courtiers to wage war on the Treasury, such as had surrounded Harold Wilson. Aides such as Charles Powell, Bernard Ingham and Robin Butler were executors of her will, not wielders of separate influence. Such ideological mentors as found room-space at Number Ten, such as John Hoskyns or Alan Walters, seldom stayed for long. She used Walters to goad and infuriate the Treasury, not to supplant it. There was nothing approaching a Prime Minister's Department under Thatcher. As Pliatsky observed, 'In terms of the allocation of functions, the Treasury and the Cabinet Office are now once again the only two fully-fledged central departments in Whitehall'.[22] Nor did this change under Major. The Treasury was the only department in which he had served any length of time, as Treasury Whip, Chief Secretary and as Chancellor. At one point his principal private secretary, press secretary, home affairs secretary and head of the civil service were all drawn from his former department.

This concentration of power failed to find a response in the public-spending aggregates. In the next chapter I discuss possible reasons for this additional paradox of Thatcherism. Certainly as the Treasury entered the 1990s recession, the prime indicator of control, the public borrowing requirement, rose to heights not seen since the mid-1970s. It topped 7 per cent of gross domestic product in 1993–4, only exceeded in the awful years of 1974–6.[23] Government statisticians wrestled to refine their tools and redefine their categories. The planning total became the control total. Local spending was shifted into, out of and round different categories. Cyclical expenditure, such as demand-led social-security payments, were reclassified to imply that they were beyond departmental discipline. Yet 'general government spending' proved immune to reduction. At £100 billion in 1980, it broke through £200 billion in 1990 and £300 billion by 1995 (in cash terms; it roughly doubled in real terms). By 1995 few Treasury officials could think of new ways of making controls more severe without overriding cabinet government. There was no new administrative technique that might restrain public spending, only a new political will.

Yet there are more ways of killing a cat than by wringing its neck. Throughout this period the Treasury saw itself as more than just bank manager to the state. One of its senior officials, Anthony Rawlinson, told the BBC that in addition to its 'traditional and proper concern to hold a sceptical attitude towards public expenditure in general', the Treasury was also 'conscious of our duty to the government and to the taxpayers to promote value for money'.[24] He could have fooled most observers of the Treasury at the time. Value for money was not a traditional concern of that department, whose task was primarily to keep down each year's overall spending so as to balance the budget. Value for money was the concern of spending departments, who were in business to squeeze what value they could from their budgets. Indeed the outside perception of the Treasury was of a department so fixated on 'annualized' spending that it dare not consider the longer-term consequences of its discipline. Much-quoted instances from the 1980s were capital projects such as the Nimrod aeroplane and the British Library. In both cases, Treasury officials tolerated an ever-longer completion date and a rising eventual cost in return for reducing each year's outgoings. It was as if the Treasury regarded £4m a year over ten years as a better deal than £5m a year over five years.

Treasury officials vigorously refute any suggestion that they were short-termist, as they refute all substantive criticism of their custodianship of public money. Yet they felt that they could only be reactive rather than creative in their responses to requests for extra money. They were in business to manage the government's cash, not promote its investment. They were not macro-economic strategists. Few were accountants or had any accountancy training. Few were scientists or economists. As laymen they were sceptical of the language of investment analysis or value-for-money audit. If they were short-term in outlook, it was because politics gave them only short-term problems to solve. What the 1980s did was present them with new intellectual challenges from spending departments. The Treasury had to confront efficiency audit, agency corporate plans, 'reinvented government' and fundamental expenditure reviews, all bombarding them with new ways of viewing public expenditure and, more worrying, new ways of justifying it. This led to some spectacular rows.

The biggest tussle was over audit. The increased requirement within spending departments to declare objectives and quantify 'outputs' brought a new daring to public accounts. Compulsory competitive tendering, internal transfer pricing, performance contracts and annual reviews deluged Whitehall with information. As we have seen in earlier chapters, these information flows dominated departmental relations with agencies and quangos, and with local government. They also offered new weapons in the perpetual battle with the Treasury. The latter was not likely to ignore the threat. As the decade progressed its concern was not whether the new 'audit culture' would swamp its control mechanisms but whether it could control the swamping.

Nigel Lawson's memoirs well convey the flavour of some of these Whitehall turf wars. Lawson was Chancellor from 1983 to the end of 1989 and his regime set the tone of late Thatcherism. His permanent secretary throughout this time was Sir Peter Middleton. Both were uninhibited Treasury imperialists. Throughout Lawson's career, as a financial journalist, editor and minister, that department had been the focus of his interest. To run it was the greatest honour. To him this was not just a finance ministry: 'It is both in name and in reality the Central Department, with a finger in pretty well every pie that the government bakes.'[25] A Chancellor, he wrote, 'if he proceeds with care and caution, can affect the content and not merely the cost of other ministers' policies'.[26] More than any other Chancellor, he insinuated himself into every corner of Whitehall. Poll tax, health reform, energy privatization, education, mortgages, railways, no subject was too dull or too small for the Treasury not to have its 'view'. Lawson did not win every fight, but when he lost – as he did over poll tax – the Treasury went on to exact a terrible price. Small wonder that, as we have seen, Kenneth Baker's civil servants warned him not to take on the Treasury over the National Lottery for fear of 'its revenge'.[27]

Few battles were as fierce as over public-sector audit. Formal oversight of British government spending was through the Comptroller and Auditor-General (C & AG) and the Commons Public Accounts Committee. This process was little more than an accountant's report, concerned with the legality of expenditure rather than investigating its worth. For some time, reformers had sought the latter. The Heath government embarked on Programme Analysis and Review. This was abandoned in 1979 as too easily manipulated by departments. Derek Rayner of Marks and Spencer resumed the challenge, persuading Thatcher to let

231

him wage an 'anti-red tape' campaign early in the new parliament. Rayner's investigations were designed partly to eliminate bureaucratic waste, partly to scrutinize departmental performance against objectives and partly to effect more lasting civil-service reform. The Rayner Unit was set up in the Prime Minister's office and conducted formal 'surveys', over 150 of which were to claim savings of £2 billion. The 'Rayner rangers' had the virtue of not being Treasury and were thus not linked in departments' minds to automatic cuts in budgets.

Rayner was at first regarded as modest in impact, but he stimulated wider ambitions. In 1982 he produced what he hoped would be a self-sustaining chain reaction, the Financial Management Initiative (FMI). This was a process within each department for identifying its objectives, setting targets and measuring performance against them. FMI was to entrench self-audit. (A similar enterprise called MINIS had been brought by Michael Heseltine to the environment department in 1979 and later carried to defence.) Though variable in its impact, FMI began to produce information for judging bureaucratic performance. Even if performance was not quantifiable, individual administrative units were expected to declare their aims and assess their ability to meet them in claiming public money. As we saw with the police and hospitals, FMI gave spending departments new tools to measure the performance of subordinate agencies and hold them to account. Unlike previous attempts to revolutionize the processes of Whitehall, this one appeared to be sticking.

The Comptroller and Auditor-General from 1981 to 1987, Sir Gordon Downey, received a new Act of Parliament in 1983, converting his department into a National Audit Office with a remit to 'follow public money wherever it goes'.[28] Earlier a more muscular Audit Commission had been set up to offer audit and management information to local government and later to the NHS. Downey could see the way the wind was blowing. He decided to scrutinize Rayner's scrutinies, and gave them a sound bill of health.[29] He struck out boldly into value for money, hiring private consultants to help him. By the 1990s the NAO had almost a half of its work in this qualitative field.[30]

The Treasury viewed this with open alarm. In the skirmishes prior to the 1983 Act it fought Downey's wish to have the scrutiny of 'policy objectives' included in his terms of reference. The Treasury won this battle outright. Under section 2 of the Act, the C & AG was explicitly forbidden 'to question the merits of the policy objectives of any department', nor was he able to investigate nationalized industries or local government.[31] The Treasury saw such audit as embracing a dangerous subjectivity, however much its spokesmen, such as Rawlinson above, claimed to be conducting the same scrutiny themselves. The 'three Es' of the new audit, economy, efficiency and effectiveness, were full of vagueness. Value for money might prove a Trojan horse, out of which would pour battalions of consultants supporting demands for money and undermining the fragile walls of spending control.

The Treasury's Peter Middleton saw a danger that Rayner and his successor, Sir Robin Ibbs, might form an alliance with the C & AG and undermine Treasury sovereignty. He and Lawson demanded that FMI be 'fully integrated with the existing public expenditure survey process', a demand expressed in the 1983 paper entitled *Financial Management in Government Departments*. Lawson clearly distrusted Ibbs, remarking that he 'conducted himself in a wholly different fashion from Rayner'.[32] To him Ibbs was 'conscious that in the private sector it is necessary to spend money in order to make money'. To Lawson this meant he would be 'always sympathetic to the predictable complaints of the spending departments that they could . . . give much better value for money if only the Treasury was less stingy and ceased to deny them the resources they needed to do the job properly'. (Lawson ignored the possibility that the private sector and spending departments might be right in this.)

Lawson wrote to Ibbs in 1984, shortly after the latter's appointment, warning him off the Treasury's patch. 'We need to do all we can to ensure that increased efficiency shows up in lower expenditure. We cannot afford changes in financial management which become a means of institutionalizing present levels of expenditure, and then try to console ourselves that public-sector output has risen.'[33] As we saw in chapter two, Lawson believed that the only way of bringing private-sector approaches to the public sector was by total privatization. 'But so long as public services existed . . . Treasury control was essential. The alternative was no financial discipline at all.' This was Treasury paranoia in a nutshell. Lawson even cited the new Soviet Union where, deprived of the glories of Treasury control, 'the result was chaos'. Is that what Thatcher's so-called Efficiency Unit wanted to see in Whitehall?

Ibbs saw himself as firmly in the Rayner tradition. He had the support of the Prime Minister, whose interest in Whitehall management reform grew steadily after 1982. (Nothing boosted her confidence in her authority over the government machine quite so much as her victory that year over General Galtieri.) Ibbs saw in the scrutiny process the key to unlocking not just significant savings of public money, but a release of civil-service energy from the bondage of Treasury short-termism. By 1986 FMI was widespread throughout Whitehall. It now saw its apotheosis in the 'Next Steps' proposals of 1987 (published a year later). This took the FMI concept into the more radical realm of changing not just the practice of the civil service but its whole organization. It proposed hiving off up to 95 per cent of central-government activity, either into the private sector or into self-governing agencies. These were defined as covering all government activities that were not overtly 'political', chiefly those administering public services. Examples included the Stationery Office, vehicle licensing, the payment of benefits, the Meteorological Office and the management of royal parks and palaces. Budgets should be allocated by sponsoring departments. But ministerial responsibility would not extend to management or operational decisions. (This, as the 1995 Woodcock report on the Whitemoor prison escape concluded, meant little: as we have seen at the Home Office and health department, ministers continue to intervene when it suits them politically to do so.)

Lawson and Middleton were deeply sceptical of all this. Back in 1964, the Treasury had been accused of hostility to growth and enterprise, and seen a Department of Economic Affairs set up to clip its wings. That threat had been confronted and eventually crushed. Now the accusation was of narrow-minded short-termism in the control of public spending. New institutions with new ways of validating expenditure were springing up. The Treasury was so opposed to Next Steps agencies that Lawson persuaded Thatcher to suppress the 1987 report pending a review. He believed that Whitehall reform was not a central concern of hers. She had said before the 1979 election that her job was to turn the economy round, 'not muck around with the machinery of government'.[34] Certainly her first policy adviser, John Hoskyns, had been unable to interest her in the subject. After Rayner and Galtieri that clearly changed. By 1987 Whitehall and government generally were seeing a different Thatcher at work.

The argument over Next Steps was eventually concluded with a turf wars treaty. It was negotiated by Robin Butler on behalf of Number Ten and by Middleton from the Treasury. Middleton insisted that he be allowed to keep what the Treasury most coveted, control over capital spending and staff pay and conditions. He also insisted that agency targets be 'agreed with the Treasury in the first place and monitored by the Treasury thereafter'.[35] In return, a diluted version of Next Steps was announced in 1988, with nothing more specific than a promise from Downing Street to examine it further. The view at the time was that the Treasury had triumphed (with Butler in covert support). Hennessy commented, 'The centre had not yielded one ounce of real power to the periphery. One suspects that Mrs Thatcher, under whom the Treasury had enjoyed a purple patch of imperial power, did not want it.'[36] Giving evidence to the Treasury select committee in March 1988, Butler was dismissive of Next Steps. It was merely about 'general direction' and no discussion had taken place within the civil service, nor had any decisions been taken.

235

This seriously misjudged both the momentum that FMI had established in Whitehall and Thatcher's commitment to Ibbs. A senior Treasury official, Peter Kemp, was appointed to push on with the project, an appointment variously seen as showing Downing Street's commitment, indicating the Treasury's triumph or, alternatively, proclaiming its defeat. As always in Whitehall's great battles, different sources give each incident a different spin. Lawson's memory is that Kemp was appointed 'to secure the public interest', in a dig at Ibbs.[37] Whatever its genesis, Next Steps proved the biggest upheaval the British civil service had seen since the war.

Kemp told a Commons committee shortly after his appointment that he confidently expected three-quarters of the existing civil service to be in agencies within a decade. Each year the roll-call of units changing their status increased. Even Lawson became a modest convert, offering up the Stationery Office, the Royal Mint and the Central Office of Information for hiving off. New candidates sprang into being by the month, for example the Child Support Agency, the Prisons Service and the National Rivers Authority. By 1991 Kemp had overseen the creation of fifty-one executive agencies and by 1995, helped by the Department of Social Security's benefits empire, two-thirds of civil servants were working in them. There was little resistance from within the civil service. Able officials wanted to exercise their managerial skills. Social-security administrators, hospital managers, school inspectors, roads engineers responded with enthusiasm. They wanted performance pay and incentive bonuses. Civil-service morale had been low in the mid-1980s. Reform promised more responsibility, more career flexibility and more money.

The Treasury had lost a battle over Next Steps but it had not lost the war. Its aversion to the Ibbs reforms is curious in retrospect. They offered what the Treasury most wanted: better financial targeting and a clearer exposure of aims and objectives. Departments had to produce more information. By making claims for resources more explicit, Next Steps gave the Treasury a battery of tools to judge performance and thus validate, or invalidate, bids for money. In future the Treasury was to set agencies, and the more arm's-length quangos, financial targets so tight as often to vitiate their new managerial autonomy. I recall at English Heritage that the budget process was so circumscribed that officials would refer nostalgically to the old civil-service days when 'there was always a bit of money knocking about the department at the end of the year' to meet a crisis.

A much-publicized victim of the new *dirigisme* was the Child Support Agency, set up in 1991. Its external objective was to increase financial support from fathers for separated mothers. It was to this objective that the public and parliament presumed to hold it. The undeclared internal objective was to save the Treasury an annual target of money from the family support budget. This forced its staff to concentrate on 'high yielding' rich fathers and ignore difficult cases. The resulting unfairness was politically unpopular and led to the near-collapse of the agency three years later. The Treasury had used prior budget-setting in such as way as to distort the agency's behaviour. The relevant department, that of Social Security, was marginalized in the process. Yet when the policy ran into trouble, that department had to take the blame and the Treasury's role sank from view and avoided censure. This was accountable government only in the most cosmetic sense. When hapless spending ministers were put up to defend policies they had bitterly contested in cabinet, the public and parliament were not given any flavour of the original argument, or the original objective. In the case of the CSA, this was not to aid single mothers but simply to transfer subsidies for their upkeep from the Treasury to absent fathers.

Despite all this, the biggest fights between the Treasury and the rest of the public sector under Thatcher were the old familiar ones, over pay. The Treasury never relented from the 'public-sector pay policy' ethos of the pre-Thatcher years. It had to foot the public-sector pay bill, each component of which was riddled with 'knock on' effects. To the Treasury the public sector was an undivided lake of money. Controlling pay, which comprised the majority of public spending, was crucial to its sovereignty. If pay rose in one corner of the lake it rose everywhere. The débâcle of the Clegg awards in 1979, which devastated the 1980–81 planning total, led the Treasury to take control under statute of one group of public-sector workers after another. Teachers and NHS staff became subject to Treasury 'determination', as were awards from other 'independent' pay review bodies. Delegated arbitration, management discretion, cash limits, Next Steps, value-for-money were fine in theory, but once decentralize public-sector 'norms' and control would be lost, or so thought the Treasury.

A deaf ear was thus turned to all pleading that overall paybill costs or agency cash limits should be enough to isolate one group of workers from another, leaving managers to make their own decisions on individual pay. The ironic result was that the Treasury would ruthlessly cut an agency's overall budget, often implying a zero rise in its paybill, yet its civil-service negotiators would agree a pay rise with staff unions well above zero. With rate-capping and the increased centralization of all public spending, this had bizarre consequences. In 1995 school budgets were assessed by the centralized standard formula to rise by under 1 per cent. Yet the same Treasury agreed a 2.7 per cent pay rise for teachers. Given constraints on class size and open enrolment, this meant sacking staff or bankrupting some schools. As we saw with the NHS, public-sector unions were often ready to go along with this centralism to protect their own national status and negotiating rights. Nor was this centralism confined to unionized groups. The Treasury was not prepared to allow even semi-autonomous quangos to fix the remuneration of their top executives. Every pay and conditions package from a BR finance director to a concert-hall manager to a quango secretarial assistant had to be approved by the Treasury. They were rarely approved without a fight.

This relentless public-sector corporatism under Thatcher did finally begin to produce antibodies under Major. In October 1994, the head of the Treasury, Sir Terry Burns, announced that he would be cutting his own senior staff by a third, as evidence of his determination to give departments more autonomy in spending money. He said he wanted to stop 'breathing down departments' necks' on individual decisions. This was ten years after the Treasury had boasted to the BBC that they no longer did any such thing. The previous year, William Waldegrave, as civil-service minister, secured Treasury agreement to delegate pay and conditions within departmental budgets to departments themselves. Delegation was likewise promised to NHS trusts over nurses' and midwives' pay. (It was paradoxical that the unions saw decentralization as depressing pay rates, while the Treasury had always seen it as the reverse.) The Treasury was particularly nervous about public spending at the time and few observers expected an early start in honouring these oft-repeated pledges of delegation.

The arrival of Kenneth Clarke at the Treasury in 1993 brought a self-proclaimed centralist to the department. He showed little inclination to depart from the Lawson *dirigisme* or respect agency or quango autonomy. When in summer 1994 the supposedly free-standing public corporation, Railtrack, suffered a signalling strike, the management response was orchestrated by Treasury officials via a small interdepartmental committee. The transport department was treated as the Treasury's messenger boy and Railtrack was told what offer would or would not be 'tolerated by ministers', under the implicit threat of statutory direction. In another similar incident after the failure of Michael Heseltine's bid to privatize the Post Office in the same year, the Treasury publicly refused to allow it more commercial freedom, despite the express wish of the industry, an all-party parliamentary committee and a clear majority of MPs. The Post Office particularly wanted to retain and invest its surpluses. As we saw in previous chapters, the practice of 'surplus seizure' was applied by the Treasury with increasing vigour: to local-government housing accounts, railway contracts, hospital trusts and the Post Office. In the case of the last, value-for-money from investment was not uppermost in the Treasury's mind.

To an extent the Treasury was right to fear that departments fragmented into agencies would be harder to control. Next Steps agencies were being run by men and women who no longer saw their career paths decided by those paying their salaries. They would expect to move in and out of public service over their lives. Activities at a further remove from Whitehall, under 'quasi-autonomous' quangos, had the added danger of external chairmen and lay members capable of publicizing any differences with the Treasury, taking disputes direct to the Prime Minister or threatening to resign. I saw the latter technique used often to good effect: there is nothing Whitehall likes less than to have to find a new quango chairman. Other threats also appeared. The dogma that capital and current spending by public bodies is conceptually the same came under renewed attack in 1994. A committee headed by the Eurotunnel chairman, Sir Alastair Morton, was set up by the Prime Minister to seek new ways of involving private capital in public-sector projects, a search that had eluded Howe and Ryrie in 1981 (see chapter two). Proposals under the Private Finance Initiative were put forward by eager departments for joint financing of roads, Tube trains, hospitals, even schools. Treasury resistance continued, in private, and none had reached approval at the time of writing.

In truth this was little more than a shifting of furniture. The Treasury had seen some power diffused to new forms of parliamentary and internal audit. Some of its prerogatives were challenged in the 1980s as purchasers and providers separated and re-fashioned their relationships into new-fangled contracts. Treasury officials had to watch agencies, quangos and utility regulators proliferate where previously they had gazed across a landscape devoid of such dangerous obstacles. They reacted by setting their hands to a familiar plough, that of asserting and increasing control. The 'fundamental expenditure reviews' planned over the term of the 1992 parliament were a careful attempt to look at public spending long-term, at 'economy and effectiveness' and at possible public-sector withdrawal.[38] This was Lawson's ideal of a Central Department testing its strength and maturity. Combined with the cabinet spending committee, EDX, the fundamental reviews were intended both to give a 'long-term' flavour to departmental planning and to ensure Treasury oversight of that exercise.

Even as the Treasury saw public-sector management fragment, it ensured that the cash-limit regime was so draconian as to neutralize much of the freedom implied by delegation. Some agencies of government undoubtedly felt 'more free' and were more exposed to public gaze than they had been as government departments. Their staffs preferred the separate identity, the smaller units, even the publicity, of agency or quango status. As 'providers' they succeeded in shaking off some of the habits of the civil service. Yet the Great Purchaser still towered over them. By the mid-1990s, the Treasury's patronage and culture permeated government as never before. And in spite of its best endeavours, it had more public money to spend than in its entire history. The more the money, the more the need to watch over its uses and abuses, the more the need to control.

CHAPTER THIRTEEN

STRONG IS BEAUTIFUL

With the same cement, ever sure to bind,
We bring to one dead level ev'ry mind.
— ALEXANDER POPE

The claim made at the start of this book was that the 1979 Conservative administration promised to reduce the power and scope of the state but failed, and in failing damaged important constitutional freedoms. The Tory manifesto had protested that the Labour party had 'enlarged the role of the state and diminished the role of the individual . . . Attempting to do too much, politicians have failed to do those things which should be done.'[1] The Tory cabinet would reverse Labour's statist drift. We have now examined its work in the great domains of public administration: local government, the health service, the police, schools, universities, urban renewal, housing, the law, the railways and the privatized utilities. In drawing these case-histories together we must return to re-examine the thesis and test its robustness.

My intention has not been to discuss Thatcherism in the round or ponder the motivation of its advocates. It has been to describe what actually happened. In chapter two we acknowledged the government's 'rolling back' of the state where it had occurred. A quarter of the council housing stock was sold. Over half what was known as the state trading sector was transferred to private ownership — notably cars, air and road transport, steel and energy. Part of this passed into a competitive private market, part moved into a grey area of government-regulated private monopoly. The change of ownership concealed a substantial continuity in policy, especially noticeable in the railways, under the guise of regulation. As we noted in chapter two, many of these privatized-monopoly industries would be considered 'parastatals' elsewhere in Europe, despite being outside the realm of public accounts. Meanwhile, the scope of the state that is left behind has remained persistently above 40 per cent, forced upwards by a roughly doubled level of real spending on the welfare state. Add this to the government-regulated but privately owned monopolies and what might be termed the 'state penumbra' has widened rather than contracted since 1979. Thatcherism has become a Sisyphus, rolling a great stone of policy uphill each year, only to see it roll back down again.

Many analysts from the Left have been so influenced by their distaste for Thatcher's privatization as to ignore this wider public-sector context. Some on the Right are so enamoured of her leadership as to ignore it too. But in general there is agreement. The centralization of the public sector, begun in the 1930s and 1940s and continued ever since, accelerated under Thatcher. It was as if the force of her political personality created a magnetic field concentrated on Downing Street. Previous British cabinets treated the institutions of the public sector as a rough and ready confederacy. Provided they delivered a statutory service and did not cost too much public money, they were left in relative peace. The emperors of Whitehall ruled with a light, or at least a hesitant, touch. An equilibrium obtained.

This equilibrium was upset, as we saw in the last chapter, not by Thatcherism but by the experience of the last Labour government. In 1975–6, public-sector expenditure was rising towards 50 per cent of GDP, precipitating the IMF crisis and the government's eventual collapse. As I have tried to show, it was the bureaucratic reaction to this crisis that gave Thatcherism its forward drive. The Treasury's need to control public spending was the engine, the car and the fuel. For a decade and a half this was the vehicle that roared from one part of the public sector to another, destroying cosy relationships, protocols, concordats and many a racket. Complex treaties hallowed by decades of custom and practice were disregarded: treaties with the police, the schools, the universities and local government. Tight limits on spending and borrowing, on staffing and investment, on policy and practice transformed public-sector management. At least until 1987, so-called Thatcherism merely scrambled aboard this zest for financial control and tried to wrest command of the steering.

Much here was worthwhile, much that does not come within the orbit of this book. Trade-union legislation brought a new discipline to the labour market. Sanity came to personal taxation. Thatcher fought and won a war, with all that did for the unquantifiables of national self-confidence. She established for Britain a role in international affairs during the collapse of the Soviet Union, though she spoiled much of the aftermath with her obsessive anti-Germanism. Many citizens found in the 1980s and 1990s a new freedom to act and spend their money in ways not permitted to them before. Tens of thousands of former public-sector workers now own shares in their own companies. Most are more productive and better paid as a result. The buyers of council houses feel the same. The holders of privatized company stock have, for the most part, done well out of their investment. Over these years, the British people were shown for the first time that the public sector was not the sole custodian of political or economic virtue.

Closer to our theme, we must realize that much centralization was part and parcel of a wider change in the character of public administration. Thatcher was never a political libertarian but she did mean to give institutions within the public sector greater scope to spend within allocated resources. She re-educated government to be more responsive to its consumers, less in thrall to its producers. The purchaser/provider split delivered a productivity dividend, noticeable in the case of hospitals, schools and many subcontracted public services, whether contracts were won by public or private undertakings.[2] Trust-hospital status improved cost control, as did Local Management of Schools. The duplication of university research was questioned. The concepts of efficiency audit, declaring objectives and setting performance targets all produced a new tautness in public administration. There are few public servants who would like to go back to the habits and indisciplines of government before 1979.

The credit side can be lengthened. The new 'audit culture', coupled with the Citizens' Charter, served to inform citizens of the quality of their services. The Charter minister, William Waldegrave, in an elegant exposition of its virtues and those of agency government generally, said that they made government more 'realistic'. By making agency heads and other subsidiary executives more responsible (and presumably ministers less so), accountability was increased. He declared this accountability to be 'more sensible and soundly based'.[3] From the railway to the health service and the courts, customers were treated more like customers and less like recipients of public charity. Even the storms that surrounded the gas and water regulators led to a debate unheard of under nationalization. Much local and institutional autonomy was a cover for waste and a disregard for the public. Any delegated authority can be abused. The battery of reforms introduced in the most productive years of Thatcherism, roughly 1987–92, exposed that abuse and called it to account. There was undoubtedly a revolution in the management of the public sector.

These gains need to be put in the balance against the centralization thesis. In particular I must meet the accusation that I have been unduly selective. Certainly important areas of government have been omitted. They include defence and foreign affairs, social security, agriculture, training and employment. But most of these were already centralized functions of government at the start of the 1980s. All became more so by the end. We could cite the minutiae of agricultural set-aside agreements; the cash-limited Training and Enterprise Councils; the 'spoon counting' of Foreign Office expenditure; the frequent changes in social-security entitlements. In 1995, under the new job-seeker initiative, local benefits offices were given a list of rules for judging an applicant's sincerity in looking for work, including hair cut, tie, dress and wage requirements. In the 1994 spending round the Treasury asserted control over the biggest area of delegated spending, defence. This had long been protected by the right of appeal of the chiefs of staff to the Prime Minister.

The largest return earned by centralization of management, according to the theorists,[4] is short-term and once-for-all. 'Downsizing' and 'delayering' any organization will yield large immediate savings but at a cost in the increased bureaucracy required by the new discipline. Avoiding this requires organizational 're-engineering', putting in place new delegated responsibilities and incentives. Like Edward Heath before her, Thatcher had no experience of private business, yet a naïve faith in it as a managerial exemplar of good government, sometimes yielding pride of place to a well-budgeted household: like any conglomerate or household, government must operate to stringent financial controls, with an orderly pattern of delegation and clear reporting lines.

The trouble is that politics vitiates these models. It turns the spotlight on any and every action and demands accountability. This accountability in turn leads to defensive administration, becoming ever more complex as the line of that accountability lengthens. Politics erodes the autonomy of managers and leads them to refer all decisions upwards. The Treasury's annual public-spending tables contain an ever-lengthening list of 'ring-fenced' grants: money for breast screening, hill-farming, cathedral restoration. The annual reports of government department are filled with boasts of what has been achieved. From cheese safety rules to railway line closures, from the specification of a legal-aid adviser to the composition of a historic roof tile, no matter is too trivial for modern government intervention. The reason is that public administration is not a private business. If it were, it would not be public administration.

Size itself is not inefficient. Large companies can organize themselves into small units and operate successfully. But in government, experience suggests that size attenuates and enfeebles both

246

democratic and financial accountability. The further the point of decision drifts from its eventual 'customers', the less accountable it is likely to be, and the more ponderous become the efforts to make it so. The act of delegation requires the delegator to take a risk, especially in the short term. Yet politics is about minimizing risk, avoiding bad publicity, watching out for banana skins. By centralizing decision, a minister can give himself the illusion that he is minimizing risk. He may be, but he is blanketing decision in a fog of caution and irresolution. There is a good reason why all governments throughout history have fallen prey to a crippling bureaucracy. For all the oratory of 1979, it was never likely that Thatcherism was going to disinvent this particular wheel.

Thatcher herself defended her accretion of power in vigorous terms, as would be expected. Her view and that of her defenders is that concern over the long-term consequences of centralization is misplaced. As Sam Beer pointed out, British government prior to the 1980s was blighted by 'pluralistic stagnation, class decomposition and a revolt against authority'.[5] As a result government properly so-called had become impossible, witness the 1970s under both the Tories and Labour. This analysis sees a modern democracy as inherently centrifugal, undisciplined, irresponsible. To bring it to order, a government must be centripetal. For Thatcher, the assertion of control over the public sector was vital to her programme. Pitt (and after him Lord Acton) was wrong. Concentrated power does not corrupt. In a democracy it counterbalances that of domestic pressure groups always baying for extravagance.

We examined earlier in this book the democratic paradox: a public expecting government to be a responsible custodian of its money, yet persistently demanding more be spent on individual expenditures. The Thatcher government inherited a total for public spending and borrowing in 1979 that was rising fast. Over the next decade the Treasury evolved the most detailed framework of control: cash limits, rolling-targets, 'cyclical social security' and the isolation of demand-led spending. It was regarded as the world's most sophisticated machine for controlling

247

spending. Yet there was no point in owning a Rolls-Royce and never taking it on the road. Whenever this vehicle was taken out of Downing Street it crashed into the first political lamp-post – especially the one directly opposite at the Department of Health. To restrain the spending commitments of Tory cabinets the Treasury had to control intensively and relentlessly. It cut what it could not directly control (such as universities) and controlled what it could not directly cut (such as the police). Runaway spending had not only rotted public finances in the 1970s, it had undermined respect for government. If early-period Thatcherism was about nothing else, it was about trying to end this rot. The resistance from within the public sector, indeed from within the cabinet, was fierce. This 'drag' on spending control exasperated Thatcher and demoralized her cabinets. Hence, so her defenders say, her need for more power, even at the risk of bureaucratic gigantism. Strong is beautiful.

Yet it is at this point that the centralist's case begins to weaken. Of course government needs strong institutions at its core to limit extravagance. The growth of unstable deficits in democracies as constitutionally diverse as America, Italy and Scandinavia is evidence of that. Yet the tools evolved by British governments in the 1980s were no more successful. Thatcher's budgetary discipline worked in the late 1980s not because spending was restrained but because revenues were boosted by a boom. When recession returned in 1990, the cabinet's failure to limit demand-led transfers – social security, mortgage tax relief, housing benefit, legal aid – drove it into the highest borrowing in its history.

The single overwhelming fact of public expenditure in Britain since 1979 is that the greatest indiscipline lay not with sub-national administration – local government, nationalized industries and quangos – but with programmes directly under the control of ministers. Throughout the period covered by this book, the fastest rising items were health, law and order, social security, agriculture and (initially) defence. All were areas in which ministers felt vulnerable and found themselves drawn into spending commitments. Items not the direct concern of ministers tended to lag, such as education, housing and public transport. Even within departmental budgets, items for which ministers felt personally answerable were treated more generously than those supposedly run by others: motorways rather than railways, grant-maintained rather than council schools, the Housing Corporation rather than local-authority housing. Urban renewal was starved of money until ministers set up their own appointed Development Corporations, and the money flowed. All governments are unpopular between elections. Where they have taken to themselves the power to be generous, the cost is all the greater.

The Treasury intervened constantly in public-sector pay in the belief that it was a tougher negotiator than anybody else. Yet pay rises were highest for those closest to the politics of the cabinet. Nurses, policemen, soldiers, senior civil servants did better than, say, teachers, lecturers or local-government officers. For many sub-national employers, centralized pay bargaining caused desperate problems. The Treasury thought that by declaring agencies quasi-autonomous yet keeping control of pay and conditions, it was able to keep a lid on public-sector pay. The opposite tended to be the case, since centralization made it easier for unions to plead comparability. The Treasury would cash-limit a subordinate budget to, say, inflation minus 1 per cent but then concede a pay rise to the relevant staff group of inflation plus 1 per cent. Ministers were happy to cash-limit education or health authorities, but reluctant to be seen as mean to nurses or teachers.

Centralization gave the Treasury more power but also increased cabinet pressure for more spending. The nationalization of public-sector pay encouraged a drift of national rates towards the top end of the market. Areas that need not pay top rates found themselves having to do so by agreement if not by law. This phenomenon long predated Thatcher, but she was reluctant to end any control over pay that might in theory hold down spending. Geoffrey Howe had constantly to deny a pay 'norm' yet enforce one in practice. This inflationary drift was persistently denied by the centralizers. Yet as we saw with local authorities, while overspenders might be kept within bounds by the nationalization of pay policy, possible underspenders were under intense union pressure to spend up to the norm. The same applied to local-government spending. All evidence after the introduction of central capping in the mid-1980s indicates that it increased rather than reduced local spending overall (see chapter three). In other respects, the removal of local democratic accountability for a quarter of public-sector spending was a disaster for the Treasury. The public sector lost two taxes for which central government was not responsible – domestic and business rates – and got in return two for which it soon became all too responsible – council tax and the centralized business rate. Concentrating control of public spending directly on the Treasury failed to reduce it. It laid it open to raw cabinet politics.

Many politicians claim that centralization is nowadays a governmental response to a public demand for potency in its rulers. As prosperity and national security are taken for granted, government is seen as an insurance policy against accident.[6] People crave more health and safety laws, with the media in eager collusion. They tear apart ministers who 'allow' listeria to infect eggs or dogs to savage children. We saw in chapter ten the list of interventionist laws passed by the Thatcher and Major governments as a result of public pressure. The modern citizen is ever more risk-averse, and wants government to be so too. For every libertarian lobby against government meddling there are ten for it. Such expectations cannot be met by diminished central control. That is why no minister can say of an incident within his area of concern: 'I may have the power to intervene but do not wish to deprive any citizen of the freedom to take risks.'

Allied to this is said to be an increased demand for a uniform standard of services, abetted by the decline in localism and greater economic mobility. Seen from Westminster and Whitehall, the United Kingdom consolidated as a nation during the 1980s. As industries shrank in size, families moved. Provincial cities were losing their pride and their commercial cores to out-of-town housing, shopping and entertainment. Commuting and car ownership were expanding the boundaries of traditional communities. Local identity and culture were diminishing. Students in Britain went to residential universities and colleges away from home. People were dropping their regional accents. The media, and television in particular, all looked to London. England, if not Scotland, Wales and Northern Ireland, was acquiring a 'nationalized' personality. It expected nationalized service delivery.

Of much of this there can be no doubt. Value-for-money audit and performance league tables increased public awareness of variations between services in different parts of the country. They made people more critical and more demanding. A question in parliament about the most trivial aspect of public administration – a train service withdrawn, a prisoner escaped, a hospital ward closed, a by-pass delayed – would embarrass ministers. Any stick would do to beat that dog. Nothing was more potent than an 'average' performance. Journalists and politicians became obsessed with these averages: average poverty rates, average unemployment, average ambulance waiting times, average crime rates, average truancy, average maths scores. This drift towards uniformity had a number of consequences. There was in Britain no 'lobby for diversity'. While American states or German *Länder* might take pride in their prisons or police or forests or schools, little such pride was possible in Britain. The political energies of local authorities went as much into blaming government for the inadequacy of their services as into defending them to their electors. Despite the apparent 'localism' of the one-member constituency system, national politicians in Britain do not need a local political base as in other democracies.

The diminished freedom of local authorities in Britain is reflected in the large size of electoral units and the paucity of democratic participation. In the United Kingdom the ratio of councillors to electors is 1:1,800. In Sweden it is 1:270 and in France 1:110.[7] This disempowers the local electorate and makes local and central government administrators more

251

sensitized to nationally audited norms than to local political pressures. Hitherto, the citizens of Truro may have been happy with a different waste-disposal system from that in Inverness. Patients in Bournemouth may want faster hip replacements than those in Dundee. Blackpool may want more police stations, Norwich more bobbies on the beat. The nationalization of service standards makes no allowance for these divergences. Time and again we have come up against this conundrum. Comparison is information and information is good. Yet comparison can only compare what is quantifiable. It cannot cope with the diverse traditions, characteristics, demands and accountabilities of what is still a 'United Kingdom' of disparate regions, shires and cities.

Nor can crude statistics measure the true efficiency of service delivery. They cannot measure the good relations between a police force and its community. They cannot reflect the 'personalized' atmosphere of a cottage hospital as against the anonymity of a general one. A league table can quantify GCSE results but not the spirit of a school shown in extra-curricular achievements. As Andrew Likierman wrote in 1988, 'It is easier to determine how many students in higher education finished their courses last year than it is to measure the quality of their education.'[8] A prison service has the dual task of keeping prisoners in custody and of rehabilitating them. 'It may do well on the first objective, but badly on the second. Does this mean it is effective or ineffective?' A government which governs by statistics becomes rigid, loses its political 'give'. It shifts accountability from the diverse assemblies of local and national democracy to a list of tables. The accountability of ballots, meetings, publicity and democratic surgeries is supplanted by accountability to a statistical norm. This in turn demotes those qualities in public administration which many believe to be its essence: those of professional trust, community cohesion and institutional loyalty.

Successive editions of the compendium, *The Changing Constitution*,[9] have recorded the growing role played by quantitative comparisons in not just the monitoring but also the subsidizing of the British public sector in the 1990s. In 1994, John McEldowney argued that centralized audit blights enterprise. The imposition of norms by any organization on its subsidiaries 'militates against innovatory ideas and encourages over-cautious strategies'.[10] The stifling of diversity in local government was one example of this. 'Undoubtedly auditors have a worthwhile contribution in the development of policy. But democratic institutions might wish to determine different priorities and policies beyond purely economic objectives.'[11] Many commentators have also pointed out that the growth of audit has led to a shift of power away from people in day-to-day contact with the public, such as social workers, doctors and policemen, towards accountants, administrators and inspectors.[12] This shift, according to Michael Power, is away from professions that the public claimed in opinion polls to trust more and towards those it claimed to trust less.

The would-be reformers in French regional and departmental government in the early 1980s debated precisely these points of local discretion and innovation. Under the 'loi Deferre', mayors and other elected leaders demanded the freedom to set their budgets independent of the prior approval of the central prefects. Under a roughly similar block grant regime to that being introduced in Britain, they won that right. Prefectorial audit was exercised at the end of the budgetary year, not the start. The 'loi Deferre' granted wide powers over both social security and economic development to mayors and departments. Such powers are unthinkable in modern Britain. The characterization of France as a centralized public administration, to which Kenneth Baker and others loved to refer, is simply wrong. Even the most centralized French service, education, has been devolved to a greater extent than is now the case in Britain.

The Treasury and the defenders of the 'audit function' respond that this is all an absurd caricature. League tables and other tools of audit are no more than aids to democratic participation. They help correct the more lunatic claims of lobbyists, and make welfare decisions more equitable. The torrent of comparative statistics that flows from league tables of police forces, schools and hospitals is there, says the Audit Commission, merely to inform debate. 'You should not assume that a high figure is always better than a low one,' says the Commission of its police performance indicators. The figures show differences but 'do not explain why differences may arise'.[13] This is naïve. League tables might be harmless were they not the raw material of cash-limited budgets. Money flows to the average performer, not the risk-taker or the innovator. A head teacher, a chief constable, a health authority executive will always be safe if he spends the norm. If a police force is to be judged on responding to 999 calls, it will concentrate resources on that. A school will select those pupils likely to pass exams; a hospital will cut operation waiting times rather than care for the sick; a university will hire a lecturer who writes copiously rather than who teaches comprehensively.

The Treasury argues that the pre-1979 model of devolved government in Britain was deficient. It both allowed local councils, institutions and professions to form their own judgements on public-sector priorities and subsidized them almost without limit, on a percentage basis, to do so. That model ran up against the wall of diminished resources. But the Conservative government was unwilling simply to cash-limit these claims on the central taxpayer's generosity, as did the French government. It did not hold to the 'block grant' principle, sometimes referred to as 'fund and forget'. It seemed professionally, intellectually, instinctively unable to keep its hands off every corner of the public sector. Standardized spending, value-for-money audit, accountability to parliament, crisis management, all drew the Whitehall net ever tighter. Treasury officials sometimes plead with their critics that, harsh though life at the top may seem, there is no alternative model of public-expenditure control. To that there is a simple reply: the old model was better able to deliver what ministers want – maximum discipline overall with minimum personal and political risk. And there are many other models elsewhere in the democratic world at least worth a second look.

When the British government refused to sign the European Charter of Local Self-Government, permitting local councils to act in their electors' interest unless stopped by statute, it did so out of just this fear of loss of control. As Vernon Bogdanor has pointed out, this charter was intended to 'buttress the concept of local government as representative of the community, encouraging the citizen to see in the local authority not just one agency amongst others . . . but the voice of the local community'.[14] This representational role for local government, roughly paralleling that of parliament, was rejected by ministers. Yet, apart from Ireland, no other European governments had any such difficulty in signing. A decentralist culture does not pose a natural conflict between the centre and the localities. In France, for instance, a collaborative basis for overall local spending has been established, and now works reasonably well. In Britain, as a survey for the Commission for Local Democracy found, an attitudinal gulf separates local and national government, summarized as 'civil servants believing that they possess Rolls-Royce minds and local government officers motor cyclists' minds'.[15]

There is a wide literature on comparative local government. Historically it was British local councils that led the way in their independence, indeed insularity, from central government. They formed the template for civic democracy in the United States, from the eighteenth century to this day, and used to be contrasted with, for instance, the centralism of France and Spain. Since 1980 Britain has moved in the opposite direction from the rest of the world, including the post-communist states. Every one of the European countries covered in a recent study of their local government by Batley and Stoker has moved in the direction of decentralization to subordinate democratic bodies.[16] The most determined programmes of constitutional devolution have been in countries as widely scattered as Sweden, Norway, Denmark, France, Spain and Portugal. In all cases the most marked divergence was not so much in the practice of devolution as in the theory. As Richard Batley pointed out, 'the British debate was dominated by a view of local authorities as agents for the provision of public services. In contrast [the foreign cases] emphasized their view of local government as a system by which a community governs itself, chooses its own leaders and direction and acts as a local forum.'[17]

What most surprised continental observers of the British scene was the extent of political conflict with the centre, indeed its exhausting relentlessness. The centre saw local government not as a component of the constitution but as a political enemy. This was not just because of the tendency of local elections to run against national governments. Examples cited included the attempt by government to stop the Urban Development Corporations from forging links with local councillors and the attempted exclusion of elected representatives from any role in school, police or health authorities. In Britain, local government in the 1980s was seen as a managerial activity rather than an expression of political will. The authors of the European study concluded that Britain risked being submerged in precisely the 'bureaucratic, prefectorial supervision which other governments have found to be costly and stultifying, and from which they were now seeking to escape through decentralization'.[18] This supervision was well illustrated by Michael Heseltine, a normally sympathetic observer of British local government, in his book *Where There's A Will*: 'There can be only one Chancellor of the Exchequer. There is an obligation to intervene where a local authority's performance prejudices social conditions, the local economy or the stability of local industry. Central government must ensure that local authorities . . . do not provoke political confrontation with central government.'[19] The crushing logic of that final sentence is typical of the modern government minister.

Local polls undertaken for Sir John Banham's Local Government Commissioners in the course of 1994 indicated that most people were relatively content with their local government. They identified most strongly with towns and cities, where they lived in them, and in rural areas with counties rather than county subdivisions. On the whole they supported local government as a check on the centre and did not want to see it lose power.[20] These loyalties seemed unrelated to changes in commuting, land-use or industrial location. Where former counties and boroughs had been abolished in 1974, as with Hereford, Rutland or East Riding, people wanted them restored. New administrative units, such as Merseyside, Humberside and Tyne and Wear, were unpopular and rejected. The message was that local identity remained vigorous and was related to representative local democracy.

The centralization of British government traced in this book is wholly exceptional. The oft-cited case of France is no longer relevant. Communes and their mayors enjoy wide discretion in planning and local budgets, and central government is currently delegating more powers under a programme of agreed departmental and regional devolution. French prefects have lost their power to veto local-council decisions. The same is true in Italy, Spain and Portugal. Every other state of the European Union has all or most of the following features: local discretionary taxes; freedom to buy and sell property without government permission; freedom to raise commercial loans; discretion to fix pay and conditions for its staff; the administration of public health. German *Länder* can veto national legislation if they do not like it. Italy's new regions can levy income and transport taxes.

Under the Scandinavian 'free commune' system, communities big and small can 'opt out' of central government oversight and run their own affairs. The result has been an increase in local participation, innovation and diversity. Indeed the free commune system is likely to prove the most imitated model of public administration throughout northern Europe. It embodies the subsidiarity much preached by British ministers in Europe, delegating authority to the lowest tier relevant to effective service delivery. Other political systems see in local democracy, especially the institution of the elected mayoralty, an antidote to the centripetal tendency of modern government. Elites are not ashamed to recognize this and take action to curb their own bureaucratic excesses. British ministers can hardly plead a natural decline of localism as justifying their approach to devolution. They are out of step with what appears natural everywhere else.

I believe that one reason why other European states feel less threatened by co-operative supranational authority is precisely this phenomenon: they diffuse political activity more widely than does Britain. A Basque, a Corsican, a Bavarian or a Tuscan enjoys a geographical autonomy unthinkable to a resident of York or Bristol. His resistance to superior authority is constitutionally protected by an array of local representatives. British central government feels less secure. Since its status in relation to both supra- and sub-national government is a matter of constant negotiation and conflict, it is never quite sure where it stands. It therefore distrusts those who wish to trespass on its territory. There is no coherent reason for the British government to feel it must suppress local autonomy so as to help it fight external threats to its sovereignty. Yet it does so feel. Fighting is its instinctive mode. Jim Bulpitt quotes one local councillor on the propaganda war conducted against local government by the centre: 'It's like a Great War artillery bombardment. It goes on and on and destroys everything above ground.'[21]

This perpetual combat mode is the best explanation for much of what I have been describing in this book. We have witnessed not a rational argument over the best distribution of constitutional power in a modern state. We have witnessed a turf war. The debate over centralization is not about efficiency, democracy or uniformity, but about power. As long as Britain has no written constitution and concentrates all governmental power in the hands of the leadership of a Commons majority, that leadership will always seek more.

CHAPTER FOURTEEN

WHY IT MATTERS

Politics remains a baffling art, full of inexactitude, prejudice and mystery. In Britain, it is performed on a stage that enhances this mystery, that of the British constitution. The principal observers of this stage, from Burke and Bagehot to Dicey and Jennings, have accepted its centralism, under the Crown then under parliament, as a fact of history. The scenery has been shifted, usually peacefully, back and forth along a few hundred yards of the Westminster bank of the Thames in London. But in the view of most authorities it has delivered the goods. Despite recent polls showing dissatisfaction with their system of government, British citizens are on the whole an admiring audience.[1] They see unstable assemblies, indecisive executives and corrupt administrations in virtually every other democratic state. The British way of government may be bad, but all the others seem worse. Centralism may be full of dangers, but they are surely dangers in the right direction. If the centre cannot hold, then surely Yeats was right: 'mere anarchy is loosed upon the world'. I am inclined to agree. I accept the view of the American scholar, Lawrence Lowell, who wrote in 1908 that 'measured by the standards of duration, absence of violent commotions, maintenance of law and order, general prosperity and contentment of the people . . . the English Government has been the most remarkable in the

259

world'.[2] But Lowell was writing of the nineteenth century, and he used the past tense. We now approach the twenty-first.

For me the most trusty guide over this territory is still the man who led generations of statesmen to understand the nature of democracy. He is the Frenchman, Alexis de Tocqueville, who observed its emergence in Europe and America in the early nineteenth century. Tocqueville witnessed the extremes of social and economic turmoil in revolutionary and post-revolutionary France. He was a man of political intelligence and intuition, who bravely tackled democracy's central challenge: how can a modern state combine stable administration with genuine freedom of association? He dissected autocratic France and aristocratic England. He criticized Montesquieu and Rousseau. He travelled to British America and compared it favourably with French Canada. He himself practised administration. Every conclusion he drew from life, not from theory. His pragmatic vision of political economy was widely read and accepted, and was unchallenged until the rise of Marxism. The demise of Marxism has left that vision unchallenged.[3]

Tocqueville noted that the French Revolution had shattered the 'intermediate institutions' of France. It had wiped out the feudal aristocrats and civic communes, with their local autonomy, in the cause of democracy. Yet the Revolution supplanted one centralist bureaucracy with another. A monarchical dictatorship was replaced by an elected dictatorship. The new democratic citizen might have the vote, but it was an 'atomized' vote. Under the Directorate, Frenchmen were privatized. They withdrew from public affairs into the realms of their private concerns. Tocqueville described the new despotism emerging in France in eerily modern terms: 'I see each citizen standing apart, like a stranger to the destiny of others; his children and personal friends forming for him the entire human race. As for the remainder of his fellow citizens, he is beside them but he does not see them . . . Above these people rises an immense and tutelary power. It looks after their security, foresees and assures their needs, facilitates their pleasures, regulates their principal affairs, directs their industry, controls their legacies, divides their bequests.'[4] The coming of welfare socialism, Tocqueville realized, risked creating an overpowering central paternalism, making 'general indifference a sort of public virtue'.

To counter this Tocqueville regarded individualized democracy as inadequate. The newly emerging capitalism gave the consumer power and choice, but it was only as much power as his income permitted, and only as much choice as was left by the tendency to monopoly. Promoting consumer choice, like offering a ballot, was a necessary but not a sufficient condition for democratic freedom. Tocqueville would have cheered Thatcherism's privatizing of state corporations and competitive tendering. But he could see further. He would have deplored the stripping out of intermediate democracy, the 'withering of the habit of association'. He would have warned against giving so much power to a centralized élite.

Civic spirit was Tocqueville's guardian of true democracy against false democracy, and he contrasted French centralism with American localism in this respect: 'I see most French communes, whose accounting systems are excellent, plunged in profound ignorance of their true interests and overtaken by such invincible apathy that society seems to vegetate rather than live. On the other hand I see in American townships, with their untidy budgets lacking all uniformity, an enlightened, active and enterprising population.'[5] He noted that these American communities were anything but parochial. They were proud and self-confident, able both to rule themselves and yet look outwards and, in particular, westwards. He was shocked by the insularity and lack of colonizing zeal of the French Canadian communes to the north. They did not move and did not grow, their prefects always waiting for instructions from Paris. They let Britain conquer the West. The French way was the 'deadliest enemy of citizenship'.

British government under Thatcherism ran precisely this risk. It was run by a small élite of politicians who shared with their predecessors a belief in the worth of their vocation and a reluctance to change its parliamentary framework. They held not only that theirs was the Mother of Parliaments but that British democracy was the finest in the world and needed no updating. The political community in Britain was averse to outsiders. Few gained access to the inner counsels of government who had not served a conventional apprenticeship in parliament or the central civil service. Those who lost this access seldom returned.[6] The system was and remains obsessively conservative. There was no substantial change in the lines of government accountability in the 1970s or 1980s, with the modest exception of parliamentary select committees. The much-vaunted Citizens' Charter, initiated under John Major, was concerned with the citizen as a consumer of public services, not as a participating democrat. Both the institutions of local democracy and the regulators of privatized utilities were blessed with nothing new by way of accountability. An ever widening range of public-sector activity had to be scrutinized through the tarnished needle's eye of the parliamentary dispatch box.

The most elegant critic of Thatcherism during the 1980s was the former minister, Sir Ian Gilmour. In a series of books he attacked Thatcher's neglect of pluralism, a pluralism which he maintained was the essence of Toryism. 'In the Conservative view,' he said, 'economic liberalism à la Professor Hayek, because of its starkness and its failure to create a sense of community, is not a safeguard of political freedom but a threat to it.'[7] The longer they were in office, the more Thatcher's ministers came to believe that, provided they could win elections, even on minorities of the popular vote, they had met their obligation to democracy. They became oligarchs with no interest in enhancing democratic control over public administration. They were Bagehot's 'minist-erialists', hostile to an inconvenient democracy, not part and parcel of it. Countervailing power to that of the executive was supplied by the five-yearly franchise. No more was needed.

I have detected in many ministers who served in government in this period a dim awareness that they were transgressing some ideological boundary, betraying Gilmour's ancestral rite of Toryism. Yet they could not admit this – often not even to themselves. They would profess to be decentralizers, not centralizers. Their utterances achieved an Orwellian dysfunction. Kenneth Baker declared that his local-government and school reforms were meant to give power back to local democracy. Nicholas Ridley proclaimed that poll tax would give local councils more discretion, even as he capped their revenue-raising power.[8] Michael Howard said he was releasing police and prisons from central bondage, despite enforcing ever more stringent cash limits and performance targets. John Gummer described his 'Integrated Regional Offices' as a 'shift from the centre' which would make government 'more responsive to local needs and acceptable to local people'.[9] It was as if a new Thatcherspeak had vested words with new and contradictory meanings. Somehow the gods of Toryism past had to be appeased, even as they were abused.

The greatest ideological illusion was that the 'social democratic settlement' initiated by the wartime coalition and entrenched by the Attlee government had been torn up. This view was expressed by many of Thatcher's critics on the Left as well as by her admirers on the Right. Certainly the custodianship of this settlement changed. Attlee had put in place a rough and ready tripartitism. Public services were authorized by the national government, their level fixed and partly financed by local councils, and they were administered by the professions. Until 1979, Whitehall ministries ran no schools, built no houses, employed no scholars and commanded no police (except in London). Even the health service was mostly delegated to the medical profession. The public sector operated on the basis of a wide range of treaties, between tiers of government, institutions and occupational groups.

Thatcherism tore up these treaties. For compacts it substituted contracts. Some, as in the privatized utilities and competitive tendering, were genuine contracts between purchasers and providers of a service. Others were more in the nature of 'unequal treaties', between the Treasury as keeper of the nation's purse and spending departments and agencies. At the heart of these treaties lay strict budgetary control. With the exception of some demand-led outlays such as pensions and unemployment benefit, each item of public spending had by 1995 been brought within the cash-limit regime. Standardized performance measures and assessments of personal and collective need brought the Treasury nearer to that goal of twentieth-century socialism, the equitable, national unit of welfare, the perfectly efficient state.

At some stage in this process, various forms of democratic activity must become superfluous. Institutions atrophy when their structure no longer accords with their functions or powers. As we saw in chapter three, a vigorous debate took place in cabinet in 1991 on whether to continue with what some ministers regarded as the charade of local government, given the continuance of council-tax capping and the dominance of central grant. The intervention of local councillors had perhaps become superfluous to good government. With 'one-stop' offices in the regions for the administration of central-government services, local democracy was an irritant. It would be simpler to bring all its functions under central executive control. Local democracy survived 1991 by the skin of its teeth, but its powers and functions continued to wither. The only two areas in which it continued to show vitality were those in which it had been left some discretion, the care of the elderly and bidding for 'challenge' grants for urban development.

If there was little role left in public administration for local democracy, the role of lay members on centrally appointed executive bodies was no less open to question. Central government still felt it appropriate to appoint outsiders to monitor its managerial hierarchy. School governors, prison visitors, museum councils, hospital trusts, funding council boards comprised a substantial quangocracy, estimated at 30–50,000 people in England and Wales, depending on definition.[10] This was a large body of participation. Ministers seemed to accept that lay 'validation' of executive decisions had a virtue, if only in protecting them from parliamentary or press criticism. What was extraordinary was the lengths to which ministers went to ensure that the membership of these bodies was loyal to them, and distant from any link with local democracy. Not until the Nolan Committee report in May 1995 on standards in public life did they begin to concede that they might have gone too far in this respect, being forced to accept an independent monitor of quango appointments.

The Thatcher and Major governments struggled, unsuccessfully, to rid schools of education committees. They went on to limit the budgets of school governors. By 1995 many were questioning the role of lay people on health district and police authorities, in any role other than a 'cheer-leader' one. University councils had become powerless over resource allocation. Government was in danger not just of centralizing but of de-professionalizing and de-politicizing British public administration. Observers such as Bernard Crick and Jerry White noted this growing 'fear of politics' among politicians.[11] To ministers the phrase 'business experience' became code for being both 'one of us' and uncontaminated by local politics. To have been elected came to seem a disqualification for appointed office. There was no end to the paradoxes of Thatcherism.

The concentration of accountability on ministers alone became more than a necessity consequent on centralization. It became a habit of mind. In May 1995 the Prime Minister found himself explaining at the dispatch box why an emergency patient had been moved from London to Leeds, and his health secretary why part of an Edgware hospital accident department should close. A sports minister negotiated a special payment for teachers for one games period a week. Alternative conduits of accountability had either been stripped out of government or rendered impotent. The minister stood alone, exhausted, battered, usually confused, defending decisions of which he had little knowledge and over which he had little direct control. His defence weapons were Treasury budget-capping and performance audit. His praetorian guard was a swelling army of managers, consultants and auditors. Waldegrave's thesis that new managerial tools would diffuse and pluralize accountability across a range of consumer conduits might pass muster at a Whitehall presentation, but it was not politically realistic.[12] Accountability still lay where it always had, to the half-baked badinage of the House of Commons.

At this point I can do no more than restate the article of faith that has run through this book. Democratic politics is endangered where the 'habit of association' is allowed, indeed encouraged, to degenerate. Citizenship is not a matter of exercising consumer choice of products and services where permitted, and voting once every four or five years. The ceaseless exercise of political freedom is not just a right: it is an obligation on every member of any sophisticated community. Some have attributed the centralization of British government in the 1980s and 1990s to the arrogance of ministers too long in power, who have lost sight of the compacts of the British constitution and of the virtues of pluralism. There is much truth in this. Public administration is not lacking in controversy in Britain, but the controversy is largely internal to itself, an argument within the élite.

The greatest damage has been done to local democracy, damage that, as we have seen, began under Attlee. Courage must be found to return to local democracy much of the autonomy taken from it in the past two decades. In virtually all the spheres of government discussed in this book, functions and powers could revert to elected rather than appointed bodies – power to raise revenue, set service standards and monitor them locally. No country in Europe, indeed few in the world, have as little autonomy vested in subordinate local institutions as has Britain. Even Thatcher's favourite philosopher, Hayek, was emphatic on this: 'Nowhere has democracy worked well without a great measure of local self-government, providing a school of political training for the people at large as much as for their future leaders.'[13] Many have put the astonishing revival of the post-war German economy down to the vigour of its self-governing cities. To Hayek, as to Tocqueville and the framers of the American constitution, local government was the true forum of democratic activity. There is no worse comment on democracy in Britain than the 30–40 per cent turnouts at local elections, less than anywhere else in Europe. This is not the 'fault' of local government, but of a constitution that has casually left it unreformed and denuded of power, and of a custodian of that constitution, the British cabinet, that has revelled in so denuding it.

Like so many leaders before her, Thatcher found that the magnetism of power overwhelmed any ideological disposition to repel it. She shared with Lord Hailsham a familiar syndrome among British politicians: an aversion to 'elective dictatorship' when out of office and a sudden conversion to its glorious subtleties when in power.[14] The libertarian in Opposition became the absolutist in office. As we saw in chapter one, Thatcher had considered modern government the enemy of freedom. Once in Downing Street, events caught her in a swirl. She had to have more power, not less, to confront them. Ferdinand Mount pointed out that this was outrageously at variance with Tory philosophy, however tentative the lip-service paid to that philosophy by previous Tory leaders. 'The dispersal of power and responsibility was well understood to be the foundation of civic virtue; it was what distinguished us from the irresponsible sloth which was bred by the unpredictable and - overweening caprice of oriental despots.' He deplored Thatcher's 'clinging to a geographical and administrative centralization of a sort which, when encountered elsewhere, we disdain as brutishly Napoleonic'.[15]

This phenomenon was more than Napoleonic. I have sought to show how much it had in common with what Tories would once have denounced as statist, corporatist, even social-ist. Tocqueville feared that socialism would enervate incon-venient, cantankerous citizenship and put in its place a uniform welfare centralism. Conservatives feared this too. Yet how else are we to view the 'national performance indicators' drawn up by the Audit Commission, or Whitehall's lengthening list of national league tables? What is presented as useful information to guide citizens in (non-existent) local democratic choices has become the backbone of Whitehall budgetary control. Of all the paradoxes of Thatcherism, none is greater than this: that more open government should have been used, not to enable the public to participate more fully in democracy, but as a tool of state centralism in its quest for national efficiency.

The customary response to this ostensibly gloomy state of affairs is to advocate that constitutional pluralism should in some sense be entrenched. Checks and balances on executive power should be written down, enacted by parliament and enforced by a supreme court of judges. This court should enjoy a measure of sovereignty over the House of Commons. Britain now stands alone among democracies, indeed among sovereign states, in not having such a text.[16] (One exception to this generalization is Israel, whose constitutional future is still pending. Another is New Zealand.) To Mount, a written constitution 'can animate society with a sense of what is right, and instil into government an understanding of the proper limits to the exercise of power; above all, it can inform the conversation of politics with a sense of dispersed responsibility'.[17]

This is not the moment to begin a quite different book, on the reform of the British constitution. I can only say that I agree with Mount, and with Lord Hailsham and Margaret Thatcher in their early incarnations. I subscribe to what can be called the alarmist tendency. Both governing parties in post-war Britain have had their chance to expand the range of democratic participation and diversify the accountability of government. Both have rejected that chance. They have proved susceptible to the tendency to bureaucratic centralism which I believe to be innate in all public administration and all political systems. They have become its tools and ultimately its apologists. The irony is that one of Europe's great liberal institutions, the Tory party, should find itself in this bind, at the same time as wrestling to come to terms with an even greater centralism, that of the European Union.

The only defence against all these threats to plural democracy is constitutionalism. Constitutionalism is a power greater even than democracy, since it ordains democracy. Without constitutionalism nations fall back on cynicism, which is the path to anarchy.

NOTES

CHAPTER ONE: ACCOUNTABLE TO ONE

1 See James Bulpitt, 'The Discipline of the New Democracy: Mrs Thatcher's Domestic Statecraft', *Political Studies*, 34:1, 1985.

2 Richard Rose and Phillip Davies, *Inheritance in Public Policy*, Yale, 1994.

3 Margaret Thatcher, *The Downing Street Years*, HarperCollins, 1993, p. 8.

4 Quoted in Maurice Mullard, *The Politics of Public Expenditure*, Routledge, 1993, p. 148.

5 Nigel Lawson, *The View from No. 11*, Bantam, 1992, p. 64.

6 Shirley Letwin, *The Anatomy of Thatcherism*, Fontana, 1992, p. 30.

7 Andrew Gamble, *The Free Economy and the Strong State*, Macmillan, 1994, p. 209.

8 Restrained versions of this thesis can be found in Hugo Young, *One of Us*, Macmillan, 1991, and William Keegan, *Mrs Thatcher's Economic Experiment*, Allen Lane, 1984.

9 For the revisionist viewpoint, see Mullard, op. cit.; Peter Riddell, *The Thatcher Era and Its Legacy*, Blackwell, 1991; Martin Holmes, *Thatcherism: Scope and Limits*, Macmillan, 1989; Stephen Savage, Rob Atkinson and Lynton Robins, *Public Policy in Britain*, Macmillan, 1994.

10 Richard Cockett, *Thinking the Unthinkable*, HarperCollins, 1994, p. 314.

11 Quoted ibid., p. 295.

12 See *The Omega File*, Adam Smith Institute, 1985.

13 Samuel Beer, *Britain Against Itself*, Faber and Faber, 1982, p. 14.

14 Quoted in Peter Hennessy, *Whitehall*, Fontana, 1989, p. 628.

15 Kenneth Harris, *Attlee*, Weidenfeld and Nicolson, 1995, p. 568.

16 Letwin, op. cit., p. 30.

17 Thatcher, op. cit., p. 7.

18 Ibid., p. 14.

19 Quoted in *The Conservative Party*, Conservative Political Centre, 1970.
20 Thatcher, op. cit., p. 13.
21 Lawson, op. cit., p. 718.
22 In an interview in *The Times*, 2 November 1990.
23 Gamble, op. cit., p. 251.
24 Ferdinand Mount, *The British Constitution Now*, Heinemann, 1992, p. 27.
25 Mullard, op. cit., p. 220.
26 Speech in Anglesey, 23 January 1976, quoted in Mullard, op. cit.
27 Thatcher, op. cit., p. 6.
28 Letwin, op. cit., p. 350.
29 Lawson, op. cit., p. 718.
30 Ibid., p. 601.
31 Nicholas Ridley, *My Style of Government*, Hutchinson, 1991, p. 86.
32 See Simon Jenkins in *The Times*, 28 June and 1 July 1995, for an analysis of the Redwood manifesto.
33 Richard Rose and Phillip Davies, op. cit., chapter 2.
34 Quoted in Mullard, op. cit., p. 166.
35 Michael Power, *The Audit Explosion*, Demos, 1994.
36 Lawson, op. cit., p. 586.
37 Ibid., p. 383.
38 Leo Pliatsky, *The Treasury under Mrs Thatcher*, Blackwell, 1989.
39 See Clive Gray, *Government Beyond the Centre: Sub-national Politics in Britain*, Macmillan, 1994.

CHAPTER TWO: THE FAMILY SILVER

1 Margaret Thatcher, *The Downing Street Years*, HarperCollins, 1993, p. 676.
2 See Matthew Bishop and Mike Green, *Privatization and Recession*, Centre for Study of Regulation Industries, 1995.
3 See *The Economist*, 11 March 1995.
4 David Howell, *A New Style of Government*, Conservative Political Centre, 1970.
5 Nigel Lawson, *The View from No. 11*, Bantam, 1992, p. 198.
6 Geoffrey Howe, *Conflict of Loyalty*, Macmillan, 1994, p. 254.
7 Thatcher, op. cit., p. 678.
8 Nicholas Ridley, *My Style of Government*, Hutchinson, 1991, p. 83.

9 Howe, op. cit., p. 254.

10 *Political Quarterly*, No. 55, 1984.

11 Oliver Letwin, *Privatizing the World*, Cassell, 1988, p. 41.

12 Howe, op. cit., p. 255.

13 *The Economist*, 11 March 1995.

14 Hyman Howard in Cento Veljanovski (ed.), *Privatization and Competition*, Institute of Economic Affairs, 1989, p. 191.

15 Lawson, op. cit., p. 205.

16 *Nationalized Industries Legislation – Consultation Proposals*, H.M. Treasury, 20 December 1984.

17 Energy Select Committee Report, House of Commons, 276, 1983–4.

18 Quoted in Tony Prosser, *Public Law*, January 1986, p. 24.

19 Ibid., p. 19.

20 John Moore, *The Value of Ownership*, Conservative Political Centre, 1986.

21 Thatcher, op. cit., p. 682.

22 Ibid., p. 684.

23 See David Marsh, *Public Administration*, vol. 69, 1991, p. 465.

24 Ibid., p. 469.

25 John Kay, *Privatization and Regulation*, Oxford University Press, 1986.

26 Lawson, op. cit., p. 239.

27 See Tony Prosser, *Nationalized Industries and Public Control*, Blackwell, 1986.

28 Speech to Charter 88, reported in *The Times*, 15 March 1995.

29 Introduction to Letwin, op. cit., p. xvii.

30 *Daily Telegraph*, 31 July 1987.

31 See Peter Riddell, *The Times*, 16 January 1995.

32 *The Economist*, 11 March 1995.

33 See H. Abromeit, *British Privatization Policy*, Parliamentary Affairs, vol. 41, 1988, pp. 68–85.

34 Tony Prosser, 'Regulation, Markets and Legitimacy' in J. A. Cross, *Modern British Government*, University Tutorial Press, 1972, p. 254.

35 Lawson, op. cit., p. 217.

36 Ibid., p. 219.

37 Marsh, op. cit., bibliography, p. 477, with eighty entries by 1991.

38 Thatcher, op. cit., p. 677.

39 Christopher Foster, *Public Administration*, vol. 72, 1994.

40 See Ridley, op. cit., and Stephen Savage, Rob Atkinson and Lynton Robins, *Public Policy in Britain*, Macmillan, 1994.

41 Thatcher, op. cit., p. 677.
42 *The Economist*, 11 March 1995.

CHAPTER THREE: THE FIRST CASUALTY

1 Margaret Thatcher, *The Path to Power*, HarperCollins, 1995, p. 249.
2 David Butler, Andrew Adonis and Tony Travers, *Failure in British Government*, Oxford Univeristy Press, 1994; also M. Crick and A. van Klaveren, *Contemporary Record*, 5/3, 1991.
3 Margaret Thatcher, *The Downing Street Years*, HarperCollins, 1993, p. 643.
4 Ibid., p. 644.
5 *Alternatives to Domestic Rates*, Department of the Environment, Cmnd 8449, 1981.
6 *Local Government Finance*, Department of the Environment, Cmnd 6813, 1977.
7 Butler *et al.*, op. cit., p. 32.
8 *Methods of Financing Local Government in the Context of the Government Green Paper*, House of Commons Papers, 217, 1982.
9 Butler *et al.*, op. cit., p. 37.
10 Nigel Lawson, *The View from No. 11*, Bantam, 1992, p. 565.
11 Butler *et al.*, op. cit., p. 38.
12 *Rates*, Department of the Environment, Cmnd 9008, 1983.
13 Ibid., p. 14.
14 Lawson, op. cit., p. 564.
15 Speech to Association of Metropolitan Authorities, 21 September 1983.
16 Butler *et al.*, op. cit., p. 44.
17 Thatcher, *Downing Street Years*, p. 646.
18 Speech to the Social Market Foundation, 1 December 1993, quoted in Butler *et al.*, op. cit., p. 223.
19 Lawson, op. cit., p. 570.
20 Thatcher, *Downing Street Years*, p. 642.
21 Lawson, op. cit., p. 574.
22 Thatcher, *Downing Street Years*, p. 649.
23 *Paying for Local Government*, Department of the Environment, Cmnd 9714, 1986.
24 Thatcher, *Downing Street Years*, p. 656.
25 Ibid., p. 651.

26 Butler *et al.*, op. cit., p. 139.
27 Lawson, op. cit., p. 581.
28 *Spectator*, 8 April 1995.
29 *Sunday Times*, 15 November 1989.
30 Kenneth Baker, *The Turbulent Years*, Faber and Faber, 1993, p. 127.
31 Thatcher, *Downing Street Years*, p. 663.
32 Thatcher, *Path to Power*, p. 247.
33 Baker, op. cit., p. 111.
34 Thatcher, *Downing Street Years*, p. 284.
35 Geoffrey Howe, *Conflict of Loyalty*, Macmillan, 1994, p. 460.
36 Thatcher, *Downing Street Years*, p. 642.
37 Ibid., p. 667.
38 Butler *et al.*, op. cit., p. 180.
39 Ibid., p. 182.
40 Tony Travers in Colin Crouch and David Marquand, eds., *The New Centralism*, Political Quarterly/Blackwell, 1989, p. 3.
41 Quoted in Butler *et al.*, op. cit., p. 230.
42 See Christopher Foster, *Public Money*, CIPFA, 1981.
43 For options see Rita Hale and Tony Travers, *The Future of the Non-domestic Rate*, Hale Associates, 1994.
44 See *Treasury Financial Statement*, HMSO, January 1995, table 4A.1.

CHAPTER FOUR: NATIONALIZATION AT LAST

1 Kenneth Morgan, *Labour in Power 1945–51*, Clarendon, 1984.
2 Ministry of Health memorandum to Commons Committee on Health, 15 July 1950, NH(50)17.
3 *National Health Service Reorganization*, DHSS, Cmnd 5055, 1972.
4 Margaret Thatcher, *The Downing Street Years*, HarperCollins, 1993, p. 606.
5 *Patients First*, Department of Health and Social Security, 1979.
6 See Gerald Wistow, in David Marsh and R. A. W. Rhodes, *Implementing Thatcherite Policies*, Open University, 1992.
7 Rudolf Klein, in P. Jackson (ed.), *Implementing Government Policy Initiatives*, Royal Institute of Public Administration, Gower, 1985.
8 Report of the House of Commons Social Services Select Committee on the NHS, 1980–1 session, para. 25.
9 Nigel Lawson, *The View from No. 11*, Bantam, 1992, p. 613.
10 Wistow, op. cit., p. 103.

11 Norman Fowler, *Ministers Decide*, Chapman, 1991.

12 Roy Griffiths, *NHS Management Inquiry*, Department of Health and Social Security, 1983, para. 5.

13 See Brian Edwards, *A Manager's Tale: 1946–92*, Nuffield Provincial Hospitals Trust, 1993.

14 Patricia Day and Rudolf Klein, *Accountabilities*, Tavistock, 1987, p. 87.

15 Mark Exworthy, *Policy and Politics*, vol. 22/1, 1994.

16 Edwina Currie, *Life Lines: Politics and Health, 1986–88*, Sidgwick and Jackson, 1989.

17 Thatcher, op. cit., p. 571.

18 Ibid.

19 Ibid., p. 608.

20 Ibid.

21 Alain Enthoven, *Reflections on the Management of the NHS*, Nuffield Provincial Hospitals Trust, 1985.

22 For a review of the reviews, see Edwin Griggs, *Political Quarterly*, October 1991; see also David Green, *Everyone a Private Patient*, Institute of Economic Affairs, 1988.

23 Thatcher, op. cit., p. 609.

24 Griggs, op. cit., p. 427.

25 Thatcher, op. cit., p. 612.

26 *Working for Patients*, Department of Health and Social Security, Cm 555, 1989.

27 Malcolm Balen, *Kenneth Clarke*, Fourth Estate, 1994, chapter 10.

28 Ibid., p. 180.

29 Thatcher, op. cit., p. 609.

30 Kenneth Stowe, *Caring for the National Health*, Nuffield Provincial Hospitals Trust, 1988.

31 Hansard, House of Commons, 17 January 1990.

32 David Hughes, *Journal of Social Welfare Law*, 1990, p. 303.

33 Hansard, House of Commons, 17 January 1990.

34 David Hughes, *Modern Law Review*, January 1991.

35 David Hughes and Robert Dingwall, *Journal of Social Welfare Law*, 1990, p. 304.

36 Julian le Grand, *Evaluating the NHS Reforms*, King's Fund Institute, 1994.

37 *The Times*, 11 March 1995.

38 *Spectator*, 21 May 1994.

39 Diana Longley, *Public Law*, 1990.

40 Quoted by Hughes and Dingwall, op. cit., p. 297.
41 *Managing the New NHS*, Department of Health and Social Security, 1994.
42 Chris Ham, *Health Director*, November 1993.
43 Quoted in B. Watkin, *The National Health Service*, Allen and Unwin, 1978.
44 See Wistow, op. cit., p. 116.

CHAPTER FIVE: ARRESTING CHANGE

1 Robert Reiner, *The Politics of the Police*, 2nd edn, Wheatsheaf, 1992, p. 61.
2 Tony Jefferson and Roger Grimshaw, *Controlling the Constable*, Muller, 1984, chapter two.
3 Ibid., p. 16.
4 Reiner, op. cit., p. 61.
5 Robert Mark, *In the Office of Constable*, Collins, 1978.
6 Ibid., p. 200.
7 Margaret Thatcher, *The Downing Street Years*, HarperCollins, 1993, p. 32.
8 Robert Reiner and Sarah Spencer, eds., *Accountable Policing*, Institute for Public Policy Research, 1993, p. 17.
9 Barry Loveday, *Political Quarterly*, July 1991.
10 Barry Loveday, 'The Joint Board', *Policing*, Autumn 1987, p. 203.
11 Reiner and Spencer, op. cit., p. 26.
12 Barry Loveday, 'Central Co-ordination, Police Authorities and the Miners' Strike', *Political Quarterly*, January 1986.
13 Thatcher, op. cit., p. 348.
14 Barry Loveday, op. cit., 1986.
15 At a Salford police seminar, 4 February 1994.
16 See Roger Graef, *Talking Blues*, Fontana, 1990.
17 Kenneth Baker, *The Turbulent Years*, Faber and Faber, 1993, p. 451.
18 *Police Papers*, Audit Commission, No. 8, December 1990.
19 Hansard, House of Commons, 23 March 1993.
20 Hansard, House of Lords, 15 February 1994.
21 See Barry Loveday, *Political Quarterly*, July 1991, p. 388.
22 See Vernon Bogdanor, *Guardian*, 1 November 1993.
23 Ibid.
24 Hansard, House of Commons, 23 March 1993.

25 *Annual Report*, Home Office, Cm 2808, HMSO, 1995.
26 Barry Loveday, *Political Quarterly*, April 1995, p. 144.
27 *Police Reform*, Home Office, Cm 2281, 1993, para. 7.5.
28 *Annual Report*, Home Office, HMSO, 1995.
29 Report on Police, Audit Commission, June 1990.
30 *Local Authority Performance Indicators*, vol. 3, Audit Commission, 1995.
31 Report in *Daily Telegraph*, 7 July 1994.

CHAPTER SIX: OPTING IN AND OUT AND IN

1 Excerpts quoted in Leslie Bash and David Coulby, eds., *The Education Reform Act: Competition and Control*, Cassell, 1989; and in full in *Education*, 22 November 1976.
2 Reported in Robert Morris, ed., *Central and Local Control of Education*, Longman, 1990.
3 Ibid., p. 15.
4 *Local Authority Arrangements for School Curriculum*, Department of Education and Science, 1979.
5 Margaret Thatcher, *The Path to Power*, HarperCollins, 1995, chapter 6.
6 See Stuart Maclure, in Denis Lawton, ed., *The Education Reform Act: Choice and Control*, Hodder, 1989, p. 35.
7 Julian Haviland, ed., *Take Care, Mr Baker*, Fourth Estate, 1988, p. 28.
8 See Geoff Whitty and Ian Menter, *Journal of Law and Society*, Spring 1989.
9 Kenneth Baker, *The Turbulent Years*, Faber and Faber, 1993, p. 167.
10 Ibid., p. 161.
11 Thatcher, op. cit., p. 166.
12 Hansard, House of Lords, 3 May 1988.
13 Nigel Lawson, *The View from No. 11*, Bantam, 1992, pp. 606–9.
14 Ibid.
15 Baker, op. cit., p. 167.
16 Quoted by Maclure, in Lawton, op. cit., p. 28.
17 Baker, op. cit., p. 191.
18 Maurice Kogan, *Political Quarterly*, April 1991, p. 229.
19 See Maclure, in Lawton, op. cit., p. 33.
20 Baker, op. cit., p. 252.
21 Margaret Thatcher, *The Downing Street Years*, HarperCollins, 1993, p. 593.

22 Ibid., p. 597.
23 Paul Meredith, *Modern Law Review*, vol. 52, 1989, p. 216.
24 Thatcher, *Downing Street Years*, p. 595.
25 Ibid.
26 Ibid., p. 596.
27 See Bash and Coulby, op. cit., p. 114.
28 Ibid., p. 123.
29 Lawson, op. cit., p. 609.
30 Thatcher, *Downing Street Years*, p. 392.
31 Baker, op. cit., p. 215.
32 Quoted in ibid., p. 230.
33 Hansard, House of Commons, 9 November 1992.
34 Meredith, op. cit., p. 222.
35 Maclure, in Lawton, op. cit., p. 14.
36 Whitty and Menter, op. cit., p. 42.
37 Ibid., p. 48.
38 Maclure, in Lawton, op. cit., p. 26.
39 Bash and Coulby, op. cit., p. 17.
40 Baker, op. cit., p. 220.
41 Thatcher, *Downing Street Years*, p. 597.
42 *Choice and Diversity*, Department of Education and Science, Cm 2021, 1992.
43 Hansard, House of Commons, 3 March 1993.
44 Thatcher, *Downing Street Years*, p. 570.
45 Paul Meredith, *Education and the Law 1994*, Longman, 1994, p. 126.
46 *Annual Report*, Department of Education, Cm 2810, 1995.
47 *The Times*, 5 May 1995.
48 Interview in the *Guardian*, 7 January 1995.
49 Peter Newsam, in Haviland, op. cit., p. 262.
50 Baker, op. cit., p. 252.
51 Thatcher, *Path to Power*, p. 174.

CHAPTER SEVEN: TAMING SHREWS

1 Quoted by John Griffith, *Political Quarterly*, January 1989, p. 51.
2 Quoted in Michael Shattock, *The University Grants Committee*, Open University, 1994, p. 25.
3 Ibid., p. 104.
4 Ibid., p. 105.

5 *Annual Report*, University Grants Committee, 1968.
6 Shattock, op. cit., p. 112.
7 Quoted in ibid., p. 133.
8 *Meeting the Challenge*, Department of Education and Science, Cm 114, 1987.
9 Nigel Lawson, *The View from No. 11*, Bantam, 1992, p. 308.
10 Quoted in Griffith, op. cit., p. 62.
11 Ibid., p. 55.
12 *Meeting the Challenge*, op. cit.
13 Graham Zellick, *Public Law*, Winter 1989, p. 521.
14 Quoted in Griffith, op. cit., p. 59.
15 Privately circulated draft of his *Political Quarterly* article.
16 In Denis Lawton, ed., *The Education Reform Act: Choice and Control*, Hodder, 1989, p. 75.
17 Ibid., p. 68.
18 Jarratt report, *Report of the Steering Committee for Efficiency Studies in Universities*, Committee of Vice-Chancellors and Principals, 1985.
19 See Lal, *Nationalizing the Universities*, 1989.
20 *Meeting the Challenge*, op. cit.
21 Quoted in Stuart Maclure, *Education Re-formed*, Hodder, 1989, p. 91.
22 *La Guide Libération: Les 100 Meilleurs Universités en Europe*, Libération, December 1989.
23 Shattock, op. cit., p. 154.
24 See Michael Power, *The Audit Explosion*, Demos, 1994, p. 50.
25 Hugo Young and Anne Sloman, *But Chancellor*, BBC, 1984, p. 45.
26 Power, op. cit., p. 36.
27 See the *Financial Times*, 20 March 1995.
28 Margaret Thatcher, *The Downing Street Years*, HarperCollins, 1993, p. 598.
29 Ibid., p. 599.

CHAPTER EIGHT: LANCING BOILS

1 Quoted in Malcolm Balen, *Kenneth Clarke*, Fourth Estate, 1994, p. 147.
2 See Nigel Lawson, *The View from No. 11*, Bantam, 1992, p. 564; and speech by Jack Straw, Hansard, House of Commons, 4 November 1993.
3 Quoted in Andy Thornley, *Urban Planning under Thatcherism*, Routledge, 1993, p. 181.

4 Hansard, House of Lords Select Committee on the Environment, 1981 session.

5 Quoted in Thornley, op. cit., p. 172.

6 Geoffrey Howe, *Conflict of Loyalty*, Macmillan, 1994, p. 110.

7 Lawson, op. cit., p. 52.

8 Howe, op. cit., p. 110.

9 See Simon Jenkins, *The Selling of Mary Davies*, John Murray, 1993.

10 Balen, op. cit., p. 150.

11 Jerry White, *Fear of Voting*, Rowntree, 1994, p. 20.

12 Ibid., p. 11.

13 *Streamlining the Cities*, Department of the Environment, Cmnd 9063, October 1983.

14 Quoted in Simon James, *Public Administration*, vol. 68, 1990.

15 Hansard, House of Commons, 5 June 1991.

16 See Norman Flynn, Steve Leach and Carol Vielba, *Abolition or Reform? The GLC and the Metropolitan Councils*, Allen and Unwin, 1985, p. 1.

17 Hansard, House of Commons, 3 December 1984.

18 Ibid., 5 June 1991.

19 Ibid., 4 December 1984.

20 See Steve Leach, *Local Government Studies*, vol. 16, 1990.

21 Tony Travers with George Jones, Michael Hebbert and June Burnham, *The Government of London*, Rowntree, 1991.

22 For a lively account of the LRB's dull work see Michael Hebbert and A. Dickens Edge, *Dismantlers: The London Residuary Body*, Suntory-Toyota International Centre, 1994.

23 Hansard, House of Commons, 5 June 1991.

24 Hebbert and Edge, op. cit., p. 179.

25 James, op. cit., p. 495.

26 Andy Thornley, ed., *The Crisis of London*, Routledge, 1992, p. 142.

27 'Yet it Moves', *The Economist*, 20 August 1994.

28 See Travers *et al.*, op. cit.

29 *London Pride*, London First, 1995.

30 Tony Travers and Stephen Glaister, *An Infrastructure Levy for London*, LSE, 1994.

31 See Travers *et al.*, op. cit., p. 42.

32 Ibid., p. 18.

33 Kenneth Baker, *The Turbulent Years*, Faber and Faber, 1993, p. 102.

34 White, op. cit., p. 17.

35 Thornley, op. cit., p. 146.

CHAPTER NINE: TORY SOCIAL ENGINEERING

1 Margaret Thatcher, *The Downing Street Years*, HarperCollins, 1993, p. 599.
2 See Ray Forrest and Alan Murie, *Selling the Welfare State: The Privatization of Public Housing*, Routledge, 1988, p. 103.
3 See A. Murie, 'The Nationalization of Housing Policy', in M. Loughlin *et al.*, *Half a Century of Municipal Decline*, Allen and Unwin, 1985.
4 Quoted in Michael Foot, *Aneurin Bevan*, MacGibbon and Kee, 1962.
5 Thatcher, op. cit., p. 599.
6 Ibid., p. 605.
7 See Peter Malpass and Alan Murie, *Housing Policy and Practice*, Macmillan, 1990, pp. 87–90.
8 Quoted in Forrest and Murie, op. cit., p. 213.
9 See Malpass and Murie, op. cit.
10 Nigel Lawson, *The View from No. 11*, Bantam, 1992, p. 566.
11 Geoffrey Howe, *Conflict of Loyalty*, Macmillan, 1994, p. 280.
12 Lawson, op. cit., p. 821.
13 John Hills, ed., *The State of Welfare*, Clarendon, 1991, p. 147.
14 *Housing: The Government's Proposals*, Cm 214, HMSO, 1987, p. 12.
15 Bill Randolph, in Peter Malpass and Robin Means, *Implementing Housing Policy*, Open University, 1993, p. 57.
16 Mike Langstaff, in Johnston Birchall, ed., *Housing Policy in the 1990s*, Routledge, 1992, p. 43; and see Julian le Grand, *The State of Welfare*, Oxford University Press, 1990.
17 Thatcher, op. cit., p. 603.
18 *Annual Report*, Department of the Environment, Cm 2807, HMSO, 1995, p. 35.
19 Thatcher, op. cit., p. 606.
20 Lawson, op. cit., p. 566.
21 Peter Kemp, in David Marsh and R. A. W. Rhodes, *Implementing Thatcherite Policies*, Open University, 1992, p. 75.
22 *The Government's Expenditure Plans*, Cmnd 9702, HM Treasury, 1986.

CHAPTER TEN: FORMING A JUDGEMENT

1 Margaret Thatcher, *The Downing Street Years*, HarperCollins, 1993, p. 632.
2 Quoted in Stephen Savage, Rob Atkinson and Lynton Robins, *Public Policy in Britain*, Macmillan 1994, p. 141.
3 See Simon Jenkins, *Against the Grain*, John Murray, 1994, chapter ten.
4 See Mike Nash and Stephen Savage in S. Savage *et al.*, op. cit., Macmillan, 1994, p. 160.
5 Thatcher, op. cit., p. 628.
6 Personal records.
7 Michael Zander, *The International Lawyer*, The American Bar Association, 1990.
8 *Work and Organization of the Legal Profession*, Home Office, Cm 570, 1989.
9 *The Times*, 2 February 1989.
10 *The Times*, 10 March 1989.
11 *Report of the Royal Commission on Criminal Procedure*, Cmnd 8092, 1981, para. 6.3.
12 Ibid., para. 9.4.
13 Francis Bennion, *Criminal Law Review*, 1986, p. 9. The government response was in the Home Office White Paper, *An Independent Prosecution Service*, HMSO, 1983.
14 Andrew Ashworth and Julia Fionda, *Criminal Law Review*, 1994, p. 903.
15 Hansard, House of Lords, 22 February 1994.
16 Hansard, House of Commons, 26 April 1994.
17 Ibid.
18 Ibid.
19 *The Times*, 17 March 1995.

CHAPTER ELEVEN: MR MAJOR'S POODLES

1 For the best survey, see Stephen Glaister and Tony Travers, *New Directions for British Railways*, Institute of Economic Affairs, 1993.
2 Reported in John Redwood, *Signals from a Railway Conference*, Centre for Policy Studies, 1988.
3 Ibid.

4 Margaret Thatcher, *The Downing Street Years*, HarperCollins, 1993, p. 686.
5 *The Conservative Manifesto*, The Conservative Party, 1992, p. 35.
6 *New Opportunities for the Railways*, Department of Transport, Cm 2012, 1992.
7 Hansard, House of Commons, 2 February 1993.
8 *Developing the Structure of Charges*, Ofrail, November 1994.
9 See letter from Richard Hope in the *Independent*, 11 May 1995.
10 Glaister and Travers, op. cit., p. 13.
11 See Adam Ridley, *Charities in the 21st Century*, Goodman Lecture, Charities Aid Foundation, 1991.
12 Kenneth Baker, *The Turbulent Years*, Faber and Faber, 1993, p. 463.
13 Ibid.
14 Ibid., p. 464.
15 Ibid.
16 Hansard, House of Commons, 25 January 1993.
17 Ibid.
18 Hansard, House of Lords, 31 January 1994, speech of Lady Trumpington.
19 *The National Lottery Act*, HMSO, 1993, section 26(1).
20 Hansard, House of Commons, 5 January 1993.
21 Ibid.
22 Ibid., 20 October 1993.

CHAPTER TWELVE: THE MAGPIES' NEST

1 Leo Pliatsky, *Getting and Spending*, Blackwell, 1982, p. 149.
2 Denis Healey, *The Time of My Life*, Penguin, 1990, p. 430.
3 Ibid., p. 427.
4 Andrew Likierman, *Public Administration*, Penguin, 1988, p. 73.
5 James Callaghan, *Time and Chance*, Collins, 1987, p. 426.
6 Hugo Young and Anne Sloman, *But Chancellor*, BBC, 1984.
7 Ibid., p. 41.
8 Ibid., p. 43.
9 Peter Hennessy, *Whitehall*, Fontana, 1989, p. 629.
10 See Maurice Mullard, *The Politics of Public Expenditure*, Routledge, 1993, p. 147.
11 *Financial Statement and Budget Report 1995–96*, H.M. Treasury, January 1995, table 6A.1.

12 Nigel Lawson, *The View from No. 11*, Bantam, 1992, p. 301.

13 *The Government's Expenditure Plans*, Cmnd 7841, H.M. Treasury, 1980.

14 *The Government's Expenditure Plans*, Cmnd 8175, H.M. Treasury, 1981.

15 Geoffrey Howe, *Conflict of Loyalty*, Macmillan, 1994, p. 189.

16 *The Government's Expenditure Plans*, Cm 2817, H.M. Treasury, March 1995.

17 Young and Sloman, op. cit., p. 35.

18 Simon Jenkins, *Political Quarterly*, 1985.

19 See Hennessy, op. cit., Chapter 15.

20 Colin Thain and Maurice Wright, *Public Administration*, vol. 70, 1992, p. 218.

21 Hugh Heclo and Aaron Wildavsky, *The Private Government of Public Money*, Macmillan, 1981.

22 Leo Pliatsky, *The Treasury under Mrs Thatcher*, Blackwell, 1989.

23 *Financial Statement and Budget Report 1995–96*, H.M. Treasury, January 1995, table 4A.8.

24 Young and Sloman, op. cit., p. 61.

25 Lawson, op. cit., p. 586.

26 Ibid., p. 273.

27 Kenneth Baker, *The Turbulent Years*, Faber and Faber, 1993, p. 463.

28 See Michael Power, *The Audit Explosion*, Demos, 1994.

29 Hennessy, op. cit., p. 600.

30 See Likierman, op. cit., p. 178, and John McEldowney in Jeffrey Jowell and D. Oliver, *The Changing Constitution*, 3rd edn, Clarendon, 1994, p. 199.

31 See Michael Elliott in Jowell and Oliver, op. cit., 2nd edn, 1989, p. 185.

32 Lawson, op. cit., p. 391.

33 Ibid.

34 Hennessy, op. cit., p. 645.

35 Lawson, op. cit., p. 392.

36 Hennessy, op. cit., p. 620.

37 Lawson, op. cit., p. 392.

38 *Annual Report*, H.M. Treasury, Cm 2817, March 1995.

CHAPTER THIRTEEN: STRONG IS BEAUTIFUL

1 *The Conservative Manifesto*, The Conservative Party, 1979.
2 See survey in Oliver Letwin, *Privatizing the World*, Cassell, 1988, pp. 32–9.
3 William Waldegrave, *The House Magazine*, 1993.
4 See Peter Drucker, *The Theory and Practice of Management*, Harper, 1955.
5 Samuel Beer, *Britain Against Itself*, Faber and Faber, 1982.
6 For a study of this phenomenon see John Adams, *Risk*, UCL Press, 1995.
7 See Commission for Local Democracy, *Taking Charge*, Municipal Journal, June 1995.
8 Andrew Likierman, *Public Administration*, Penguin, 1988, p. 111.
9 Jeffrey Jowell and D. Oliver, *The Changing Constitution*, Clarendon, edns 1989–94.
10 Ibid., 3rd edn, p. 175.
11 Ibid., p. 206.
12 See Michael Power, *The Audit Explosion*, Demos, 1994, p. 40.
13 *Introduction to Local Authority Performance Figures*, Audit Commission, vol. 1, HMSO, 1995.
14 Vernon Bogdanor, *Local Government and the Constitution*, Society of Local Authority Chief Executives, March 1994.
15 George Jones and Tony Travers, *Attitudes to Local Government in Westminster and Whitehall*, Commission for Local Democracy, 1994, p. 17.
16 Richard Batley and Gerry Stoker, *Local Government in Europe*, Macmillan, 1991.
17 Ibid., p. 214.
18 Ibid., p. 220.
19 Michael Heseltine, *Where There's a Will*, Hutchinson, 1987, p. 132.
20 See successive reports of the Local Government Commission, 1994–5.
21 Jim Bulpitt, in Colin Crouch and David Marquand, eds., *The New Centralism*, Political Quarterly/Blackwell, 1989, p. 61.

CHAPTER FOURTEEN: WHY IT MATTERS

1 *State of the Nation 1995*, Joseph Rowntree Memorial Trust/MORI, May 1995.

2 Lawrence Lowell, *The Government of England*, New York, 1908.
3 Larry Siedentop, *Tocqueville*, Oxford University Press, 1994.
4 Quoted in ibid., p. 93.
5 Quoted in ibid., p. 64.
6 See Peter Riddell, *Honest Opportunism*, Hamish Hamilton, 1993.
7 Ian Gilmour, speech to Cambridge Union, 7 February 1980.
8 See Nicholas Ridley, *The Local Right*, Centre for Policy Studies, 1988.
9 See Brian Hogwood, *Commission for Local Democracy Research Report no. 15*, Commission for Local Democracy, Municipal Journal, 1995.
10 Stuart Weir and Wendy Hall, *Ego Trip*, Demos, 1994.
11 See Bernard Crick, *In Defence of Politics*, Penguin, 1964; and Jerry White, *Fear of Voting*, Rowntree, 1994.
12 Weir and Hall, op. cit., p. 43.
13 Friedrich von Hayek, *The Road to Serfdom*, Routledge, 1944.
14 Lord Hailsham, *Dimbleby Lecture*, BBC, 1978, and interview in *Who's Who Magazine*, Summer 1991.
15 Ferdinand Mount, *The British Constitution Now*, Heinemann, 1992, p. 264.
16 See S. E. Finer, *Comparative Government*, Allen Lane, 1970.
17 Mount, op. cit., p. 266.

BIBLIOGRAPHY

(Government publications, academic journals and periodicals are referenced in the Notes. Relevant pamphlets and other documents not referred to in the Notes are listed here.)

Adams, John, *Risk*, UCL Press, 1995.

Anderson, Bruce, *John Major*, Fourth Estate, 1991.

Anderson, Digby and Gerald Frost, *Hubris: The Tempting of Modern Conservatives*, Centre for Policy Studies, 1992.

Baker, Kenneth, *The Turbulent Years*, Faber and Faber, 1993.

Balen, Malcolm, *Kenneth Clarke*, Fourth Estate, 1994.

Barnett, Joel, *Inside the Treasury*, Deutsch, 1982.

Bash, Leslie and David Coulby, eds., *The Education Reform Act: Competition and Control*, Cassell, 1989.

Batley, Richard and Gerry Stoker, *Local Government in Europe*, Macmillan, 1991.

Beer, Samuel, *Britain Against Itself*, Faber, 1982.

Bell, David, ed., *The Conservative Government*, Croom Helm, 1985.

Birchall, Johnston, ed., *Housing Policy in the 1990s*, Routledge, 1992.

Bogdanor, Vernon, *The Blackwell Encyclopaedia of Political Institutions*, Blackwell, 1987.

Booker, Christopher and Richard North, *The Mad Officials*, Constable, 1994.

Brownhill, Sue, *Developing London's Docklands*, Paul Chapman, 1990.

Bruce-Gardyne, Jock, *Mrs Thatcher's First Administration*, Macmillan, 1984.

Butcher, Hugh, *et al.*, *Local Government and Thatcherism*, Routledge, 1990.

Butler, David, Andrew Adonis and Tony Travers, *Failure in British Government*, Oxford University Press, 1994.

Callaghan, James, *Time and Chance*, Collins, 1987.

Cockett, Richard, *Thinking the Unthinkable*, HarperCollins, 1994.

Commission for Local Democracy, *Taking Charge: The Rebirth of Local Democracy*, Muncipal Journal, 1995.

Cope, Helen, *Housing Associations: Policy and Practice*, Macmillan, 1990.

Cosgrave, Patrick, *Thatcher: The First Term*, Bodley Head, 1985.

Crick, Bernard, *In Defence of Politics*, Penguin, 1964.

Cross, J. A., *Modern British Government*, University Tutorial Press, 1972.

Crouch, Colin and David Marquand, *The New Centralism*, Political Quarterly/Blackwell, 1989.

Currie, Edwina, *Life Lines: Politics and Health, 1986–88*, Sidgwick and Jackson, 1989

Davis, H. and John Stewart, *The Growth of Government by Appointment*, Local Government Management Board, 1993.

Day, Patricia and Rudolf Klein, *Accountabilities*, Tavistock, 1987.

Drewry, Gavin and Tony Butcher, *The Civil Service Today*, Blackwell, 1991.

Drucker, Peter, *The Theory and Practice of Management*, Harper, 1955.

Duncan, Alan and Dominic Hobson, *Saturn's Children*, Sinclair-Stevenson, 1995.

Dunleavy, Patrick, *et al.*, *Developments in British Politics*, Macmillan, 1988, 1990, 1993.

Dynes, Michael and David Walker, *The Times Guide to the New British State*, The Times, 1995.

Finer, S. E., *Comparative Government*, Allen Lane, 1970.

Flude, M. and M. Hamner, *The Education Reform Act of 1988*, Falmer, 1990.

Flynn, Norman, Steve Leach and Carol Vielba, *Abolition or Reform? The GLC and the Metropolitan Councils*, Allen and Unwin, 1985.

Foot, Michael, *Aneurin Bevan*, vol. 1, MacGibbon and Kee, 1962.

Forrest, Ray and Alan Murie, *Selling the Welfare State: The Privatization of Public Housing*, Routledge, 1988.

Foster, Christopher and M. Perlman, *Local Government Finance in a Unitary State*, Allen and Unwin, 1980.

Fowler, Norman, *Ministers Decide*, Chapman, 1991.

Gamble, Andrew, *Britain in Decline*, Macmillan, 1990.

Gamble, Andrew, *The Free Economy and the Strong State*, Macmillan, 1994.

Gilmour, Ian, *Britain Can Work*, Martin Robertson, 1983.

Gilmour, Ian, *Dancing with Dogma*, Simon and Schuster, 1992.

Glaister, Stephen and Tony Travers, *New Directions for British Railways*, Institute of Economic Affairs, 1993.

Graef, Roger, *Talking Blues*, Fontana, 1990.

Graham, C. and T. Prosser, *Waiving the Rules*, Open University, 1988.

Gray, Clive, *Government Beyond the Centre*, Macmillan, 1994.

Gray, John, *Limited Government: A Positive Agenda*, Institute of Economic Affairs, 1989.

Green, David, *The New Right*, Wheatsheaf, 1987.

Hall, Stuart and Martin Jacques, eds., *The Politics of Thatcherism*, Lawrence and Wishart, 1983.

Harris, Kenneth, *Attlee*, Weidenfeld, 1995.

Harris, Kenneth, *Thatcher*, Weidenfeld and Nicolson, 1988.

Harris, Neville, *Law and Education: Regulation, Consumerism and the Education System*, Sweet and Maxwell, 1993.

Harrison, Anthony, *The Control of Public Expenditure*, Transaction Books, 1989.

Harrison, S., D. J. Hunter and C. Pollitt, *The Politics of British Health Policy*, Unwin Hayman, 1990.

Haviland, Julian, ed., *Take Care, Mr Baker*, Fourth Estate, 1988.

Hayek, Friedrich von, *The Road to Serfdom*, Routledge, 1944.

Healey, Denis, *The Time of My Life*, Penguin, 1990.

Hebbert, Michael and A. Dickens Edge, *Dismantlers: The London Residuary Body*, Suntory-Toyota International Centre, 1994.

Hebbert, Michael and Tony Travers, *The London Government Handbook*, Cassell, 1988.

Heclo, Hugh and Aaron Wildavsky, *The Private Government of Public Money*, Macmillan, 1981.

Hennessy, Peter, *Cabinet*, Blackwell, 1986.

Hennessy, Peter, *Whitehall*, Fontana, 1989.

Heseltine, Michael, *Where There's a Will*, Hutchinson, 1987.

Hill, Michael, *Social Security Policy in Britain*, Elgar, 1990.

Hills, John, *Unravelling Housing Finance*, Clarendon, 1991.

Hills, John, ed., *The State of Welfare*, Clarendon, 1991.

Hirst, Paul, *After Thatcher*, Collins, 1989.

Holmes, Martin, *The First Thatcher Governments*, Wheatsheaf, 1985.

Holmes, Martin, *Thatcherism: Scope and Limits*, Macmillan, 1989.

Howe, Geoffrey, *Conflict of Loyalty*, Macmillan, 1994.

Jackson, P., ed., *Implementing Government Policy Initiatives*, Royal Institute of Public Administration, Gower, 1985.

Jefferson, Tony and Roger Grimshaw, *Controlling the Constable*, Muller, 1984.

Jenkins, Peter, *Mrs Thatcher's Revolution*, Cape, 1987.

Jenkins, Simon, *Against the Grain*, John Murray, 1994.

Jenkins, Simon, *The Selling of Mary Davies*, John Murray, 1993.

Johnson, Christopher, *The Economy under Mrs Thatcher*, Penguin, 1991.

Jones, George and John Stewart, *The Case for Local Government*, Allen and Unwin, 1983.

Jones, George and Tony Travers, *Attitudes to Local Government in Westminster and Whitehall*, Commission for Local Democracy, 1994.

Jowell, Jeffrey and Dawn Oliver, *The Changing Constitution*, Clarendon, 1985, 1989, 1994.

Kavanagh, Dennis, *Thatcherism and British Politics*, Clarendon, 1990.

Kavanagh, Dennis and Arthur Seldon, eds., *The Thatcher Effect*, Oxford, 1989.

Kay, John, *Privatization and Regulation*, Oxford University Press, 1986.

Kay, John, *The State and the Market: The UK Experience of Privatization*, Group of Thirty, 1987.

Keegan, William, *Mr Lawson's Gamble*, Hodder, 1989.

Keegan, William, *Mrs Thatcher's Economic Experiment*, Allen Lane, 1984.

King, Anthony, ed., *The British Prime Minister*, Macmillan, 1985.

Klein, Rudolf, *The Politics of the National Health Service*, Longman, 1989.

Klein, Rudolf and M. O'Higgins, *The Future of Welfare*, Blackwell, 1985.

Lawson, Nigel, *The View from No. 11*, Bantam, 1992.

Lawton, Denis, ed., *The Education Reform Act: Choice and Control*, Hodder, 1989.

le Grand, Julian, *The Strategy of Equality*, Allen and Unwin, 1982.

Letwin, Oliver, *Privatizing the World*, Cassell, 1988.

Letwin, Shirley, *The Anatomy of Thatcherism*, Fontana, 1992.

Likierman, Andrew, *Public Administration*, Penguin, 1988.

Loughlin, M., *Local Government in the Modern State*, Sweet and Maxwell, 1986.

Loughlin, M. *et al.*, *Half a Century of Municipal Decline*, Allen and Unwin, 1985.

Maclure, Stuart, *Education Re-formed*, Hodder, 1989.

Malpass, Peter, *Reshaping Housing Policy*, Routledge, 1990.

Malpass, Peter and Robin Means, *Implementing Housing Policy*, Open University, 1993.

Malpass, Peter and Alan Murie, *Housing Policy and Practice*, Macmillan, 1990.

Mark, Robert, *In the Office of Constable*, Collins, 1978.

Marsh, David and R. A. W. Rhodes, *Implementing Thatcherite Policies*, Open University, 1992.

Maynard, Geoffrey, *The Economy Under Mrs Thatcher*, Blackwell, 1988.

Meredith, Paul, *Education and the Law*, Longman, 1994.

Minford, Patrick, M. Peel and P. Ashton, *The Housing Morass*, Institute of Economic Affairs, 1987.

Minogue, Kenneth and M. Biddiss, eds., *Thatcherism: Personality and Politics*, Macmillan, 1987.

Moore, John, *Why Privatize?*, H.M. Treasury, 1983.

Morgan, Kenneth, *Labour in Power 1945–51*, Clarendon, 1984.

Morris, Robert, ed., *Central and Local Control of Education*, Longman, 1990.

Mount, Ferdinand, *The British Constitution Now*, Heinemann, 1992.

Muellbauer, J., *The Great British Housing Disaster*, Institute for Public Policy Research, 1990.

Mullard, Maurice, *The Politics of Public Expenditure*, Routledge, 1993.

Newton, K. and T. J. Karran, *The Politics of Local Expenditure*, Macmillan, 1985.

Norton, Philip, *The Constitution in Flux*, Oxford University Press, 1982.

Norton, Philip and Arthur Aughey, *Conservatives and Conservatism*, Temple-Smith, 1987.

Osborne, David and Ted Gaebler, *Reinventing Government*, Penguin, 1993.

Parkinson, Cecil, *Right at the Centre*, Weidenfeld and Nicolson, 1992.

Patten, John, *Political Culture, Conservatism, and Rolling Constitutional Changes*, Conservative Political Centre, July 1991.

Patten, John, *Things to Come*, Sinclair-Stevenson, 1995.

Pearce, Edward, *The Quiet Rise of John Major*, Weidenfeld and Nicolson, 1991.

Pliatsky, Leo, *Getting and Spending*, Blackwell, 1982.

Pliatsky, Leo, *The Treasury under Mrs Thatcher*, Blackwell, 1989.

Pollitt, C., *Managerialism and the Public Sector*, Blackwell, 1990.

Power, Michael, *The Audit Explosion*, Demos, 1994.

Prior, James, *A Balance of Power*, Hamish Hamilton, 1986.

Prosser, Tony, *Nationalized Industries and Public Control*, Blackwell, 1986.

Pryke, Richard, *The Nationalized Industries*, Policies and Performance, Martin Robertson, 1981.

Redwood, John, *Signals from a Railway Conference*, Centre for Policy Studies, 1988.

Reiner, Robert, *Chief Constables*, Oxford University Press, 1991.

Reiner, Robert, *The Politics of the Police*, Wheatsheaf, 1992.

Reiner, Robert and Sarah Spencer, eds., *Accountable Policing*, Institute for Public Policy Research, 1993.

Rhodes, R., *Beyond Westminster and Whitehall*, Allen and Unwin, 1988.

Riddell, Peter, *Honest Opportunism*, Hamish Hamilton, 1993.

Riddell, Peter, *The Thatcher Era and Its Legacy*, Blackwell, 1991.

Ridley, Nicholas, *The Local Right*, Centre for Policy Studies, 1988.

Ridley, Nicholas, *My Style of Government*, Hutchinson, 1991.

Rose, Richard, *Ministers and Ministries*, Oxford University Press, 1987.

Rose, Richard and Phillip Davies, *Inheritance in Public Policy*, Yale, 1994.

Savage, Stephen, Rob Atkinson and Lynton Robins, *Public Policy in Britain*, Macmillan, 1994.

Seldon, Arthur, *The State is Rolling Back*, Institute of Economic Affairs, 1994.

Shattock, Michael, *The University Grants Committee*, Open University, 1994.

Siedentop, Larry, *Tocqueville*, Oxford University Press, 1994.

Simon, Brian and Clyde Chitty, *Education Answers Back*, Lawrence and Wishart, 1993.

Skidelsky, Robert, ed., *Thatcherism*, Chatto, 1988.

Stephenson, Hugh, *Thatcher's First Year*, Jill Norman, 1980.

Stewart, John, *The New Management of Local Government*, Allen and Unwin, 1986.

Stewart, John, Alan Greer and Paul Hoggett, *The Quango State: An Alternative Approach*, Commission for Local Democracy, 1995.

Stewart, John and Gerry Stoker, eds., *The Future of Local Government*, Macmillan, 1989.

Stewart, John *et al.*, eds, *Accountability to the Public*, European Policy Forum, 1992.

Stoker, Gerry, *The Politics of Local Government*, Macmillan, 1991.

Tebbit, Norman, *Upwardly Mobile*, Futura, 1989.

Thatcher, Margaret, *The Downing Street Years*, HarperCollins, 1993.

Thatcher, Margaret, *The Path to Power*, HarperCollins, 1995.

Thompson, Grahame, *The Conservatives' Economic Policy*, Croom Helm, 1986.

Thornley, Andy, *Urban Planning under Thatcherism*, Routledge, 1993.

Thornley, Andy, ed., *The Crisis of London*, Routledge, 1992.

Timmins, Nicholas, *The Five Giants: A Biography of the Welfare State*, HarperCollins, 1995.

Travers, Tony, *The Politics of Local Government Finance*, Allen and Unwin, 1986.

Travers, Tony with George Jones, Michael Hebbert and June Burnham, *The Government of London*, Rowntree, 1991.

Veljanovski, Cento, *Privatization and Competition*, Institute of Economic Affairs, 1989.

Veljanovski, Cento, *Selling the State*, Weidenfeld and Nicolson, 1987.

Vibert, Frank, ed., *Britain's Constitutional Future*, Institute of Economic Affairs, 1991.

Vickers, John and George Yarrow, *Privatization and the Natural Monopolies*, Public Policy Centre, 1985.

Waldegrave, William, *The Public Service and the Future*, Conservative Political Centre, 1993.

Watkin, B., *The National Health Service*, Allen and Unwin, 1978.

Watkins, Alan, *A Conservative Coup: The Fall of Margaret Thatcher*, Duckworth, 1991.

Weir, Stuart and Wendy Hall, eds., *Ego Trip*, Demos, 1994.

White, Jerry, *Fear of Voting*, Rowntree, 1994.

Willetts, David, *Modern Conservatism*, Penguin, 1992.

Young, David, *The Enterprise Years*, Headline, 1990.

Young, Hugo, *One of Us*, Macmillan, 1991.

Young, Hugo and Anne Sloman, *But Chancellor*, BBC, 1984.

Young, Hugo and Anne Sloman, *The Thatcher Phenomenon*, BBC, 1986.

Zander, Michael, *A Matter of Justice: The Legal System in Ferment*, Oxford University Press, 1988.

Zifcak, Spencer, *The New Managerialism*, Open University Press, 1994.

INDEX

298